U.S. PROPERTY
NO
TRESPASSING
BEYOND
THIS POINT

LIGHTING
THE BAY

LIGHTING THE BAY
Tales of Chesapeake Lighthouses

Text and photographs by Pat Vojtech

TIDEWATER PUBLISHERS
Centreville, Maryland

First photograph in this book: Concord Point, Havre de Grace, Maryland
Previous page spread: The two Cape Henry Lighthouses at the mouth of the Chesapeake Bay
Above: Sandy Point Lighthouse, north of the Chesapeake Bay Bridge

Library of Congress Cataloging-in-Publication Data

Vojtech, Pat.
    Lighting the bay: tales of Chesapeake lighthouses / text and
photographs by Pat Vojtech. — 1st ed.
          p.   cm.
    Includes bibliographical references and index.
    ISBN 0-87033-466-2 (hardcover)
    1. Lighthouses—Chesapeake Bay (Md. and Va.)   I. Title
VK1024.C46V65   1996
387.1′55′0975518—dc20   96-31958

Manufactured in Hong Kong
First edition

*To the keepers, their children and grandchildren,
and to all the men and women who continue to keep
the lighthouses of the Chesapeake Bay.*

*Point No Point, north of
the Potomac River.*

Contents

Preface   *ix*

Introduction: Fire on the Hill   3

1. Good Builder, Bad Light   9
2. Steering a New Course   15
3. War against the Lighthouses   23
4. Under Seige   29
5. Riding a Lighthouse   35
6. Fighting Back the Sea   39
7. Earthquake!   47
8. Stranded in the Ice   53
9. Isolation, Illness, Death, and the Law   57
10. All the Comforts of Home   63
11. Killer Caissons   69
12. Lighting the Way to Baltimore   73
13. The Unlucky Lighthouse   83
14. Rescues: All in a Day's Work   89
15. The Long Sail Home   93
16. Imprisoned by Fog   99
17. Automating the Lighthouses   105
18. Death on a Lighthouse: Murder or Madness   111
19. Rescue in a Hurricane   119
20. Lady Keeper of the Lamp   125
21. Bombing the Lighthouses   131
22. Tearing Down the Screw Piles   135
23. Point Lookout: The Haunted Lighthouse   141
24. The Forgotten Lighthouses   147
25. The Renaissance   151

Appendix: List of Lighthouses, Lightships, and Tenders   159

Sources   183

Index   189

Chesapeake Bay Lighthouses

Numbers indicate approximate location of original sites of Chesapeake Bay Lighthouses.

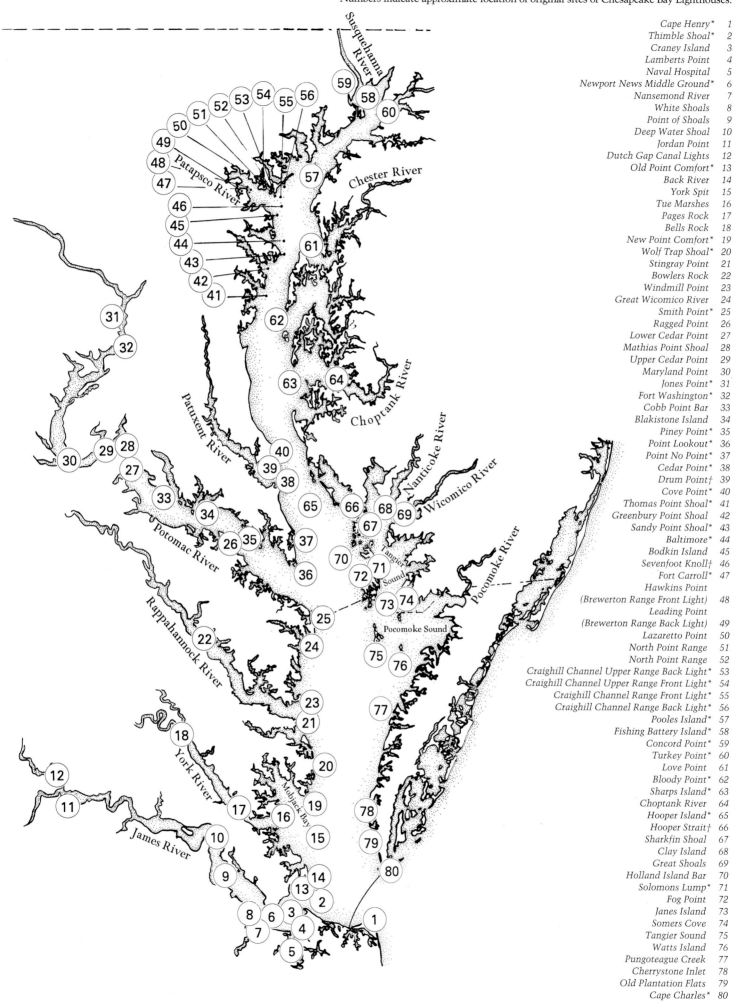

Cape Henry*	1
Thimble Shoal*	2
Craney Island	3
Lamberts Point	4
Naval Hospital	5
Newport News Middle Ground*	6
Nansemond River	7
White Shoals	8
Point of Shoals	9
Deep Water Shoal	10
Jordan Point	11
Dutch Gap Canal Lights	12
Old Point Comfort*	13
Back River	14
York Spit	15
Tue Marshes	16
Pages Rock	17
Bells Rock	18
New Point Comfort*	19
Wolf Trap Shoal*	20
Stingray Point	21
Bowlers Rock	22
Windmill Point	23
Great Wicomico River	24
Smith Point*	25
Ragged Point	26
Lower Cedar Point	27
Mathias Point Shoal	28
Upper Cedar Point	29
Maryland Point	30
Jones Point*	31
Fort Washington*	32
Cobb Point Bar	33
Blakistone Island	34
Piney Point*	35
Point Lookout*	36
Point No Point*	37
Cedar Point*	38
Drum Point†	39
Cove Point*	40
Thomas Point Shoal*	41
Greenbury Point Shoal	42
Sandy Point Shoal*	43
Baltimore*	44
Bodkin Island	45
Sevenfoot Knoll†	46
Fort Carroll*	47
Hawkins Point (Brewerton Range Front Light)	48
Leading Point (Brewerton Range Back Light)	49
Lazaretto Point	50
North Point Range	51
North Point Range	52
Craighill Channel Upper Range Back Light*	53
Craighill Channel Upper Range Front Light*	54
Craighill Channel Range Front Light*	55
Craighill Channel Range Back Light*	56
Pooles Island*	57
Fishing Battery Island*	58
Concord Point*	59
Turkey Point*	60
Love Point	61
Bloody Point*	62
Sharps Island*	63
Choptank River	64
Hooper Island*	65
Hooper Strait†	66
Sharkfin Shoal	67
Clay Island	68
Great Shoals	69
Holland Island Bar	70
Solomons Lump*	71
Fog Point	72
Janes Island	73
Somers Cove	74
Tangier Sound	75
Watts Island	76
Pungoteague Creek	77
Cherrystone Inlet	78
Old Plantation Flats	79
Cape Charles*	80

* Lighthouses that still exist
† Lighthouses that have been moved from their original locations and still exist

Preface

*I*n the early 1800s, the United States was plagued with poorly built lighthouses, primarily because the man who oversaw lighthouse construction was a bookkeeper, not an engineer. Stephen Pleasonton, the fifth auditor of the U.S. Treasury, knew nothing about lighthouses or construction, but the job of overseeing lighthouse construction and maintenance lay on his shoulders for thirty-two critical years when the country was just beginning to light its waters. Unfortunately, Pleasonton liked to save money, and he routinely compromised construction techniques to return a few dollars to the treasury. Consequently, many lighthouses built during Pleasonton's reign crumbled and fell. Yet, despite problems nationwide during this era, the Chesapeake Bay was blessed with perhaps the country's finest early lighthouse builder—John Donohoo.

Donohoo was an honest, hard-working entrepreneur who insisted on high quality and yet was able to stay within the tight budgetary requirements of the fifth auditor. Between 1823 and 1854, he built almost every lighthouse on the Bay. Historians disagree on the exact number, but it was about thirteen, including Concord Point at Havre de Grace on the Susquehanna River, which still stands 170 years later as an example of his excellent work. With the exception of several lighthouses built on islands and those destroyed by fire or erosion, every Donohoo lighthouse still stands today—architectural gems for Chesapeake inhabitants and visitors to enjoy. For years, however, historians cast a cloud over Donohoo's early attempts at lighthouse construction, claiming that poor workmanship was the reason his first—Thomas Point Lighthouse—was taken down.

Most of us know Thomas Point Light as the cottage-style lighthouse on the shoal stretching from the entrance to the South River, near Annapolis, Maryland. But long before this screw-pile lighthouse was built over water, there were two constructed on land. Donohoo received the contract to build the first in 1825. In fact, it was his first lighthouse from start to finish. (He had completed another lighthouse when a contractor failed to meet performance standards.) Unfortunately, Thomas Point Lighthouse had to be taken down and rebuilt after just a few years. Historians repeatedly used this as evidence of Donohoo's early failure at lighthouse construction. The truth is that erosion, not poor construction, caused the demise of the first lighthouse. This is made quite clear in a letter written in the mid-1800s by Fifth Auditor Stephen Pleasonton to the Honorable John P. Kennedy, chairman of the House of Representatives Committee on Commerce. In the letter, Pleasonton notes that a seawall had to be built around the Thomas Point Light, "and in 1838 the tower was taken down and rebuilt, at a cost of $2,500." He goes on to explain the need for rebuilding the lighthouse.

> This light was placed upon a clay bank at least 30 feet high, and about 500 feet from the water. Such was the action of the water upon the bank that in a few years it was washed away to within 50 feet of the light; upon being informed of which, I directed a quantity of rubble stone to be placed at the base of the bank. This arrested the water but in a slight degree, and in 1838 it had approached within 15 feet of the lighthouse, when I contracted with Winslow Lewis to take down the tower, and rebuild it in a secure place for $2,000.

This letter, along with many others, is preserved in an 1871 government publication, *U.S. Light House Board Compilation of Public Documents and Extracts from Reports and Papers Re-*

lating to *Light-Houses, Light-Vessels, and Illuminating Apparatus, and to Beacons, Buoys, and Fog Signals, 1789–1871*, which I found at the Nimitz Library of the U.S. Naval Academy in Annapolis.

Having cleared John Donohoo's good name, I hope I do not misrepresent other historical facts. In researching this book, I sifted through thousands of documents, newspaper articles, and recorded histories and conducted many personal interviews with wives, children, and grandchildren of keepers who once lived in lighthouses. *Lighting the Bay: Tales of Chesapeake Lighthouses* contains tens of thousands of facts gathered from hundreds of sources. When facts contradicted one another, I chose the most reliable source. For example, when Thimble Shoal Lighthouse at the mouth of Hampton Roads burned in 1909, various newspapers had differing accounts of how many men were in the lighthouse at the time and how they were rescued. I chose what I believed was the most credible story.

Writing history is very much like detective work. Granted, nobody will hang when all is said and done, but a reputation, like Donohoo's, may suffer. Consequently, in the course of researching this book, I looked for clues to support stories I had heard or read along the way in an effort to uncover the truth of what happened 50, 100, 150, or 200 years ago. For example, did a one-legged man really operate Drum Point Light for a while, creating the need to provide an easier access up the center of the hexagonal light station? After finding two references to his existence (supplied by Robert Hurry at the Calvert Marine Museum), I would have to say yes. And speaking of facts, are all the so-called screw-pile lighthouses in the Bay actually standing on screws? The answer is no. Seven or eight, and perhaps more, of the forty-two cottage lighthouses built on piles in the Bay did not have screws to hold them in the ground. In fact, Pungoteague Creek Lighthouse, lauded as the Chesapeake's first screw pile, was almost certainly not built on screw piles. Screw piles had to be literally screwed or turned into the earth, but the annual reports of the Lighthouse Board state that Pungoteague's piles had conical bases and were "pneumatically driven" into the ground.

While I feel certain that this description of Pungoteague Creek Lighthouse is accurate, sometimes the Lighthouse Board's reports, which gave detailed accounts of construction, did not reflect what was finally built. This is because the decision of the Board on what to build often changed. Consequently, in one annual report the Board would describe in detail how a lighthouse would be constructed, only to change the plans completely before or during construction. Such was the case with both the current Thomas Point Shoal Light, a screw-pile lighthouse which was originally designed as a caisson lighthouse, and Sandy Point Lighthouse, a caisson originally designed as a screw pile.

While getting the facts, I tried to bring history alive for the reader by placing some of the great moments in lighthouse history in the context of what was happening around the Chesapeake. For example, the same ice that carried away a lighthouse in 1877 also crippled ports, destroyed merchant vessels, and locked hundreds of dredgers in ice around the Bay. Lighthouse keepers on the Chesapeake dutifully recorded the tremors of the second worst earthquake in United States history in 1886, but the earthquake did its biggest damage south of the Bay. The great August Storm of 1933 that set the stage for one of the most heroic rescues in Chesapeake lighthouse history called upon many other lighthouse keepers to perform less publicized, though no less important, acts of heroism and bravery.

When I started to research this book, I thought lighthouses and their keepers were relatively isolated, but I soon discovered that there was nothing in American history that did not reach out across the lonely waters and swampy peninsulas of the Chesapeake and touch the lives of lighthouse keepers on the Bay. From war to advances in technology, lighthouse keepers were in the midst of everything, despite their lonely outposts. They were on the cutting edge of technology, as lighthouses were employed in the early development of communications, power, sound transmission, radio transmission, geological survey, construction technology, and, of course, advances in optics and lighting. Lighthouse keepers dealt with the latest in erosion prevention 150 years before the

The two Cape Henry Lighthouses, towering over the tree-covered dunes of Cape Henry, represent different styles of lighthouse architecture: the old is built of sandstone blocks, while the new is of cast iron. The rooftop near the new Cape Henry is the keeper's dwelling.

ordinary property owner on Kent Island had heard about a jetty of stone to counter nature's advances. The latest techniques were employed in lighthouse construction, sometimes (but not always) as quickly as they were invented. Early masonry and brick lighthouses, which were exposed to the worst natural environments, including salt, water, sand, and high winds, were used as experiments for improving on the early ingredients of cement and mortar. Some of the first modular homes were lighthouses. The superstructure, or living quarters, of the lighthouses built on piles in the Chesapeake were almost all built in wall sections on land before being hauled to the site and assembled, usually in less than a month.

In my readings, I even ran across a very detailed account of what must well have been one of the first uses of a circular saw in the 1870s, some twenty or thirty years before its widespread use. The saw was used in construction of the front light of the Craighill Channel Range, and the Lighthouse Board determined that it was a failure—at least for underwater work.

War left the lighthouses irrevocably changed: in some cases, they were damaged or destroyed; in other cases, they were equipped to the hilt with the latest in communications equipment so that keepers could help the government identify the enemy.

Today, only 34 original lighthouses, of 106 built, remain on the Chesapeake. Fortunately, every type of lighthouse built on the Bay is still represented. The first lighthouses were conical towers of stone or brick with a detached dwelling for the keeper. The old Cape Henry Light in Vir-

A full moon rises over Drum Point Lighthouse at the Calvert Marine Museum in Solomons, Maryland.

ginia, Piney Point in St. Marys County, Maryland, and Concord Point in Havre de Grace, Maryland, are excellent examples of this style. In some cases—usually to save money—the lighthouse cupola was built atop the keeper's dwelling. This style is represented by Point Lookout Lighthouse at the mouth of the Potomac River. A third early style was a small wooden structure with a detached dwelling. This structure was sparce, economical, and usually found up rivers where there was little need for height or heavy-duty construction. Representative of this style is Fort Washington Fog Tower on the Potomac River. The wooden tower originally housed only the fog bell, but a light was later placed in the tower when the lighthouse was blocked by other buildings at the fort. Several Chesapeake lighthouses, including Jordan Point Lighthouse, were originally housed in such simple towers.

In the 1850s, the pile lighthouse was introduced to the Bay, allowing lighthouses to be built over water in the muddy Chesapeake for the first time. The most typical pile lighthouse was the screw pile, but there were also sleeve piles—wooden piles driven into the substrata and encased with hollow iron piles—as well as iron pilings without screws, such as at Pungoteague Light. Examples of pile lighthouses can be found at both the Chesapeake Bay Maritime Museum in St. Michaels, Maryland, which owns the second Hooper Strait Lighthouse, and the Calvert Marine Museum in Solomons, which has Drum Point Lighthouse on display. Most people believe that all pile lighthouses were picturesque hexagonal cottages, but many were square or rectangular buildings, which were no less picturesque. In fact, the square cottages had quite a bit of gingerbread trim, which added to their beauty. Unfortunately, none of the four-sided cottage lighthouses survived. They were all torn down and replaced by automated beacons. The most unique screw pile built on the Bay was Sevenfoot Knoll, which is a round, metal structure. In the late 1980s, it was moved from the mouth of the Patapsco River to the Inner Harbor at Baltimore.

When ice began to damage many of these pile houses, a fifth style of lighthouse emerged on the Bay—the caisson lighthouse. A wooden or iron cylinder was lowered to the Bay bottom and usually embedded in the substrata until it reached solid earth, and a house of iron or brick (and in one case, wood) was built atop this foundation. The caisson proved to be the most sturdy lighthouse that could be built in Chesapeake Bay waters, and all twelve that were constructed still exist in their original location. However, Solomons Lump, a caisson topped with a wooden dwelling, was stripped of its dwelling after it was converted to automatic status, most likely because of rot and decay.

A sixth style of lighthouse on the Bay is the cast-iron lighthouse. This style emerged in the 1880s and allowed for much taller structures. Two different styles of the cast-iron lighthouse are found at Cape Henry and Cape Charles. The new Cape Henry Light is a free-standing cast-iron light-house, while that at Cape Charles has a narrow cylinder center which houses a circular staircase, supported by a web of iron rods around the light-house exterior. Cast-iron lighthouses were built in sections in a factory and shipped to the site, where they could be quickly and easily assembled. This was a great advantage on the wind- and storm-whipped capes where anything that could go wrong did go wrong during construction, includ-ing, in one instance, hordes of mosquitoes that forced construction to stop.

Erosion and shifting soil are by far the biggest culprits in the loss of Bay lighthouses; ice, how-ever, destroyed at least eleven pile lighthouses. In the end, men gave up the battle with nature and disassembled, removed, and for the most part de-stroyed almost every cottage lighthouse built over water. Likewise, a number of land-based towers were either abandoned and left to crumble or dismantled because they were threatened by the sea and too expensive to maintain.

Before I began my research, I tended to blame the men who gave the orders to destroy the light-houses for the loss of so many of our guiding lights. In researching the struggles of man and nature, however, I've come to realize that the real villain is the beautiful Chesapeake, whose constantly swelling and ebbing tide and legendary squalls and ice floes have never ceased to move the earth below and the ice above, making lighthouse pres-ervation a constant, uphill battle. In time, we'll

almost certainly lose a few more lighthouses. For example, Cedar Point's days are numbered. This lighthouse off the mouth of the Patuxent may well be gone by the time you read this account. But as long as there are people who care about the light-houses and work to preserve them, there will be a few left to admire.

I owe a great deal of thanks to the many lighthouse enthusiasts who have given hundreds of hours to research and compile the local history of their favorite beacons. Much of their work ap-pears in the pamphlets that are handed out to visitors at the various lighthouses that are now museums. When I wrote *Chesapeake Bay Skip-jacks*, I found only one person who had done extensive research on skipjack history, and I felt that I was treading on virgin territory. When I researched this book, however, I discovered that a tremendous amount of work had already been done by these often-unnamed local historians who have combed records and picked the memories of local residents, many of whom are no longer with us and whose stories would have been lost. For their work, I am extremely grateful.

Likewise, I owe a great deal to the careful work of newspaper reporters who recorded (as early as the 1860s) some of the details of life at the lighthouses, as well as harrowing accounts of ice, storms, and fires that threatened the lighthouses over the past two hundred years. I have to admit, however, that there are a few reporters whose necks I would like to wring because, after going back to original sources, I discovered that their stories were more the product of a creative mind than of accurate reportage.

I am also in debt to the many children, grand-children, and other relatives of the lighthouse keepers who have spent years researching their work. In particular, I wish to thank Olga Crouch, the daughter of Turkey Point Lighthouse keeper Fannie May Salter, the last female lighthouse keeper in America. Mrs. Crouch wrote a detailed and loving account of her parents' long careers in the lighthouse business, starting with her father, Clarence Salter, who died in 1925 after more than twenty years of lighthouse keeping, leaving his wife to tend the Turkey Point Light. Mrs. Crouch's personal, hand-written account is full of fascinating, insightful, and often humorous details of growing up in a lighthouse. She recalls that as a child she hid in a closet so the inspector wouldn't discover that the family of the keeper was visiting him on a water station, a violation of law in the 1920s. She climbed the towering Cape Charles Light with her sister, some 180 feet to the top... and they swore never to tell their parents, who certainly would have punished them. And she played "pretend" fishing games on a water station, accidentally pulling out her sister's teeth!

I also owe special thanks to Spencer Tracy of Salisbury, Maryland, who doggedly pursued, through the Freedom of Information Act, records of his grandfather's death on a lighthouse in the 1930s. His grandfather, Ulman Owens, died on Holland Island Lighthouse, sparking a full investigation by the Federal Bureau of Investigation, which was concerned that rumrunners may have killed him during those years of Prohibition. Despite the exhaustive report, we may never know if it was murder or madness or, for that matter, a love triangle that brought about Owens's untimely death in 1931.

Other relatives of lighthouse keepers who shared their stories with me and to whom I am much in debt are the relatives of Thomas J. Steinhise, keeper of Sevenfoot Knoll Lighthouse, who performed the most daring rescue ever recorded in Chesapeake lighthouse history during the height of the August Storm of 1933. His relatives, including Bernadette Gesser, researched his years in the lighthouse business and were able to supply me with ample newspaper clippings and personal accounts of the grandfather they so loved.

I wish also to thank the many relatives of the keepers of Point Lookout and Piney Point lighthouses, who still live in the area and who shared their stories with me. They include Alma Gatton, a granddaughter of one Point Lookout keeper and wife of another; and Harry Yeatman, the son of William Yeatman, Jr., and grandson of William Yeatman, Sr., both keepers at Point Look-

out. I also want to thank another Yeatman descendant, Geraldine Bracken, who shared some of her research into family history with me, including an early newspaper account of her grandfather.

Later inhabitants of and visitors to Point Lookout recounted haunting stories of ghosts and supernatural occurrences at the nineteenth-century lighthouse. I particularly appreciate the stories of Alan Manuel, who was noticably shaken, even twenty years after the fact, telling of an incident in which he believes a ghost held his infant child. I am not a believer in ghosts, but he and Mike Humphries, director of the St. Clement's Island–Potomac River Museum, in St. Marys County, told convincing stories of how the old lighthouse is haunted.

Historians who offered their expertise include Jane Jackstite, of the Friends of Concord Point Lighthouse, who filled me in on some of the details of John Donohoo's life, as well as facts about the lighthouse. I am also grateful to Pete Lesher, curator of the Chesapeake Bay Maritime Museum, and Robert J. Hurry, museum registrar at the Calvert Marine Museum, as well as others who assisted me at both museums. And I'm particularly in debt to Archivist Richard Peuser at the National Archives, who provided me with quick assistance and helpful information when I was doing research there.

The public affairs departments of the Naval Air Station at Patuxent River and the Aberdeen Proving Ground generously offered their time and services in taking me to lighthouses on restricted army and navy bases. I would also like to thank the Rukert Terminals Corporation of Baltimore, which built a replica of Lazaretto Point Lighthouse and allowed me access in order to photograph it.

Finally, I want to thank the U.S. Coast Guard at Baltimore, Hampton Roads, and Gwynns Island, whose men and women were gracious enough to organize trips to some of the lighthouses I had not been able to reach in travels around the Chesapeake in my sailboat, *Athena*.

LIGHTING THE BAY

The first Cape Henry Lighthouse, built in 1791, sits atop the highest sand dune at the cape. Rising ninety feet, the sandstone tower was a work of art, as well as a navigational aid. It was abandoned in 1881 after cracks developed in four of the eight walls and a new tower was built. However, the cracks failed to bring about the tower's collapse, as nineteenth-century engineers had predicted.

Fire on the Hill

The light tower is now threatened with destruction and requires an extension of its foundation. Strong north and northeasterly gales have hollowed out the sand.

Nathaniel F. Williams, collector for the port and district of Baltimore, speaking of Cape Henry Light in 1843.

For two days, the crew of the sloop *Tryal* had struggled to deliver its heavy cargo to Cape Henry. Heading out from the stone quarries of the upper Rappahannock River in 1773, the men had sailed 135 miles to the mouth of the Chesapeake where they were to unload tons of stone for the construction of the first lighthouse on the Bay. The heavy ballast in the sloop's hold had not made the journey an easy one.

Now, as the captain scanned the Bay, turned frothy with whitecaps, he realized with dismay that unloading the stone would be even more difficult than he had expected. The wind had been picking up all morning, and a steady breeze blew across the bow of *Tryal*. In such heavy surf, transferring stones from one boat to another would be tricky, the captain surmised.

On the wild, lonely beaches of Cape Henry there was no pier to tie up to, nor was there a deep-water cove to protect the boats from the increasingly rough seas. Since *Tryal* was too deep of draft to reach the shore, the crew would have to work in the open waters of the Bay, unloading their cargo, stone by stone, into smaller, flat-bottomed vessels, which were already heading out to meet the sloop. The captain had hoped for calm seas, but that would not be the case today.

After the stones reached the beach, the job became even more frustrating, for the stones were so heavy, they often sank right into the sandy shore. When the men could successfully reload them onto horse-drawn carts, the spindly wheels dug so deep into the sand that the horses could not pull their carts. Special carts finally had to be made to move the stones inland.

Construction of Cape Henry Light, on a tall sand dune, required six thousand tons of stone, and even at this early stage of construction, things were not going well at all. If the original contractors had known anything of the long, troubled history of Chesapeake Bay's first lighthouse, they would have expected the worst, for the project had been riddled with delays and problems ever since it was proposed by Governor Alexander Spotswood of Virginia in 1721.

The Chesapeake Bay had a greater volume of shipping than any other region in colonial America, thanks in part to the tobacco trade. Spotswood envisioned a lighthouse that would safely guide ships between the capes at the entrance to the Bay at night and during inclement weather, attracting even more trade to the region.

At the time, ship captains had basic, rudimentary tools to help guide them into harbors. They took compass bearings and used prominent sites on land—such as a big tree or a house—as navigational aids. To check water depth, they dropped a lead line—a piece of lead tied to a line—until it

The sturdy base of the original Cape Henry Lighthouse was sometimes inundated with sand, sometimes scoured clean by the high winds that plagued the cape.

touched bottom, then hauled it up and measured the portion of line that had been underwater. At night, however, or when weather conditions curtailed visibility, captains were often forced to ride out a storm or heavy wind in the open ocean, rather than take the chance of being driven onto a shoal.

It would take seventy years for Spotswood's dream to become reality. In the meantime, colonists who shared his concerns organized an effort to keep a fire burning on the highest sand dune at Cape Henry to guide ships at night.

"Keeping a fire" was the earliest method used to light the entrance to harbors for mariners. Historical records show that fires were commonly used around the Chesapeake Bay and along the coast. In 1774, John Daines began keeping a fire at Old Point Comfort to help guide ships into Hampton Roads. Daines was the caretaker of Fort George, which had stood during colonial days on the grounds where Fort Monroe now stands. (The original fort, built in 1728, was destroyed by a hurricane in 1749.) Daines's fire became important enough to the colony that the House of Burgesses awarded him twenty pounds annually for his effort.

Farther up the Chesapeake on the Potomac River, Jesuit priests in the Newtown Manor House, a brick dwelling that sat on a narrow peninsula between Breton and St. Clements Bays, regularly placed a midnight lamp in a window as a beacon for mariners seeking a safe harbor.

At Cape Henry, the fire was contained inside a large metal basket filled with pine knots gathered in the "desert," as the swampy area of the cape was known. The light was important enough that a man, called a "keeper," watched over the fire throughout the night.

In the decades to come, lighthouses along the coast and in the Chesapeake Bay would become targets for warring factions, and even this early "fire on the hill" had to be defended against enemies. The keepers of this rustic type of beacon were threatened more than a few times by pirates, who stood to benefit from a darkened bay. Pirates, including the legendary Blackbeard, preyed on vessels that were forced to wait at the mouth of the Chesapeake for daylight to guide them in, so they occasionally tried to snuff out the fire. This early light was so important to colonial navigation that lookouts patrolled the shore between Lynnhaven and Cape Henry, and organized efforts were made to apprehend the pirates.

Not all pirates went after their prey. Some preferred to lure merchant ships by setting their own fires where ships would be sure to go aground. Then the ships could easily be plundered.

While historically the division of the Chesapeake Bay into two colonies is blamed for the delay in building a lighthouse on the cape, other reasons certainly contributed. For one, it was felt that the Chesapeake was far more forgiving than harbors to the north. The Bay has almost no submerged rocks, like those in New England. But shoals can be as treacherous as rocks, particularly when wind and sea drive a vessel onto them. Many early vessels were lost in the sudden squalls and driving northeasters that plagued the estuary.

In 1750, Virginia again pursued the dream of a lighthouse. Thomas Lee, then president of the Virginia Council, proposed moving the fort at Point Comfort to Cape Henry, where both a fort and a lighthouse could be built.

Nothing was done until 1767, when Virginia took the lead toward drafting proposals for the lighthouse. By 1773, Maryland had taken similar action and the project was ready to go forward. Some six thousand tons of sandstone were ordered from quarries on the Rappahannock River. A sloop was purchased, and four flat-bottomed boats were bought for moving the stone to shore.

Now that all the parties were finally in agreement, the wind, sea, and sand would bog the project down once again. The monies allocated for the project were quickly used just trying to move the stone to the site. A bill to increase funding for the lighthouse passed in the Virginia Legislature in 1775, but by then the political climate was heating up. Virginia Governor Lord Dunmore, a British sympathizer, had fled the colony and was aboard HMS *Fowey* in the York River. The Revolutionary War had begun, and the lighthouse project was abruptly abandoned.

Yet even in the midst of the war, the colonists recognized the need for a guiding light. In 1777, a white flag, striped with red, was ordered to be raised on a pole fifty feet high at Cape Henry. It was kept hoisted in the day when no enemy was within the capes and taken down when an enemy appeared. The order also called for a light to be hoisted up the pole and kept constantly burning in the nighttime when no enemy was within the capes. After the war, however, there was no money in the colonies for such an ambitious project as a lighthouse, and the long-awaited Cape Henry Light was formally abandoned in 1782.

It would be almost another decade before the construction of the Cape Henry beacon began again. By 1791, the thousands of tons of stone that had taken so much effort and money to move had disappeared into the sand and the surf. The job of

This view from the copper-domed cupola of old Cape Henry Lighthouse reveals a clear view of ships traversing the mouth of the Chesapeake. Today, tourists can climb the steep circular staircase and look down on ocean and Bay.

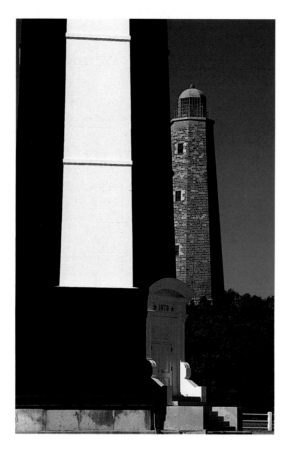

Today, the old Cape Henry is dwarfed by the new Cape Henry Lighthouse.

That first year, 1792, the lighthouse was equipped with ordinary spider lamps, which had no lenses or reflectors to direct and magnify the beam. The light, although poor, was the best available at this early period in history. Over the years, almost every kind of fuel was used in Cape Henry's lamps: fish oil, sperm oil, colza oil (oil from rapeseed or other related plants), lard oil, and, eventually, kerosene—whichever happened to be cheapest.

From the start, the constantly shifting sands of Cape Henry proved a major headache. Sometimes the wind blew too much sand around the small buildings at the station; sometimes it blew too much sand away. In 1798, six years after the lighthouse was built, so much sand had sifted inside the keeper's two-story dwelling that it "buried his kitchen to the eaves," noted B. H. Latrobe during an inspection.

But in 1843, strong winds drove the sand in the opposite direction, away from the foundation of the light. Nathaniel F. Williams, collector for the port and district of Baltimore, during a visit to Cape Henry, reported: "The light tower is now threatened with destruction and requires an extension of its foundation. Strong north and northeasterly gales have hollowed out the sand."

The troubled beginnings of Cape Henry Light hinted at the problems that lighthouses throughout the Chesapeake region would face in the coming years. In particular, the shifting, sandy terrain at Cape Henry was a foreboding sign. Of the approximately 106 lighthouses built on 80 sites over the next 125 years, at least 13 would fall victim to erosion and shifting silt, and almost every other lighthouse built on land—and even some built in the water—would be threatened by the abrading sea. The soft terrain would also make it difficult to construct lighthouses around the Chesapeake. In fact, mud would be a continuous problem until a new invention, the screw pile, was introduced in the United States in the mid-nineteenth century.

Once lighthouse construction began over water in the 1850s, however, a new type of weather problem threatened keepers: ice. When the Chesapeake Bay and its rivers began to thaw after severely cold winters, the running ice knocked down everything in its path, including

digging them out and moving more stone would have to begin. This time, however, it would be overseen by a new, zealous nation. President George Washington, whose birthplace was on the Potomac River, would take a personal interest in the project.

The top of the dune was leveled, and a fortresslike bulkhead of rough stone—some three feet thick and three feet high—with foundations sunk below the surface, was built around the side of the dune. The tower was built of sandstone blocks held together with mortar.

It had taken seventy years, but Cape Henry Light, completed in 1792, was the first lighthouse on the Chesapeake, and the first to be built by the new federal government following the Revolutionary War. This tower was more than an aid to navigation; it was a work of art. Its beautiful octagonal shape, tapering from a wide base as it rises ninety feet in the air, is crowned by a copper dome that protects the lantern room. Sitting atop the highest sand dune, it was easily spotted in the daytime by mariners beyond the capes.

lighthouses perched on iron pilings. Of the forty-two pile and screw-pile lighthouses built in the Chesapeake and its tributaries, at least eleven were destroyed by ice, and almost every other one was damaged to some degree.

Finally, flat terrain encountered at Cape Henry, so typical of almost all the lands surrounding the Chesapeake Bay, would pose continuous problems for lighthouse builders. Lights need height to be seen a distance, and many early lighthouses built on the Bay were simply not tall enough to be of much aid to the mariner. Some were abandoned because they were too short and virtually useless.

Nevertheless, construction of Cape Henry Light put the Chesapeake Bay in the lighthouse business. In the following decade, three lighthouses were built in three years, between 1802 and 1804, at other locations in Virginia—Old Point Comfort at Hampton Roads, Smith Point at the entrance to the Potomac River, and New Point Comfort on the peninsula between the Chesapeake Bay and Mobjack Bay.

Even in these first few years, erosion, combined with violent hurricanes, proved to be the biggest enemy of Chesapeake lighthouses. Smith Point Light had been standing only three years when on August 10, 1805, keeper William Nelms wrote to his authorities that the lighthouse was in danger of being undermined by the sea. The bank on which it stood was caving in because of erosion. By July 1806, the government had built a seawall around the tower, but within two months, a hurricane damaged the wall. On January 4, 1807, the new keeper, Elsey Borroughs, reported that the lighthouse was unsafe. Finally convinced, in May 1807 the government began taking proposals for the rebuilding of Smith Point Light farther from the abrading sea. A year later, another hurricane swept through the area, further damaging the seawall and threatening the tower.

Five years after it was first lighted, the second Smith Point Lighthouse was in operation. But in only twenty years, the sea would encroach again, requiring construction of a third lighthouse, built ninety yards inland in 1828. Still, it was not far

enough inland for the fast-eroding banks of Smith Point. In 1848, a report called attention to the washing away of the base. By 1853, the annual report of the Lighthouse Board pleaded for yet a fourth light at Smith Point, this time, one built in the new screw-pile style. The fourth Smith Point Light was completed in 1868.

Such rapid erosion was not at all uncommon on the Chesapeake. In the relatively short period of lighthouse history on the Bay—just two hundred years—giant islands have disappeared completely. Many of them were important enough to be marked by lighthouses, including Sharps Island, where farms and communities once existed.

During the 150 years or so that lighthouses were manned on the Chesapeake Bay, life went on inside these dwellings just as it did everywhere else. They were the scenes of birth and death, and at least one honeymoon. They housed children, a dozen at one lighthouse! Their keepers performed dramatic rescues and were, in turn, rescued themselves. Illness and loneliness touched the lives of the men and women who kept the lights, but there were also many moments of happiness shared inside these unique homes, as families enjoyed the company of each other and the peace of living on the water.

Over the years, technology made the manned lighthouse obsolete. The last one, Thomas Point Shoal, was finally automated in 1986. Many lighthouses succumbed to the elements, but even more were torn down to save the cost of repairing the obsolete dwellings. Today, only thirty-four lighthouses remain on the Chesapeake, a far cry from the sixty-eight that had illuminated the Bay's horizon at the height of manned lighthouses at the turn of the twentieth century.

Changing topography, changing technology, and changing lifestyles on the Bay eventually sounded the death knell for the manned lighthouse. But for more than one hundred years, powerful beams winked on almost every major shoal, making this vast estuary the most lighted body of water in America . . . if only for a brief moment in history.

Turkey Point Lighthouse,
built by John Donohoo.

Chapter One

Good Builder, Bad Light

Something should be left to the knowledge and judgment of the navigator, or otherwise every shoal, river, and creek must be lighted, an expense too enormous to be tolerated.

Alexander Claxton, a member of the Honorable Board of Navy Commissioners, criticizing requests for a lighthouse at York Spit in 1838.

*I*n 1812, as the government of the United States negotiated a deal that should have vastly improved the country's lighthouse system, Great Britain's mighty navy slipped out of port with the intention of bringing the feisty rebel colonists back under British control. As it turned out, war proved a lot easier to resolve than the troubles that would plague the government in the decades after it purchased Winslow Lewis's patent for a new lighting system.

The immediate problem, though, was the British, whose first act after sailing into the Chesapeake Bay was to commandeer one of the very few lighthouses in existence there.

British commander Adm. George Cockburn, aboard *Marlborough*, led a British fleet of five ships of seventy-four guns and ten frigates. The fleet fired on Hampton, Virginia, and damaged much of the city in March 1813. After taking over the city, Cockburn ordered two companies of soldiers to encamp at Old Point Comfort. He then commandeered the lighthouse, which served as his watchtower for the remainder of the war.

After his success at Hampton, Admiral Cockburn headed north, bombarding and burning towns along the way. By May, his fleet had reached the head of the Bay and on May 3, 1813, they attacked the small town of Havre de Grace on the

Susquehanna River. At this time, there were no lighthouses anywhere in Maryland waters. When Concord Light was finally built fourteen years later, however, the man who distinguished himself by defending the town single-handedly in the battle with Cockburn's fleet of ships would be remembered and rewarded with the post of lighthouse keeper.

Later nicknamed the "fighting Irishman," John O'Neill was a simple nail maker in Havre de Grace. During the War of 1812, he also held the position of lieutenant in command of a company of Harford County militiamen. It would prove to be no easy task to hold his men at their posts. When nineteen British barges began a fifteen-minute bombardment of the town, the militiamen fled for their lives...all, that is, except O'Neill. As the British overran the town, looting and torching buildings, Lt. John O'Neill, standing alone at his post, manned the town's pitifully small "Potato Battery," so-called because of the size of the shot hurled by its two six-pound and one nine-pound cannons.

O'Neill loaded, primed, and fired the cannons by himself in the face of flying cannonballs until one of his own cannons recoiled and injured his thigh. Then he limped away, using a musket for a crutch, stopping occasionally to fire the musket at the pursuing British. He fired one last time, wounding a British officer, before being taken prisoner. O'Neill was forced to board the British flagship *Maidstone,* where he was told he would be shot at dawn.

On learning of her father's fate, O'Neill's sixteen-year-old daughter, Matilda, rowed out to the flagship and pleaded with the admiral to spare her father's life. Cockburn was reportedly so impressed by the young girl's courage that he released O'Neill.

In 1827, when the thirty-nine-foot granite stone lighthouse was completed at Concord Point in Havre de Grace, O'Neill assumed the post of lighthouse keeper, which he kept until his death in 1838. The post stayed in the family throughout the history of the light, which became one of the earliest automated lighthouses on the Chesapeake Bay in 1920.

Prior to the War of 1812, lighthouses numbered just forty-nine in the United States, only four of which were located on the Chesapeake Bay. The lights that shone from these early towers were very poor, for they were furnished with only a common spider lamp and had no lens or reflectors to magnify the beam.

In 1812 a significant improvement was made in the lighting apparatus when the U.S. secretary of the treasury entered into a contract with Winslow Lewis of Boston for his "patent-right to the plan of lighting lighthouses by reflecting and magnifying lanterns." For the sum of twenty thousand dollars, Lewis agreed to outfit all the existing lighthouses in the United States with his new lighting apparatus, as well as those that would be built in the next two years. The lighting system was the catoptric system, consisting of an Argand wick lamp, or series of lamps, fitted with parabolic reflectors.

Unfortunately, Lewis, an unemployed ship captain with no engineering background, had not really designed the lighting system. He had simply "borrowed" the lamp and parabolic reflector design of Jean Robert Argand of Switzerland, then sold it as his own patent. Historians not only portray Lewis as a patent thief, but also lambast his reflectors as very poor copies of the real thing. One critic described them as being "as close to a parabola as a barber's basin."

Nevertheless, the catoptric system of using reflectors to increase candlelight power was a vast improvement over the simple lamp that had been in service. However, in a few brief years, Lewis's growing influence over the man who ran the lighthouse system in the United States would serve to hold the country back from embracing and using significant advances in lighthouse lighting apparatus.

During the early years, the job of overseeing construction of lighthouses in the young nation was shifted from one person to another. In 1820, the job was finally put under the authority of the fifth auditor within the Treasury Department. Historians see this move as the worst in the history of U.S. lighthouses, for it put engineering decisions in the hands of a mere accountant. Specifically, it fell on the shoulders of a man named Stephen Pleasonton, who knew nothing about lighthouses.

Pleasonton reigned over lighthouse matters for the next thirty-two years, a period when many new innovations advanced lighthouse technology around the world. Unfortunately, Pleasonton refused to embrace the new technology, which included the invention of a fantastic lens by a Frenchman named Augustin Jean Fresnel (pronounced Fray-nell) in 1822 that literally revolutionized navigational aids in Europe. The Fresnel lens consisted of a series of simple concentric lenses that allowed great magnification of a light source.

A man of extremely limited vision, Pleasonton is also blamed for authorizing many poorly built, inadequate lighthouses. To save money, the fifth auditor cut corners on important points such as the height of a tower, the materials, and, most importantly, the lighting apparatus.

Lewis's optical system was in use when Pleasonton took over lighthouse matters, and Pleasonton continued to rely on these optics, even though the Fresnel lens was invented two years into his tenure. According to Lewis's original contract, he was supposed to fit his own optics into all the U.S. lighthouses built within two years of the contract. As it turned out, he continued to fit the country's lighthouses with his optics for almost forty years.

Their low installation cost may have influenced Pleasonton's decision, but he was truly penny-wise and pound-foolish. While the initial cost of a Fresnel lens was greater than a reflector system, in the long run it was considerably less expensive to operate. Most reflector systems required many lamps—as many as twenty-four for a seacoast light, and eight to sixteen for Chesapeake Bay lights—and each lamp required fuel to burn. By comparison, a Fresnel lens required only a single lamp. Thus, it saved considerably on fuel, as well as wick material and lamp replacements.

By the 1820s, commerce was on the increase, and so was lighthouse construction on the Bay. The number of lighthouses in the United States had expanded to seventy before Maryland got its first tower under way in 1822. The thirty-five-foot lighthouse was built on Bodkin Island, a tiny island off Gibson Island that has since eroded into the Bay. The Bodkin Light was to help guide mariners into the Patapsco River to Baltimore.

Two men named Evans and Coppuck won the bid to construct Bodkin Island Light. They proved to be incompetent, however, and were fired from the job after building just the foundation. Capt. Willis B. Barney of the Fifth U.S. Naval District was overseeing the project, and when the original contractors failed to do the work, he looked around for someone dependable to complete the important task. He naturally thought of John Donohoo of Havre de Grace.

Donohoo was already a well-known man in the big town on the Susquehanna River. He served on the town council, overseeing such matters as the construction of roads, and was an important businessman, running a tavern, a commercial warehouse, and a fishing fleet. He was also a major landowner in town; in fact, he was a speculator in land—an early developer—in the business of buying and selling lots. Almost certainly he also built the big houses that went up on the lots, which would have given him a reputation as a builder. Obviously, he had never built a lighthouse; nobody had in his day. But when Captain Barney approached Donohoo, he agreed to finish Bodkin Island Lighthouse. He did so in 1823. The lighthouse was always plagued with a poor foundation, thanks to its original contractors, but it put Donohoo on the path to becoming the most important builder of lighthouses on the Chesapeake Bay.

The rough stone walls, still held together by the original mortar, of Pooles Island Lighthouse, built by John Donohoo in 1825.

Bodkin Island Lighthouse was the first new lighthouse site since the three Virginia towers were built in the first few years of the nineteenth century. Bodkin Island, along with North Point Range, completed the following year on the northern side of the Patapsco River, ushered in a new age for lighthouse construction on the Chesapeake Bay. In the ensuing two decades, seventeen new lighthouses would be built around the Bay (and, of course, Smith Island Light would be rebuilt for the third time as lighthouse officials tried to stay ahead of the high-water line). The vast majority of them were Donohoo's work.

For the most part, Donohoo built his northern conical towers out of Port Deposit granite, which was barged down the Susquehanna River. Farther south, he used bricks for his construction. The walls were tapered as they rose in order to give the tower stability. The higher the tower, the wider the base had to be.

Early lighthouse builders did not possess the knowledge to build towers over ninety feet, the height of Cape Henry. Inside the mouth of the Chesapeake, and particularly north of the Potomac River, where the Bay begins to narrow, there was little need for lighthouses even this tall. Consequently, all the early towers built in Maryland were rather short, somewhere between thirty-four and fifty feet.

Donohoo built at least thirteen lighthouses, including Bodkin Island, completing almost one a year over the next decade. His second project was the first Thomas Point Lighthouse, which was a tower built on a bank in 1825. Unfortunately, the bank eroded rapidly and in thirteen years, Donohoo's solid tower was dismantled and rebuilt far-

The Fresnel lens, shown here in Concord Point Lighthouse, was patented in France in 1824, but the United States did not adopt this advanced lens until the 1850s, when a scandalous report on the conditions of the nation's lighthouses resulted in the creation of the U.S. Lighthouse Board and the removal of Stephen Pleasonton as overseer of lighthouses.

From 1836 to 1851, only two new lighthouses were built on the Chesapeake Bay. Donohoo was summoned back to lighthouse construction in 1851 to build Blakistone Island Light. In 1853, he completed Fishing Battery Island Lighthouse. He died a year later.

Most of Donohoo's structures were similar in style: small stone or brick towers that rose about thirty-five to forty-five feet and had detached dwellings built of similar material. Several, however, were houses with lanterns mounted on top. Point Lookout was supposed to be a tower when first proposed, but because of cost overruns in purchasing the land, it was built as a house with the lantern on top. Blakistone also had its tower atop a two-story brick house.

Many of Donohoo's lighthouses are still standing, including Turkey Point, Concord Point, Cove Point, Piney Point, Pooles Island, Point Lookout, and Fishing Battery Island Light. Their survival is testimony to his good work. Annual reports conducted over the years often praised the good construction of his lighthouses. However, there is evidence that at least one of his towers may have been a flop. A congressional inquiry in 1838 described the Fog Point tower on Smith Island as in deplorable condition just ten years after construction. "This tower [is] built of bad materials; the cement has already been affected by the atmosphere, and [the tower] is crooked in many places." In defense of Donohoo, however, Fog Point was a remote, marshy island. His tower may well have been affected by soft ground settling beneath it, encroaching tides that notoriously wash across Smith Island, and salt spray, which damaged the mortar in many early lighthouses.

With Donohoo as its primary builder of lighthouses, the Chesapeake region suffered less from the effects of poorly constructed lighthouses than most areas of the country under the reign of the fifth auditor. Beyond Pleasonton's poor decisions involving the lighting apparatus of the lighthouses, he made bad decisions about their construction. To save money, he often chose to build towers that were too short or simply in the wrong place. The first lighthouse at Cape Charles, a brick tower built in 1828, was considered too short. Greenbury Point, a house with an eight-sided

ther from the encroaching sea. The same year he completed Thomas Point Light, Donohoo built Pooles Island Lighthouse, another stone conical tower rising forty feet. This lighthouse, on an island above the Patapsco River, separated the Chesapeake Bay into two shipping channels: a shallow channel to the west of the island, where the lighthouse stood, and a deeper channel to the east.

Captain Barney came to depend on Donohoo and awarded him the contract to build Concord Point Light in his hometown of Havre de Grace. Donohoo completed the project in 1827. Other lighthouses that Donohoo built over the next ten years included Fog Point on lonely Smith Island, Maryland, in 1827; Cove Point near Calvert Cliffs, in 1828, which is still lighted and used as a navigational aid; Point Lookout at the mouth of the Potomac River, in 1830; Lazaretto Point in Baltimore, in 1831; Watts Island on the Eastern Shore, in 1833; Turkey Point at the head of the Chesapeake, in 1833; and Piney Point on the Potomac River, in 1836.

tower on the roof, was also of little use to mariners shortly after it was built in 1849.

For at least three Chesapeake lighthouses, Winslow Lewis not only supplied the optics, but also built the structure. The second Smith Point tower, the second Thomas Point Light, and the Back River tower, north of Old Point Comfort in Virginia, were all examples of his inferior handiwork. Years later, all three towers received scathing remarks about their poor construction in the annual reports of the U.S. Lighthouse Board. The 1853 annual report stated that the Smith Point tower, made of sandstone, "is badly cracked; the iron frame which supports the lamps is so weak that no great effort would be required to shake it down." The light was discontinued in 1859, only thirty years after construction.

Not surprisingly, all three lighthouses have since disappeared. Lewis evidently was no better a lighthouse builder than he was an optics designer.

One innovation that Pleasonton did embrace, however, was the light-vessel, or lightship. In 1820, the first permanent lightship in the United States was put into service at Craney Island in Hampton Roads, at the mouth of the Elizabeth River. Within a year, three more lightships were anchored in the Chesapeake: at Willoughbys Spit at the southern approach to Hampton Roads; on Wolf Trap Shoals off the western shore of Virginia; and at Upper Cedar Point on the Potomac River, some forty-four miles below Mount Vernon.

The fact that the Chesapeake Bay was the first location in the country where lightships were employed points to the unique problem of lighting this shallow estuary. Primarily a drowned river, the Chesapeake has a relatively narrow deepwater channel that in some places reaches well over one hundred feet. The vast majority of the Bay, however, is twenty feet or less in depth, and many shoals less than eight feet deep protrude a mile or more from land. Add to this problem the flatness and marshiness of the land surrounding the Bay, and it is easy to see that engineers had difficulty providing adequate navigational aids in the Bay from the shores.

Lightships appeared to be the perfect answer. A vessel could be anchored at the tip of a dangerous shoal, removing the guesswork for captains navigating in the waters. A lantern was hoisted up the mast, or sometimes two lanterns were hoisted up separate masts. The vessel was often painted in such a way to distinguish it from vessels under sail. At first, ordinary sailboats, such as schooners, were used as light-vessels, but eventually the government developed a unique ship whose characteristic high profile allowed it to ride rough seas more easily and be seen at a distance by passing vessels.

Lightships were expensive to maintain, however, since they required a full crew to handle the vessel in case it should break away from its mooring in a storm. Consequently, lighthouses, which could be manned with one or two keepers, were still the preferred method of lighting navigated waters.

Despite Pleasonton's many mistakes, lighthouse construction thrived under his tenure. By 1838, there were 204 lighthouses and 28 lightships in the country, including 19 lighthouses and 8 lightships on the Chesapeake. Pleasonton was beginning to attract outspoken critics, however, and the first of several scathing reports on the country lighthouse system was issued in 1838.

That year, Lt. George M. Bache of the U.S. Navy wrote to the Honorable Levi Woodbury, secretary of the treasury, to complain about the lighthouse system under Pleasonton: "Lighthouses have been . . . placed in situations where the service rendered by them has not warranted the expense of their construction and maintenance; . . . the comparatively safe shore of populous districts are seen in many instances studded with lights, while on the unsettled though much frequented and dangerous portions of our sea coast they are of much rarer occurrence."

Alexander Claxton, a member of the Honorable Board of Navy Commissioners, also criticized Pleasonton. In writing against a proposed lighthouse at York Spit at the mouth of the York River, he noted, "It will be seen that this part of the bay is almost in a blaze of light establishments. Something should be left to the knowledge and judgment of the navigator, or otherwise every shoal, river, and creek must be lighted, an expense too enormous to be tolerated." (Claxton's predictions, of course, eventually came true, as boaters today

A full moon rises over the Chesapeake, as Cove Point Lighthouse flashes its warning light twelve miles out across the Bay. One of the many lighthouses built by John Donohoo, it is as sturdy today as it was when constructed in 1828.

find lighted buoys on every creek and every bend in the river. However, at the time, the "blaze" he refers to consisted of New Point Comfort Light marking Mobjack Bay, Wolf Trap Light-Vessel, and Back River Light.)

For some reason, Congress chose to ignore or overlook the inadequacies in the lighthouse system outlined in the 1838 report. Whether it was because of the criticism or for other reasons, however, lighthouse construction almost disappeared on the Chesapeake after the report was filed. Only two lighthouses were built on the Chesapeake between 1839 and 1851, the year that marked the end of Pleasonton's reign over lighthouse matters.

In 1851, as Congress initiated another probe into lighthouse issues, there were still only twenty-one lighthouses and nine lightships serving the entire two-hundred-mile length of the Chesapeake Bay. Their numbers would grow dramatically over the next half century as a new, better-educated body of men took control of lighthouses. In less than a half dozen years, the U.S. Lighthouse Board, by embracing many innovations that Pleasonton had refused to accept, would greatly improve and expand navigational aids on the Chesapeake and elsewhere. Unfortunately, this giant step forward would come at a high price in human suffering.

Chapter Two

Steering a New Course

The number of marine disasters which are annually reported is truly frightful.

The Lighthouse Board, 1868, urging construction of more lighthouses.

As the inspector steamed up the Chesapeake on a warm night in June 1851, what he couldn't see disturbed him.

"We passed Sharp's Island light within about three to four miles. It was not visible through the lightest green glass.... Smith's Island [Fog Point off the Eastern Shore] was not seen. Smith's Point Lighthouse was exceedingly dim. Cove Point also was dim, though better than Smith's Point," he wrote in his report in 1852.

It had taken a congressional inquiry to bring about this official trip up the Chesapeake, which was part of a far-reaching study of every significant lighthouse in the country. After decades of complaints about the fifth auditor's spending habits, elected officials were finally listening. . . and looking.

Now, what the inspector could not see in the dark confirmed what he had seen by daylight. Chesapeake lighthouses, like many other lighthouses around the country, were in deplorable shape. In some cases, the lucky cases, the light was simply too weak, a problem that could easily be remedied by upgrading the lighting apparatus. But many lighthouses had far more serious problems. Many were built on eroding banks and were threatened by encroaching seas. Others were too short to cast their beams far enough out into the Bay to be of much benefit to mariners. A few lighthouses were simply badly built and falling apart just a few short decades after having been lighted. There were even lighthouses built in entirely the wrong place to aid maritime traffic.

In 1851 Congress had chosen a group of qualified men to gather facts and make reports on the condition of the country's lighthouses. Their job was to go from lighthouse to lighthouse in their specific region, checking on the conditions of the structures, hearing comments and complaints from the keepers, and gathering facts for their reports. What inspectors wrote was not a pretty picture of the condition of Chesapeake beacons.

The hollow walls of Back River Light were full of bats; the tower itself was threatened by the encroaching sea. At Old Point Comfort, the driving rain beat in. At Bodkin Island, a blacksmith was in charge of the light and kept it so dirty, he might as well have been in the midst of his old blacksmith shop.

"The burners were so full of carbonized wick and dirty oil, that it would not be possible to produce a reasonably good combustion; the chimney was very much smoked, showing clearly that the light is not perfectly kept," wrote one inspector, who also noted that the keeper's little children rushed to clean up the mess when they realized who he was.

The inspector noted that one of the two rubble stone towers that composed the North Point Range Lights leading into the Patapsco River was "badly built; the stucco bad." The foundation of the tower also required immediate repair.

Concord Point Lighthouse was one of many that were finally equipped with a Fresnel lens in the mid-1850s, after the U.S. Lighthouse Board took over the job of overseeing improvements to the country's lighthouse system.

Smith Point Lighthouse was virtually useless: "The tower is too low," the report stated, and the light itself "exceedingly dim." The Craney Island light-boat, a seventy-two-ton schooner and the first vessel ever put to such service, was "in bad order," with too small a lantern and a "miserable lamp."

When the *Report of the Officers Constituting the Light-House Board* was published in 1852, it was a scathing, detailed analysis of Stephen Pleasonton's thirty-two-year reign. The report concluded that America's lighthouse system was more expensive and far less adequate than that of Great Britain or other European countries.

"The cost of American lights of the same minimal class is but little less than that of Great Britain, while the quality is quite inferior. In fact, if all matters relating to maintenance were fairly compared, the American lights would prove the most expensive," an early report on the Fresnel lens concluded. "A defective organization leads to a waste in construction, in supplies, and in illumination. The system of inspection and superintendence is insufficient; the illumination apparatus nearly obsolete; the seacoast lights defective in range and power, without proper distinctions and without regulation."

In the wake of these revelations, Congress established a permanent Lighthouse Board, composed of nine knowledgeable members, some of whom had prepared the 1852 report. The board was committed to making the lighthouse system in the United States the best in the world. To this end, it wasted no time reorganizing the entire lighthouse system in the country. The board created lighthouse districts, each supervised by an inspector who saw to it that the lighthouses were kept in top working condition, that keepers did their jobs, that supplies, particularly fuel, were of top quality, and that problems were addressed immediately. The inspectors also kept the board abreast of storm damage, erosion, and sea encroachment so that it could make long-range plans for building new structures to replace lighthouses endangered by the sea. The board funneled money into structural repairs and upgrading of the lighting apparatus. By the close of 1857, every lighthouse in the Fifth District, which encompassed the Chesapeake Bay

and North Carolina, had a new lighting system. In most cases, a Fresnel lens of the fourth or fifth order replaced Lewis's old reflecting apparatus with its eight to sixteen lamps. The new lenses, which were sized from the largest, a first order, to the smallest, a sixth order, used only one lamp. Consequently, they would save on fuel, as well as time spent by the lighthouse keepers, who were often dubbed "wickies" because of the trimming required of the many wicks in the old lighting system.

It had taken more than thirty years for the United States to adopt the Fresnel lens, but at the close of the 1850s, the Chesapeake Bay finally had a first-rate lighthouse system in place. The Lighthouse Board saw its lighthouse system as the first measure by which foreigners judged the United States, and rightly so.

"Nothing indicates the liberality, prosperity or intelligence of a nation more clearly than the facilities which it affords for the safe approach of the mariner to its shores," the board wrote in one of its early reports.

Along with aggressive improvements at existing lighthouses, the new board also immediately initiated an aggressive construction program on the Chesapeake. Increased import and export shipping, increased fishing and harvesting of shellfish, and the invention of the steamboat all contributed to the rapidly expanding maritime travel on the Bay. The board, fortunately, was not as narrow-minded as naval officer Alexander Claxton when he suggested in 1938 that "something should be left to the knowledge and judgment of the navigator."

The board would become increasingly concerned with the safety of passengers, as steamboat lines developed a healthy business operating daily routes between major towns and cities on the Chesapeake. Loss of goods due to maritime accidents was also of increasing concern. "The number of marine disasters which are annually reported is truly frightful," the board wrote in one of its reports. "The introduction and improvement of [lighthouses] are every year becoming more and more important, since the number of lives and the amount of property exposed to the dangers of the sea are increasing with time. . . ."

In 1850, there were only twenty-one lighthouses and nine lightships serving the entire two-hundred-mile length of the Chesapeake. Improving lighting on the Bay was an immediate concern for the board, which by 1854 had new construction under way at numerous locations. In seven years, the board built another thirteen lighthouses on the Chesapeake. This time, however, construction was not limited to land; the board had embraced a new concept of building lighthouses over water.

Between 1791 and 1852, all of the Chesapeake's lighthouses had been built on land. In other regions of the country, workers constructed lighthouses on shoals, closer to deep-water channels, by building up the shoal with rock. But the Chesapeake's soft, muddy, constantly shifting bottom was much too soft to support such structures. Stones simply disappeared into the mud and sand, or washed away in the tide.

In 1850, however, a new technique for building lighthouses on soft bottom was introduced to

Screw piles, like this one on display at the Chesapeake Bay Maritime Museum in St. Michaels, were commonly used to hold lighthouses snugly in the muddy bottom of the Chesapeake.

the United States. It would revolutionize lighthouse construction on the Chesapeake more than on any other body of water in America. The new technology was the screw pile, a simple, yet ingenious device that employed a huge screw, eighteen inches or more in diameter, on the end of a pole. The screw pile was literally screwed into the river or bay bottom by workers using a huge lever.

The device was invented by a blind engineer, Alexander Mitchell, who first used it as a mooring for ships at anchor. Mitchell described his invention as "a bar of iron having at its lower extremity a broad plate or a disk of metal in a spiral. . . on the principle of a screw, in order that it should enter into the ground with facility, thrusting aside any obstacles to its descent, without materially disturbing the texture of the strata it passed through, and that it should at the same time offer an extended base, either for resisting downward pressure or an upward strain."

For the first time, a lighthouse could be constructed out in the waters of the Chesapeake, close to channels. Such a light promised to give shipping considerably better guidance around the many shoals lying far, sometimes miles, beyond land.

The pile and screw-pile lighthouses, often referred to as cottage lighthouses, were distinctive and beautiful. Built atop wrought-iron foundations, most of these cottages were wooden houses with ornate woodwork, topped with a many-sided, all-glass lantern room perched forty feet or more above the water. A few, such as Tue Marshes Light on the York River, were simple square or rectangular houses, but most were hexagonal, perhaps to give the keepers a better view of maritime traffic approaching from all directions.

The most distinctive screw-pile lighthouse was undoubtedly Sevenfoot Knoll, built in 1855. Located in the Chesapeake on the southern approach to the Patapsco River, it was the first screw pile built in Maryland waters, and it replaced the deteriorating Bodkin Island Light. Sevenfoot Knoll was distinctive not only because it was round, but also because it was the only screw-pile lighthouse built of cast iron. Baltimore's emergence as a major center of cast-iron building may have influenced the Lighthouse Board's decision to build Sevenfoot Knoll out of cast iron, instead of wood.

A new innovation adopted by the U.S. Lighthouse Board in 1855 was the revolving lens. A system of pulleys and cables pivoted the heavy lens on a platform in order to create the first blinking lights. This one in Cove Point Lighthouse is no longer used to create the characteristic blink of the light, since lights can now be programmed.

Before work began on the water stations, engineers for the Fifth District made borings in order to examine the substrata and determine if the screw piles would penetrate the earth. Screw piles were designed to work in soft ground and were literally screwed in by four or more strong men, using a lever and their own muscle to turn the giant screw. It generally took a day to turn each screw pile six or more feet into the substrata. Most of the lighthouses stood on six or more screw piles.

The work did not always go smoothly. When building the first Thimble Shoal Light off Hampton Roads, Virginia, in the Chesapeake in 1872, workers had a difficult time turning the screws in the fine, compacted sand bottom. One of the screws and a cast-iron column broke, slowing the process.

At Lamberts Point in Hampton Roads, the problems were even more troublesome. After completing the lighthouse, workers had to return because the house settled fourteen inches out of alignment. They solved the problem by simply lowering the remaining screw piles, but Lamberts Point would prove over the years to be a tough house to keep level.

While constructing Greenbury Point Shoal Lighthouse in 1891, engineers placed huge iron disks around each screw pile. The disks lay on the bottom and helped distribute the weight of the house on very soft bottoms. It evidently worked, since no lighthouses that used the disks ever settled unevenly on the Chesapeake.

Most of the Chesapeake Bay's bottom accommodated the big screws. In a few cases, however, the substrata was too hard to allow the screws to penetrate the earth or too soft to hold the weight of the house. Engineers came up with variations on the screw pile as they encountered these problems.

One such variation was the "sleeve-pile" system. Long wooden piles were driven into the substrata. Then hollow, cast-iron sleeves were dropped over them to encase the wood. Such was the method used at Pages Rock Light on the York River in 1893. Borings showed that the foundation piles had to be driven very deep, some twenty feet beneath the ground, to reach sufficiently hard earth to support the house. This was too deep to turn a giant screw pile.

In some cases, hollow cast-iron piles were driven in with air pressure, using steam engines. The Bay's first water-station, Pungoteague Creek Light, used this method. This lighthouse has often been referred to as a screw pile, but the Lighthouse Board's annual report suggests that the foundation used no screws at all. The piles had rounded, conical bases, and were pneumatically driven into the earth. Such a procedure would not have worked with screws, which had to be turned.

Located in the lower Bay, Pungoteague Creek was one of few viable harbors on the Eastern Shore of Virginia. Consequently, it was a thriving commercial port, whose entrance through a long shoal was undoubtedly as tricky to maneuver 150 years ago as it is today. The station was completed and lighted with a fifth-order Fresnel lens on November 1, 1854. Soon afterward, the keeper was reprimanded for burning too hot a fire and endangering the safety of the lighthouse.

The construction of three more screw piles quickly followed. Deep Water Shoal, Point of Shoals, and White Shoals, all on the James River, were little screw piles that did not even warrant Fresnel lenses. They were illuminated with large, pressed-glass masthead lenses suspended in the lantern room of each house. The lighthouses were all lighted for the first time on February 6, 1855, improving navigation on the river.

Most cottage lighthouses were painted white with bright red or orange tin roofs. The dwellings were kept gleaming and immaculate by keepers who had little else to do but fish, cook, light the lamps, trim the wicks, polish the brass, and clean, clean, clean.

The screw piles were not only cheap to build and operate, but were also quick to construct. The first several superstructures were contracted out to independent builders, just as the wrought-iron foundations were. In 1863, the first lighthouse depot (a work and storage site for the Lighthouse Board) was established on the Chesapeake Bay on the grounds of Lazaretto Light in Baltimore. Most of the wooden cottages were built at the depot in wall sections, then transported by boat to the site, where they were quickly assembled. The Chesapeake's pile lighthouses may well have been among the first prefabricated houses in the country.

Many screw-pile and pile lighthouses were completed within a month after the schooners and, in later years, steamboats left port with the materials. Unfortunately, these houses sometimes came down as quickly as they went up. In fact, within two years after constructing the first pile lighthouses on the Bay, the Lighthouse Board learned just how destructive moving ice could be to these water stations.

On February 2, 1856, Pungoteague Creek Light was overturned by a large mass of floating ice. The keepers escaped unharmed, and the lantern, lens, and many fixtures and supplies were recovered from the wreck. The same year, the screw-pile lighthouse at Deep Water Shoal in the James River also suffered severe damage from ice floes, and in 1857 an entirely new superstructure had to be built. The other two screw-pile lighthouses on the James—White Shoals and Point of Shoal, both just north of Deep Water Shoal—also

Fishermen troll off Thomas Point Shoal Lighthouse.

suffered damage from ice in 1857. They were not nearly as badly damaged, however, and repairs were quickly made to put the lighthouses back in order. On January 20, 1867, Deep Water Shoal was again so severely damaged that the Lighthouse Board rebuilt it. In 1867 ice damaged the other two lighthouses on the James River, requiring both of them to be completely rebuilt in 1869.

Pungoteague Creek Light was in service only 459 days—the shortest period for any light on the Chesapeake—before ice knocked it down. Deep Water Shoal lasted a little longer, just seventeen days shy of two years, but by the time these houses were destroyed by ice, the Lighthouse Board had already committed itself to the concept of the screw pile. Four new pile houses were already standing; three more were in the works. With a little bit of ingenuity, the houses could stand up in the face of the worst ice floes, reckoned officials, who already had in mind wrought-iron icebreakers, stone riprap, and better construction techniques. Consequently, despite the bad omen of the shortlived screw-pile houses, lighthouses were built on piles at forty-two sites in the Chesapeake over the next forty years.

What started out in the 1850s as inexpensive lighthouses, costing about five thousand dollars to build, quickly escalated into much more expensive structures, as engineers realized that they had to build stronger, more ice-resistant substructures and stronger superstructures. Most of the screw piles were reinforced with rocks as icebreakers around their base, at five thousand dollars per shot, though one load was never enough. Most lighthouses needed additional rocks, sometimes every year, depending on the severity of the winter. The stones often disappeared, washed away with the tide, or sank into the mud.

Despite man's effort, severe winters continued to take their toll on these water stations. Thirteen pile lighthouses were destroyed by ice over the next eighty years, while many more suffered significant damage. In the war with nature, Chesapeake lighthouse officials always found themselves on the run, trying to stay ahead of the damage inflicted by this invincible enemy. In the end, nature would win, for with every year of heavy ice, there were repairs to be made, new superstructures to be built, new stones to be laid, until, finally, men tired of the fight and gave up.

Old Point Comfort was taken over by the British during the War of 1812 and used as their lookout post, but by the time of the Civil War, the country had built Fort Monroe around the lighthouse— one of few that were not put out of service by the Confederates.

Chapter Three

War against the Lighthouses

*The extinguishment of lights from lighthouses, removal of light vessels, and the destruc-
tion or removal of all the other aids to navigation existing from the northern boundary of
Virginia to the Rio Grande...continued until about April 24,
when the whole was accomplished.*

The Lighthouse Board, writing about the destruction of lighthouse property
by Confederates at the start of the Civil War.

K eeper Jerome McWilliams could not have
asked for a better assignment than to hold
the post of lighthouse keeper at Blakistone Island,
Maryland. Built in 1851 by an aging John Donohoo, it was a sturdy, picturesque, two-story brick
home, large enough to accommodate his growing
family. Unlike many keepers who had to trudge
out into the weather, McWilliams never had to
leave the comfort of his home to tend the light, for
the tower sat atop the dwelling. He could brag of
having the best view in St. Marys County, for from
his tower, McWilliams could look out over the
cultivated fields of the hundred-acre island and see
the mouths of St. Clements and Breton Bays to the
north. A sweeping glance around the dwelling
presented a panoramic view of the mighty Potomac, plied by paddlewheels and sailing schooners
on excursions to Washington, D.C., and other
ports along the river.

McWilliams and his family had the best of
both worlds, land and sea. The island soil was rich
enough, and the elevation high enough, to produce
plentiful crops, unlike the arid sand- and salt-
whipped land around lighthouses on the coast or
on the marshy lowlands of so many Chesapeake
peninsulas. And beyond their neatly kept yard was
the river, with its bounty of fish, crabs, and oys-

ters—all they could want for the taking. In 1851,
there were few light stations in the Chesapeake
that were as peaceful and beautiful as Blakistone
Island Lighthouse. Its perfect location in protected
water had attracted the area's first permanent
European settlers, who named it St. Clements
Island. Soon, its beauty would draw summer vaca-
tioners from surrounding areas.

But ten years after its construction, Blakistone Island no longer offered comfort and peace
to its keeper and his family. The South had se-
ceded from the Union. War was imminent. And
no one was in a more precarious situation than
the lighthouse keepers, watching over their
often-unprotected posts around the Chesapeake
Bay.

In the very first days of the rebellion, lighthouses became targets of destruction. Even before
the onset of war, Comdr. T. T. Hunter of the U.S.
Navy and lighthouse inspector at Charleston,
South Carolina, found himself caught in the midst
of the division. As he sat down to write a letter to
the Lighthouse Board, he knew that state officials
in South Carolina were already debating leaving
the Union. If they voted in favor of secession, he
was in a bad situation, being one of few top federal
employees living in the state.

Old Point Comfort Light and the keeper's dwelling are still in use today. The lighthouse is a working navigational aid, guiding boats into Hampton Roads, and the dwelling is used by officers of Fort Monroe.

"I will tender my resignation as soon as South Carolina passes her ordinance of secession," he wrote in a letter dated December 18, 1860. Inspector Hunter asked for orders on what to do with the public property in his charge within the limits of the state.

Twelve days later, he got answers to his questions, but not from the Lighthouse Board. On December 30, South Carolina Governor Pickens placed the light at Castle Pinckney in the charge of a state officer. Inspector Hunter, who evidently had dragged his feet at resigning his post, was taken prisoner by Governor Pickens two days later, January 1, 1861, and ordered to stay in port, along with all the lighthouse tenders, for the next thirty hours.

Eventually, the governor released the inspector, but all lighthouse property was seized. By January 8, "seizures had been made by the authority of the governor of South Carolina of all the lighthouse property, consisting of light vessels, lighthouse tenders, buoys, and their equipment and supplies in stores, and excluding the lighthouses at Charleston, Georgetown, Cape Romain,

Bull's Bay, and Hunting Island, in that state. The lights were extinguished without notice to mariners and in many, if not all, cases the Fresnel lenses were destroyed or removed," the Lighthouse Board noted in its report.

The takeover and destruction of lighthouses and supplies was swift and far-reaching, according to the report:

The extinguishment of lights from lighthouses, removal of light vessels, and the destruction or removal of all the other aids to navigation existing from the northern boundary of Virginia to the Rio Grande, excepting those on the Peninsula of Florida, was continued until about April 24, when the whole was accomplished. In a few instances the persons seizing the property claimed to do so by authority, and gave receipts for it; in others, the U.S. agents charged with its custody connived in the seizures, and in some instances the property was burned in mere wantonness.

Immediately upon the advent of war, the Union began a blockade of Southern ports in an attempt to keep the South from receiving supplies from sympathetic European countries. To counter this blockade, the Confederates decided on a simple plan to snuff out as many lighthouses as possible on the Chesapeake Bay, as well as lighthouses all along the Southern seacoast. This would make it more difficult for Union vessels to locate and blockade the ports at night, when Confederates believed they could sneak in and out with the supplies they needed.

Consequently, in the spring of 1861, groups of rebels systematically began an assault on the lighthouses. Marrauding bands of rebels burned light-vessels, smashed lenses, looted lighthouse grounds, and sometimes burned the buildings. The Confederates were aided by many Southern sympathizers on the Eastern Shore and southern Maryland, where the lifestyles of the local farmers were more in tune with Southern ways, including the institution of slavery.

In April 1861, in the first days of the war, the Princess Anne Militia attacked the Cape Henry Lighthouse and destroyed the lens. The sabotage of Cape Henry Lighthouse was followed by attacks farther up the Bay. The Lighthouse Board later reported on this activity:

> Between the 19th and 24th of April, 1861, the two light vessels in the Potomac were wantonly burned, and four in the Chesapeake between the mouth of the Potomac and Hampton Roads were removed and their apparatus carried off or destroyed. Two of these light vessels were subsequently recaptured, but they had been stripped of everything that could be removed.

The light-vessels and lighthouses proved terribly vulnerable to attack. The rebels went up both shores of the Chesapeake and destroyed one light after another. Craney Island Lighthouse was left in ruins. The small beacon at the Naval Hospital in Norfolk was extinguished. York Spit Lightship at the mouth of York River, Virginia, was destroyed, and Wolf Trap, a 180-ton lightship off Wolf Trap Shoals near Gwynns Island, was also attacked. The Confederates set upon New Point Comfort Lighthouse at the northern approach to Mobjack Bay, destroying the lantern, and the light-vessel at Windmill Point, off the mouth of the

The lightship Chesapeake, *stationed off the mouth of the Bay between 1933 and 1965, is now on display at the Inner Harbor in Baltimore.*

War against the Lighthouses   25

Fort Carroll Lighthouse originally sat atop the keeper's dwelling, but the light was moved often over the years as the army made improvements to the fort, situated in the middle of the Patapsco River.

Rappahanock River, was destroyed. The rebels then went upriver and destroyed the lightship at Bowlers Rock. They somehow spared Blakistone Island on this first round of assault, but boarded and burned the light-vessel stationed at Lower Cedar Point, halfway up the Potomac River. They also commandeered Smith Point Lightship and towed it several miles up the Great Wicomico River on Virginia's shore, where it was stripped. Many light-vessels that were never recovered were sunk by the rebels in the Elizabeth River as an obstruction to Union vessels.

On May 17, 1861, the Union retaliated against the onslaught on the lights. They sent one hundred men to retake the Smith Point Lightship and whatever other lightships they could find in rebel hands.

The expedition included two detachments of the New York Eighth Artillery and Captain Thome's company of the New York Thirteenth Regiment. At Annapolis, they boarded the propeller ship *William Woodward*, carrying with them down the Bay two pieces of artillery and three days' rations. They would not need even that much.

The Union soldiers quickly found the abandoned lightship in the Great Wicomico River and boarded the vessel. As the troops were leaving, a Confederate company called the Lancaster Grays fired upon them. None of the Union soldiers was hurt, although bullets were dug out of the wood-

work of the boat. Unable to use their heavy guns aboard the vessel, the New York soldiers fired several volleys into the bushes along the river, where they could see the rebels hiding, dodging from bush to bush before they finally fled. On May 20, the Union soldiers returned safely, without losing a man.

The following spring, in March 1862, the waters off Old Point Comfort in Hampton Roads became a major battleground as the USS *Monitor* and the CSS *Merrimack* (which had been rebuilt and rechristened *Virginia*) fought the battle of the ironsides. Old Point Comfort was one of two lighthouses on the Bay surrounded by a fort. In this case, it was Fort Monroe, which was armed with three hundred large guns, with a range of three miles.

Later that year, in August, Cape Charles Light was attacked. While the second tower on Smith Island off Cape Charles was still under construction, Confederate guerrillas raided the station, destroyed the light, and took everything they could carry, including many of the materials needed to complete the second tower. Cherrystone Inlet Light just north of Cape Charles was also raided and its light extinguished.

The Lighthouse Board struggled to maintain some semblance of an organization during the early months of the Civil War. The board admitted that new construction and regular maintenance had come to a standstill. Fortunately, however, lighthouses were important enough to the defense of the Union that the federal government pitched in to help with funds and vessels. The Lighthouse Board reported on these efforts in 1862:

> Strenuous efforts have been made to restore discontinued lights and in view of the numerous grave difficulties to be encountered the board has reason to congratulate itself upon the success which has attended its exertions.
>
> Immediately upon the restoration of the eastern shore of Virginia to government control by the military operations in that quarter, the lights at Cape Charles, Cherrystone, and Hog Island [a barrier island off Delmarva] were reestablished, and have rendered assistance of no small importance to

the immensely increased navigation of Chesapeake Bay and tributaries. The light at the Naval Hospital, near Norfolk, has been relighted. A temporary light has been exhibited from the ruins of the lighthouse at Craney Island, and the work of permanently restoring that structure is in progress.

A vessel has been purchased and stationed off Smith's Point, to replace the light vessel belonging to that station, which was removed and destroyed by the insurgents. Through the courtesy of the general commanding this department, a competent military guard of this vessel has been detailed for duty and is yet continued.

Various and important repairs to light vessels in the upper part of Chesapeake Bay were also made.

The rebels were not the only problem the Lighthouse Board faced that year. In 1862, the lightship marking the Tail of the Horse Shoe, off Hampton Roads, broke away from its station during a severe January storm, and "it was found necessary to place a vessel which the board had been refitting at Baltimore for another station."

Also in 1862, the lighthouses on the James River—at White Shoals, Point of Shoals, and Deep Water—were lighted after being snuffed out by the rebels. When the Union army withdrew from the peninsula, however, the Lighthouse Board, now a little smarter, removed the lighting apparatus from the lighthouses and stored them at Fort Monroe.

By 1863, the lighthouses at Craney Island, Back River, and Cape Henry had been repaired, renovated, and refitted and were in operation again. Cape Henry was protected by a military guard under the command of the general at Fort Monroe.

Throughout most of the war, the Point Lookout Lighthouse keeper found herself in the difficult position of being surrounded by a prisoner-of-war camp. Pamela Edwards had taken over the job of lighthouse keeper after the death of her mother in 1855 and was still keeper when the Civil War broke out. The Union chose the grounds around the lighthouse as its site for a prison, mainly because it was surrounded on three sides

by the Chesapeake Bay and the Potomac River, which made escape difficult. The camp quickly became overcrowded, and poor, unsanitary living conditions led to outbreaks of disease. Some four thousand Confederate soldiers died there, many from starvation. The tales of horror and death that came out of the prison gave rise, naturally, to ghost stories. Later, the inhabitants of the lighthouse and employees of the state parks department working on the grounds of the old camp would swear the ghosts were real.

By 1864, Jerome McWilliams had good reason to stare out the windows of Blakistone Lighthouse with trepidation. It was bad enough to be alone on an unprotected island in the midst of war, but making matters worse, his wife was pregnant. Her life and the life of their unborn child were in jeopardy. Little did he know how important his wife's condition would be in the fate of the lighthouse.

McWilliams knew only that it was a treacherous time to be a lighthouse keeper. He had heard the stories about the attacks on lighthouses and the burning of the lightships. Out on the Potomac, he had seen the traffic change: the excursion vessels were now replaced with warships. The mighty schooners no longer carried goods for the local markets, but guns and supplies for armies. Even small sailboats were suspect.

So when the thirty-foot sloop *Swan* landed on the island and twelve Confederate soldiers disembarked, McWilliams knew his worst fears had come true. But he felt a twinge of hope when he recognized the man in charge of the small group. Confederate Capt. John M. Goldsmith was originally from nearby St. Patricks Creek, and McWilliams had known him since childhood. Yet Goldsmith, ignoring old allegiances, set about destroying the light. McWilliams and his wife stood by helplessly as Goldsmith's men smashed the lens and lamp of the lighthouse and confiscated all the fuel oil they could find. When finally Captain Goldsmith told McWilliams of his intention to blow up the building and kidnap him, McWilliams pointed out his wife's condition and begged him to reconsider. McWilliams insisted that moving his wife at this late hour in her pregnancy would endanger her life. Goldsmith finally consented to abandon that part of his plan. He left the house intact and McWilliams behind with his wife.

The couple felt a great sense of relief as the sailboat pushed off the island with its small contingent of rebels. On the Chesapeake, where allegiances were uncertain and men often found themselves fighting onetime friends and neighbors, human kindness had in this case won out over war. They had saved themselves and their lighthouse. In the following days, Union forces from Point Lookout replaced the damaged lens and lamps and patrolled the island perimeter in gunboats until the war ended.

By December 1864, the restoration of lights along the seaboard was proceeding rapidly as the North advanced on the South. Soon, the Lighthouse Board was confidently predicting that "the same unbroken chain which was exhibited before the war will soon be reestablished along the whole coast of the United States."

When the war ended in 1865, it left the Chesapeake and the entire East Coast from Delaware south with far fewer lighthouses to guide mariners. Little did anyone know, however, that out of all this destruction would come an important advance. As the Lighthouse Board pondered the question of how to relight the Chesapeake, it would make a decision that would revolutionize the lighthouse system on the Bay. The board would finally fully embrace the concept of building lighthouses over water, abandoning all ideas of using lightships.

In the postwar years, hardly a year went by that one or more light stations were not built on the Bay. Twenty-two new lighthouses were built in the Chesapeake through 1876, including two sets of ranges, each with two lighthouses which guided vessels down narrow channels when the lights lined up, one atop the other. Of that number, a whopping nineteen were built over water on piles or screw piles. Lighthouses now marked almost every important shoal on the Chesapeake; they lit the entrance to almost every river on the Bay; and they guided side-wheeling steamboats, loaded with passengers, around every dangerous bend in the waterway. The board had set out to create a better-lit, safer Chesapeake Bay for the thousands of vessels that would ply her waters in the decades to come. Unfortunately, along the way, they had forgotten an all-too-important lesson that should have been learned in the first years of pile lighthouse construction on the Chesapeake. That lesson would be driven home again, with frightening force, in the year 1877.

Fort Carroll Lighthouse stands atop the manmade fort which General Robert E. Lee helped construct before the onset of the Civil War.

Chapter Four

Under Siege

The keepers say that for nine days the vibration of the lighthouse was so violent that sleep was impossible except at very short intervals when the ice ceased running.

From a Baltimore *Sun* article about Thomas Point Shoal Light, January 20, 1877.

No lighthouse keeper was more prepared for unpredictable weather than Capt. James T. Bolling, a veteran of the Civil War clash between the *Monitor* and the *Merrimac*, who had won the post of keeper of Sevenfoot Knoll off Gibson Island. Bolling had turned the bottom platform of his round, cast-iron lighthouse into a barnyard. On the fenced-in platform, he kept hogs, goats, and chickens, which he periodically slaughtered in order to put meat on the table for his growing family, who lived with him on the light. Occasionally, a bad storm would wash some of the animals out of the makeshift pen, into the Chesapeake, and the family would have to round them up. On a few occasions, high tides forced the family to bring the chickens and hogs into their living quarters.

Bolling was one of the more self-sufficient offshore lighthouse keepers in the nineteenth century. Not only did he keep animals, but the family also managed to raise a few vegetables in the summertime in big pots they laid out on the deck surrounding the dwelling. But they could never grow enough vegetables, so Captain Bolling would take buckets of fish that the family routinely caught on hooks and lines dropped from the lighthouse, row the six miles to shore, and barter with the farmers for the vegetables he could not grow. Once in a while, the Bollings even enjoyed a hearty waterfowl dinner. There was no need to hunt the birds, for they often flew into the big light and fell to the walkway or the water, where the family could easily retrieve them.

The Bollings were not the only family living on an offshore lighthouse in 1877. Farther down the Bay at Thomas Point Shoal, assistant keeper Captain Miller had his wife and their young son, George, aboard the lighthouse with him. In the nineteenth century it was not uncommon for the families of lighthouse keepers to live aboard the pile lighthouses in the Bay. Families had lived with the keepers at land stations, and evidently the Lighthouse Board had not yet begun to question the practicality of allowing families to join the keepers on these offshore lighthouses. (The board would later prohibit families from living aboard water stations.)

Despite the fact that ice floes had damaged and destroyed a handful of lighthouses on the Bay in the 1850s and 1860s, few keepers expected the ice to endanger their families and their stations as much as it would in the 1870s. The constant pounding ice would not only make living conditions horrendous in the fragile pile lighthouses, but would also threaten the lives of the keepers and their families.

But even veteran keepers like Bolling could not have predicted the harsh, unrelenting cold that descended on the Chesapeake Bay twice in three years, first in 1877, then again in 1879.

Thomas Point Shoal Lighthouse, standing a mile out in the Chesapeake Bay, was nearly destroyed by ice during the winter of 1877. Ice shook the lighthouse so badly that the lens fell from its pedestal.

The first onslaught of bitter cold weather settled in unusually early during the last weeks of 1876, and by December 15, the Patapsco River and Baltimore Harbor were closed to business. Some keepers were beginning to run a little low on food and supplies when the first signs of a thaw were felt three weeks later, on January 6, 1877. The temperate weather, however, quickly changed to polar conditions once again. Baltimore Harbor was open just one day, on January 7, before the cold froze it, preventing the lighthouse tender from leaving port with fresh supplies. It would be another week before ships could return to Baltimore.

The freezing weather had hung on for a solid month, paralyzing the rivers and the Bay with fourteen inches of ice or more and isolating the keepers stationed out on the pile beacons in the Bay.

The keepers, however, were not alone out on the frozen waters. Ever since January 1, more than eighty dredge boats had been solidly stuck in the ice on Eastern Bay inside Kent Island. Crews on the big pungies and schooners were used to being locked in by ice for short periods, but they, too, were running out of food and had not been able to find anything to eat in the sparsely populated farming community on the Eastern Shore. Other commercial ships were also stranded in the ice, though many of them had managed to find a safer haven inside rivers and creeks before their vessels were frozen in place.

By Thursday, January 11, slightly warmer days had loosened the tons and tons of ice around the Chesapeake, and it all began to shift and move in the tide. As the current pushed the ice, shoving it against one shore, then the other, the thick, broken slabs piled up into icebergs, some three or four feet high. The ice was now big and heavy enough to do real damage as it slammed up against everything in its path, including vessels, piers, and lighthouses that stood on slender pilings out in the Bay. The screw piles and sleeve piles, which had appeared so solid (some were actually ten-inch-thick cast iron) when the lighthouses were built in milder weather, shook and vibrated every time the ice floes struck a column.

To make matters worse for Bolling, he had an infant child to worry about. Knolie, named after the light where she was born, came into the world

The spindly iron legs of the screw-pile lighthouses—like the ones of Drum Point Lighthouse pictured here—were exposed to the elements. Often ice would form, pushing over the house or bending the pilings.

on June 23, 1876. Her mother had no doctor or assistant, except her husband, although by then, the family was somewhat experienced with childbirth, having had three children before Knolie. (Over the next decade they would gain even more experience as their family grew to include thirteen children.)

Somehow, the Bolling family survived without personal harm or damage to the lighthouse, but other keepers around the Bay did not fare so well. Hooper Strait Lighthouse became the latest victim of the ice on January 11, 1877. Located in the narrow strait between the Chesapeake Bay and Tangier Sound, a mile off Dorchester County on the Eastern Shore, the little lighthouse took the full brunt of ice bearing down on it from both bodies of water.

Northwest winds had been blowing across the Bay since January 8, pushing the loosened ice up against the lighthouse. For three days, the ice remained piled against the structure. Then on January 11, a strong southerly gale carried more ice up against the lighthouse until the sheer weight of it snapped the bolts and welds holding the dwelling to the piles. The lighthouse was a small structure, built in 1867 on sleeve piles, which were wooden pilings driven into the mud and covered with cast-iron sleeves to protect them from decay. When the house toppled over, it sank to the roof and was pushed out into the Bay on a field of ice.

The lighthouse sank so quickly that keeper John S. Cornwall and his assistant, Capt. Alexander S. Conway, barely escaped. Neither man had family, so they were alone on the beacon when it was wrecked. The two keepers managed to save one of the lighthouse boats, which they pushed across the ice. The men spent twenty-four hours in the raw wind, pushing the boat a mile and sleeping whenever they could in the tiny dory. Finally, they were rescued by Captain Murphy of Billys Island the next morning.

News of the tragedy did not reach Baltimore until several days later when Colonel Harwood, superintendent of the lighthouse department, headquartered in Baltimore, received a dispatch from citizens in Cambridge late Saturday, January 13, informing him that the lighthouse was floating in the Bay.

The house was four miles west-northwest of its proper location in about seven fathoms of water. Residents of nearby Dorchester County could see the lighthouse wedged upright in the ice but could not reach it, because of the danger of falling through the thawing ice. Meanwhile, the keepers, who were isolated on an island, could not telegraph headquarters. Lack of word from the men left the community wondering if they had survived the wreck.

Colonel Harwood immediately telegraphed his inspector at Norfolk to send assistance. It was the first time a water station had been knocked down since a small screw pile on the James River had been destroyed by ice some ten years earlier.

As night fell that Saturday, the lighthouse steamers *Heliotrope* and *Tulip* left Norfolk for Hooper Strait. Colonel Harwood, who had still received no word from the lighthouse keepers, could only hope that the men had been rescued. If not, he told newspapers inquiring into the tragedy, he believed they would be safe on the wreck until the steamers arrived.

That evening, when the two tenders reached the wreck, lighthouse inspector Captain Baker and his crew found the superstructure ice-bound, sitting straight up in the water, with almost half of the roof out. The crew recovered the lens, lantern, fog bell and machinery, the oil butts, and one boat. They also saved everything in the way of metal that could be reached, including the ventilators and copper stack. The rescue team, however, found no sign of the keepers. Despite this bad news and the lack of communication from the men, the Lighthouse Board continued to hold out hope that the two keepers had been rescued before the arrival of the steamers.

Meanwhile, the thaw was making life miserable out on Thomas Point Shoal Light. Heavy drifting ice descended on the screw pile, which was in the Chesapeake, a mile off the mouth of the South River, near Annapolis.

Thomas Point Shoal Lighthouse was the newest screw pile on the Bay, built just two years

On a cold winter day in 1877, the original Hooper Strait, built on sleeve piles, was toppled by ice. A second lighthouse was built on stronger screw piles. In 1966, the second Hooper Strait Light left the site by barge and was restored here at Navy Point in St. Michaels as one of the main exhibits of the Chesapeake Bay Maritime Museum.

earlier in 1875. But the latest in screw-pile construction did not save keeper Eugene Burchinal and the assistant keeper and his family from enduring a nine-day assault that began on January 11, 1877. Running ice left them harried and frightened. Loose objects flew around the dwelling. Even the stoves had to be lashed down to keep them from overturning and spilling hot coals on the wooden floors. At night the ice breaking against the piers sounded like the crackling of fire, the residents reported.

Keeper Burchinal, who later described the harrowing nine days of terror in his report, said the ice caused the house to vibrate with such violence that the lens, weighing five hundred pounds, was broken, the oil butts were overturned, and the structure canted to such an extent that the fog bell could not be rung. Other machinery was also thrown about, and the house was in shambles.

Throughout the ordeal, the lighthouse shook so violently that the keepers and the family could not sleep, except for very short intervals at slack tide when the ice ceased running. While the keepers were able to tie down the stoves to keep them from overturning, they could not control the revolving light in the lantern, which whirled about so rapidly that it finally dismounted from its machinery and broke. Huge blocks of ice were hurled against the ice breakers at the base of the house. Some of the ice fields were several feet thick and slammed against the pilings with terrific force, damaging one of the iron perpendicular supports.

On Wednesday night, January 17, with the lens broken, the keepers did their best to perform their duties by showing a small household lamp from an upper window. The next day, with the house canted to one side and no chance of making repairs without help from the Lighthouse Board, the keepers finally abandoned the screw pile. They boarded the lighthouse dory and, cutting a path through the ice, made it safely to shore. But they did not give up tending a light. They immediately took up quarters in the old lighthouse on shore, which still contained a lantern. It was lighted on Thursday night, January 18.

The damaged and abandoned lighthouse was a real blow to the egos of lighthouse engineers who thought they had outwitted nature by creating the ultimate screw pile. "It is considered one of the most substantial that can be built," the Baltimore *Sun* reported on January 20, after learning that it had been damaged and abandoned. "No fears are entertained by the engineers for its safety as they believe it cannot be moved from its position, but the news that the running ice had succeeded in disarranging and breaking the machinery so that the light could not be shown was unexpected by the lighthouse authorities."

By January 20, open water surrounded the lighthouse, and the structure, no longer pushed by tons of ice, stood erect again. Engineers made repairs, and within a few days, the new lens arrived by steamer. Thomas Point Shoal was lighted again.

As soon as the weather broke and the tender could leave port, Colonel Harwood, concerned about the welfare of the lighthouses and their keepers, boarded a steamer to make a personal tour of the pile lighthouses. He found heavy drift ice pounding against some of the screw piles in exposed areas. The jarring ice caused the houses to vibrate so much that the oil was actually shaken out of the lamps, making it difficult, if not impossible, to maintain the light. The experience helped the superintendent understand how difficult life had been on Thomas Point Shoal and other offshore lights.

Nevertheless, he was reportedly confident that every screw-pile beacon was solidly built and could resist all the ice thrown against it. He did, however, question the safety of one or two sleeve-pile lighthouses, similar to the one at Hooper Strait, which he predicted might be moved if the ice, when broken up in the rivers, rushed out with sudden force.

By January 21, ten days after the wreck of Hooper Strait, lighthouse authorities had still heard nothing from keepers Cornwall and Conway. A lighthouse steamer was again sent from Norfolk on the eighteenth to salvage what they could from the wrecked house. While much of the material was saved, still nothing was seen of the keepers. The crew, however, did locate a small boat about a mile from the lighthouse on the hard ice, fueling hope that the keepers made a safe escape to shore.

But as the days wore on, local Eastern Shore residents were beginning to lose hope that the men would be found alive. The Cambridge *Democrat* wrote: "Mr. Cornwall and his assistant were on the lighthouse, and it was impossible for them either to get ashore or receive assistance from the land. A belief prevailed in Dorchester county that the keepers were rescued by the steamers from Norfolk, which, however, was not the fact. Both men probably were lost."

Finally, on Thursday, January 25, two weeks after the ice had wrecked their lighthouse, the keepers transmitted a telegraph. They had suffered severe frostbite from their night out on the ice, but were otherwise safe and eager to go back to work.

The winter of 1879 again produced heavy ice floes, which toppled Janes Island Lighthouse off Crisfield on the lower Eastern Shore, on January 20.

Meanwhile, the Bolling family, which had been spared harm in the winter of 1877, would not fare so well the second time around. The weather was taking its toll on the Bolling children, who now included yet another baby, Eva, also born on the lighthouse. As the cold dragged on, the children became sick and weak. Fortunately, a tugboat was able to cut through the ice to rescue them in January of 1879. A toddler at the time, Eva Hawkins would tell a newspaper sixty years later when she returned by boat to her birthplace that

she had dim memories of being assisted, along with her sisters, across the chunks of ice to the tugboat several hundred yards away. The vessel probably saved their lives. Her sister Knolie, who also recounted to reporters her life on the lighthouse, said the family decided to spend no more winters there, and they moved to the city.

As the ice broke up and tenders again began to resupply the lighthouses in the Chesapeake Bay, one Baltimore *Sun* reporter suggested that lighthouse keepers "from their lonely perches can look out upon the Arctic scenes surrounding them, and at the same time enjoy comparative comfort."

But the events that unfolded during the horrible winters of the 1870s had proven without a doubt that there was nothing comfortable about a pile lighthouse under siege by running ice. In the years to come, ice would become the biggest fear of lighthouse keepers. Despite constant and expensive measures taken by the Lighthouse Board to protect the water stations, the incidents at Hooper Strait, Thomas Point Shoal, and Janes Island would be repeated again and again on the Chesapeake, and much sooner than anyone could have predicted.

Today, Thomas Point Shoal Lighthouse is protected by piles of riprap. Stones were often replaced, winter after winter, around pile lighthouses in the Bay, at a cost greater than that of the original construction.

Chapter Five

Riding a Lighthouse

The keeper and assistant clung to the fallen house....For sixteen and a half hours, their danger was very great, being in the midst of heavy floating ice, which would often pile upon the house and thereafter swamp it.

F. J. Higginson, inspector of the Fifth District, in a letter to
Rear Admiral, Ins. Rodgers, USN, chairman of the Lighthouse Board.

A strong southeast gale was blowing shortly after dawn on February 10, 1881, when a Sharps Island Lighthouse keeper by the name of Butler and his new, young assistant, Charles L. Tarr, felt a sudden jar. A thick fog had prevented them from seeing the danger before it hit the house. Now it was too late. Tons of ice rammed against the screw pile that stood in the middle of the Chesapeake Bay, north of Sharps Island. It took only five minutes for the ice floe to knock the wooden cottage off its iron stilts and into the ice-strewn Chesapeake waters.

Unable to reach the lighthouse dory that floated undamaged in the Bay, the two men clung to the fallen house in what would be a harrowing, sixteen-hour ride up the Chesapeake. Throughout the day and late into the night, the house floated in the freezing water amid heavy floes of ice, which often piled up against the building and swamped it during the wild, five-mile journey. Somehow, the wooden structure managed to stay afloat until one o'clock the next morning, when it finally grounded in twelve feet of water in Paw Paw Cove, off the west side of Tilghman Island.

The two keepers were shaken, cold, wet, hungry, and exhausted, yet they stood by the wrecked lighthouse through the night hours, waiting for a passing vessel that might help them salvage the lighthouse property. When fog moved in, obscuring passing vessels, they finally gave up and paddled their way to shore in the lighthouse dory.

The very next morning, the men returned and succeeded in saving the lens and pedestal, all the mineral oil, the empty oil cans, oil measures, and even the lighthouse library. The lantern had been severely damaged by water, but the lens was uninjured. In a matter of days, the house, still upright in the water, was submerged to the roof and was expected to break up soon. Fifth District Inspector F. J. Higginson was so impressed with the conduct of the two men that he asked the Lighthouse Board to send them letters of commendation.

Two days after the station was carried away, a steamer went ashore on Sharps Island, underlining the need for a hasty replacement for the wrecked lighthouse. This time, however, the Lighthouse Board would choose a caisson base for its offshore lighthouse, which had proven stronger and more ice-resistant than pilings.

The third Sharps Island Lighthouse (the first had been on the island itself) would not be the first caisson lighthouse on the Chesapeake. The Lighthouse Board had first used a caisson in 1873 in the Craighill Channel Range, near the mouth of the Patapsco River. The board's action was precipi-

This is the third Sharps Island Lighthouse. The iron caisson was quickly constructed in 1882 after ice dragged away the screw-pile lighthouse with the keepers still aboard in the winter of 1881.

tated by yet another ice-related disaster at Love Point the preceding year.

Love Point Light had stood off the northern tip of Kent Island in the Chester River for only four months when fields of heavy ice tore away two of its main iron columns on December 27, 1872. The keepers were forced to abandon their post as the lighthouse dangled on the edge of collapse. For the men who designed lighthouses on the Chesapeake, the Love Point disaster was yet another wake-up call, a warning that pile lighthouses just weren't tough enough to stand up to the Chesapeake's rugged winters.

The biggest problem created when ice destroyed lighthouses was the danger it posed to the ever-increasing maritime traffic, which was becoming more dependent on the lighthouse system to guide vessels safely into port. To build the Craighill Channel Range Front Light, therefore, the board responded by trying the caisson.

The Craighill Channel Range Lights were to mark a new channel just below the mouth of the Patapsco River. The channel had been widened and deepened in order to shorten the distance to Baltimore for deep-draft vessels. Given the growing importance of the city of Baltimore as a port, the board could not risk losing these lighthouses to ice.

In its annual report for 1873, the board said it sought "a more solid structure that could, beyond all doubt, safely withstand the heavy ice-floes" that habitually formed during the winter. Consequently, in the eleventh hour, the board scrapped plans to build the front lighthouse of the Craighill Channel Range on screw piles and opted to build the Chesapeake Bay's first caisson lighthouse.

The caisson was not a new idea, having been used as a foundation for bridges ever since London's Westminster Bridge was built in 1738, but in 1873 it was a new concept in lighthouse construction. The caisson was a hollow cast-iron or wooden cylinder that was built on land, then floated to the site and sunk into place. At the site, the caisson was usually filled with concrete to help it sink and to hold it in position.

If the seas were calm during transport to the site and while the caisson was being sunk, and if the seabed was solid, this proved to be a reliable method of building lighthouses. But this first caisson lighthouse on the Chesapeake was not destined to sail smoothly through construction. From the start, the job was difficult. The site was not at all ideal, since there were "no signs of a solid foundation within sixty feet of the water's surface," according to board reports. Nevertheless, the engineers designed the Craighill Channel Lighthouse so that the caisson sat on a cluster of pilings, driven twenty-seven feet into the substrata. The wooden caisson was also sunk beneath the bottom of the Bay floor. A hollow, cone-shaped foundation of cast iron was bolted to the caisson to form the base of the lighthouse and was filled with cement. A cylindrical cast-iron house was then placed on top of the frustum to form the actual dwelling.

Problems started with the pilings, which had to be level. The crew tried using what must have been one of the earliest circular saws. The saw was operated underwater, powered by a steam engine. A detailed account of the proceedings concluded that the circular saw was not practical for such underwater work because the crew could not cut the pilings to an even level. A diver had to be sent below to add blocks to the tops of the piles to level them off.

Meanwhile, as the caisson was towed to the site, a gale blew up, nearly sinking the cylinder. The crew was forced to take the caisson ashore before it reached its destination. There, they bolted on several more cast-iron sections to the base so that the sides would be higher and it would ride better in the water, creating less trouble under tow. The plan was a success, and workers quickly positioned the caisson and sank it on the pilings.

It took over a year to build the caisson lighthouse, which turned out to be one of the smallest on the Chesapeake. Its cost was twenty-five thousand dollars more than the planned screw-pile lighthouse, but considerably less costly than future caissons, which ran forty-thousand dollars or more. Considering how much it cost the Lighthouse Board to replace, repair, and reinforce pile lighthouses damaged or endangered by ice in the Bay, the cost was not at all prohibitive.

Nevertheless, the construction problems encountered at Craighill Channel Front Light evidently worried the board, which wavered over the next few years on whether to build the offshore lighthouses in the Chesapeake Bay on piles or caissons. During the next ten years, the board often flip-flopped on construction decisions, seemingly influenced by the most recent events, before finally moving forward.

Such was the case with Thomas Point Shoal Light and Sandy Point Light, both proposed in 1873 and 1874 for shoals off the western shore of Maryland. Thomas Point Shoal Light (discussed in chapter 4) was originally designed to have a screw-pile foundation, but when Love Point Lighthouse was damaged in the winter of 1872–73, the board made the same proposal in 1873 for Thomas Point as it had for the Craighill Channel Light. The report went into minute detail on construction details for the Thomas Point caisson. But it was not to be.

In 1874, the board declined to begin work on Thomas Point Shoal Light as it waited for the additional fifteen thousand dollars it needed to build a caisson. By 1875, however, with the funds in hand, the board decided to build an iron-pile lighthouse at Thomas Point Shoal, instead of the caisson. There is no indication in the annual reports why the board opted for the troublesome screw pile. Newspaper accounts indicate, however, that the board considered Thomas Point Shoal to be a much superior screw pile compared to Love Point Light and other water stations.

In 1874, the Lighthouse Board proposed that a new lighthouse at Sandy Point be built on the shoal to replace a land-based lighthouse that was old and ineffective because of the long distance it stood from the main channel. The original forty-thousand-dollar request indicates the board intended to build a caisson, since at that time screw piles cost only twenty-five thousand dollars or less. By 1875 the board had reduced its request to thirty thousand (which was later reduced further to twenty-five thousand) and was proposing a screw-pile lighthouse similar to the one under construction at Thomas Point. Not surprisingly, it took a few years for Congress to appropriate the funds. By the time it did in 1882, the Sharps Island disaster was fresh in the minds of the Lighthouse Board. They immediately changed their minds yet again about what to build in the fickle open waters of the Chesapeake. Sandy Point Lighthouse, with its octagonal brick dwelling and intricately detailed eaves, became one of the prettier caisson lighthouses to be built on the Bay.

Within a few short years, however, the Lighthouse Board would prove again that it had a very poor memory. By the mid-1880s, it was authorizing construction of pile and screw-pile structures on the Bay and its tributaries. By the end of the decade, the board had authorized eleven more lighthouses to be built on pilings, many of them in exposed locations in open waters.

As the 1890s unfolded, there were now a whopping thirty-eight lighthouses on pilings in the Chesapeake and its rivers. If the board had been flirting with disaster in the 1870s, it was now begging for it. As the winter of 1893 approached, survival—for the keepers, as well as the structures—would become the key concern.

Sharps Island Lighthouse—the leaning tower of the Chesapeake—is the only caisson ever moved by ice in the Bay.

Chapter Six

Fighting Back the Sea

The lower side of the point is being eroded rapidly by the current of the river.
The safety of the buildings of the light-station is threatened.

The Lighthouse Board, in an 1892 report describing Jordan Point Light.

*I*t was bad enough that ice had ripped down seven offshore lighthouses in the mid-nineteenth century, but by 1880, the Lighthouse Board also faced a crisis with its land-based lighthouses on the Bay. New or old, almost every one was threatened by the encroaching sea. Something had to be done quickly, or the board faced the real possibility of losing most of its towers on the Chesapeake.

If ice was like a lion, pouncing and devouring its victim in frightening short order, erosion was an insidious disease of lighthouses, hardly detectable at times as it wore away the shoreline with every flow and ebb of the tide. Some years, it washed away a few inches or a few feet, but occasionally, a big storm would do a hundred years worth of damage in the course of a few days.

The constantly shifting shores of the Chesapeake, which were little more than sand, silt, and mud, caused more rebuilding of lighthouses than ice ever would. By 1881, at least five lighthouses, including the first two towers at Smith Point, the first beacons at Thomas Point and Sharps Island, and Bodkin Island Light, had already been moved, abandoned, or taken down and rebuilt farther from the lapping waves, all because of erosion. Now, most other mainland and island lighthouses were in danger of sinking into the marsh or falling into the water. Between 1875 and 1895, nine more lighthouses would require drastic

measures to ensure that a light continued to shine in their corners of the horizon.

In 1878, lighthouse authorities began worrying about the security of the second Cape Charles Lighthouse on Smith Island—just fourteen years after the light was completed in 1864. The 150-foot tower, off the coast of Cape Charles, had replaced the original 1827 tower, which had been too short to serve mariners adequately.

The board noted that the sea was encroaching on the Cape Charles Lighthouse site, though the beacon was not yet in danger. But in just a few years, the board would embark on one of its biggest and most expensive property-saving efforts on the Chesapeake Bay at Smith Island in an effort to save the coastal light. It would spend more than fifty thousand dollars—one-third the cost of a new lighthouse—on shore erosion control measures, trying to save a barrier island that lay barely above sea level.

The second Cape Charles Lighthouse had been built in 1864 at what was presumably a safe six hundred feet inland, but by 1883, the property had lost three hundred feet to the sea and was eroding at the alarming rate of thirty feet per year. In 1885, as the ocean approached ever closer, the Lighthouse Board suggested that jetties be built to help catch and hold the shifting sand.

The stones were like boulders to the contractors who struggled to get them ashore, but the storm-driven sea moved them around like pebbles.

The elevation of Fishing Battery Island, on which this lighthouse sits in the Susquehanna River, was so low that even as early as 1881 its height was raised with fill dirt, and the bottom floor of the lighthouse had to be altered and cemented.

A series of jetties were built in front of the lighthouse starting in 1886, only to be partially washed away by storm waves and high tides. In April 1889, a storm washed away 75 feet of one jetty, undermined the south end of the protection wall, and created such high tides that the station was entirely surrounded by water until the tide finally retreated. By 1889, the average rate of shoreline erosion had accelerated to 40 feet per year, and Smith Island had lost another 240 feet, bringing the ocean to within 60 feet of the tower.

Alarmed, the board gave up all thoughts of saving the old structure and concentrated on protecting it for the several years it would take to plan and build yet another Cape Charles Lighthouse. This third tower would be located three-quarters of a mile inland and would be built at a cost of $150,000. Yet the old tower had to be saved long enough for the next one to be completed. This meant construction of still more jetties. In the end, the second Cape Charles Lighthouse cost almost as much to preserve as the third one cost to build.

The Lighthouse Board may well have expected that coastal islands would move and shift in the ocean storms. Unfortunately, the erosion problem on the Chesapeake reached as far north as the entrance to Annapolis Harbor, where Greenbury Point Lighthouse was threatening to fall into the Bay.

As early as 1878, the land around the picturesque cottage dwelling of Greenbury Point, with its unusually tall octagonal lantern room, was eroding rapidly. The lighthouse itself was actually rather useless on land because its beam was lost among the many lights already emanating from the Naval Academy. But since this light was instrumental in guiding vessels into Annapolis, an important early port, the Lighthouse Board urged Congress to fund a new screw-pile lighthouse. Greenbury Point Lighthouse survived another thirteen years until the screw pile was erected in November 1891. It has since fallen into the Bay and disappeared.

At many lighthouses around the Chesapeake, authorities battled the shifting sands. The waves were lapping at the foundation of the fog-bell tower at Cove Point Lighthouse in Calvert County, Maryland, in 1891 when the board finally took action. A substantial wooden seawall surrounding the lighthouse was finished in November of that year and the fog-bell tower was moved inland sixteen feet. Today a seawall still wraps around Cove Point and has, so far, succeeded in keeping the old lighthouse out of the Chesapeake Bay.

New Point Comfort, which lighted the way into Mobjack Bay in Virginia, stood on a peninsula for over one hundred years, but even in its earliest years, there was a hint of problems: seven thousand dollars was appropriated to rebuild the lighthouse in April 1816, only twelve years after it was built. Though the money was evidently never used, it points to the probability that, even this early in its history, New Point Comfort stood on marginal land.

Certainly by the early part of the twentieth century, the New Point Comfort Lighthouse was hard to reach by road. Edwin P. Young, a retired newspaperman, recalled in a July 1978 article for a Mathews County newspaper that even in 1928 the road to the lighthouse was hard to travel.

> It was not an island, as it is now, but a narrow neck, jutting from the length of sandy shore. . . . At the New Point end there was a wide, sandy beach completely surrounding the lighthouse. The light itself was set up on a pile of rocks so that it would be on a hill, well behind the beach. . . .
>
> There was no real road to the point . . . and even then the access was pretty close to the water at high tide. But an occasional car—a "tin Lizzie"—made it to the point. Other means of getting there were by horseback or by walking from Bayside Wharf or from one of the nearby settlements. However, even then, the main way of reaching New Point beach was by boat. There was a substantial pier on the point, on the Mobjack Bay side of the land, and there was a pier shed.

Young first saw the beach and lighthouse by way of the schooner *Edward L. Martin* when he was a counselor for a boys' camp, which was visiting the beach for a picnic and swim. Later, he remembered how the August Storm of 1933

Even Jones Point Lighthouse, located well up the Potomac River near Alexandria, Virginia, suffered enough erosion that riprap was needed to save the bank and the lighthouse.

washed away land behind the lighthouse, creating a stream:

> First, the land passageway to the point was breached by a heavy storm, and a small stream trickled through at high tide. But you could still wade from the mainland to the beach on New Point. A year or two later, you could run a shallow-draft boat through the beach, and it was not too deep to wade across. Came succeeding years with other storms and the gap widened. New Point was no longer a point, but an island.

New Point Comfort has so far survived the erosion of the land around it, but other lighthouses have not been so lucky.

Back River Lighthouse had struggled with the Chesapeake tides for most of its history before collapsing during Hurricane Flossy on September 27, 1956. The light was originally built on low, marshy land in 1829, and the builder, Winslow Lewis, had a tough time moving materials to the site. It was so marshy that the keeper's house was built 144 feet behind it and a footbridge over the marsh was needed to connect the two.

It seemed that storms battered this lighthouse more than any other. In the fall of 1903, a severe storm kicked up waves fourteen feet high against the side of the tower. The powerful waves even moved stones out of place, but a crew working night and day for seventy-two hours managed to save the house, light, and walkway.

Not surprisingly, given its marshy location, this lighthouse was one of the first to be automated in 1915. It was decommissioned in 1936, partly because of its dilapidated condition, and partly because Back River was no longer an important harbor. Within four years, the tower showed the signs of its battle with the sea. As early as 1940, a newspaper report noted that a large portion of one side of the tower had collapsed to an abrading sea, and the base of the lighthouse was beginning to crumble.

Despite the poor condition of the lighthouse, the old tower was purchased by a man who intended to fix it up. He had planned to repair it and build a wraparound patio. Unfortunately, nature again intervened. The lighthouse, now sitting on an island, finally collapsed in the face of Hurri-

cane Flossy on September 27, 1956. For many years, a pile of stone could still be found at the site.

Some points of lands, such as Smith Point at the southern approach to the Potomac River, were eroding so quickly that as many as three lighthouses were built, each a little farther inland. Smith Point Lighthouse originally stood 400 to 500 feet off the point of land, but erosion was so severe that it was rebuilt in 1807 and then again in 1828. By the early 1850s, even the third lighthouse was endangered. A retaining wall had been built about 30 feet from the octagonal lighthouse, but the sea had seeped around the wall, eroding the land behind it and creating a hollow space that was totally washed out. The lighthouse now stood on a bank just 10 feet from a crevice created by an abrading sea.

At this point, the tower was hardly worth preserving. It was so far from deep water that its light did mariners little good. Consequently, for quite a few years, a light-vessel, as well as the lighthouse, marked the point. As early as 1851–52, an offshore station had been mapped out to replace the shore lighthouse and the light-vessel that stood off the point. The lighthouse was finally decommissioned in 1859, though a lightship continued to mark the point until a screw-pile lighthouse was constructed in 1868.

In the short course of lighthouse history on the Chesapeake Bay, islands, some of them hundreds of acres in size and marked by lighthouses, have been eaten away by erosion. Such was the case with Sharps Island, midway in the Chesapeake Bay and believed to have been a seven-hundred-acre island in colonial days. It still was a substantial island in the 1800s, when a lighthouse was built on it. Today, Sharps Island Light guides vessels not around an island, but around a four-foot shoal in the Bay.

The island lighthouses presented unique problems for the Lighthouse Board. Many islands were not only losing land through erosion, but were generally low and susceptible to flooding, a problem that grew worse as the islands eroded. At Fishing Battery Island at the mouth of the Susquehanna River, the U.S. Fish Commission, which owned the island, took drastic measures in 1881 and actually raised the grade of the island through

New Point Comfort was originally built on a peninsula. The land became an island during the August Storm of 1933 and the light is now well offshore.

filling. When the island was raised, the lower floor of the lighthouse had to be removed. Workers filled the enclosure with clean soil and laid a concrete floor. The walls were also raised, presumably to add another floor to the dwelling.

Clay Island, marking the entrance to the Nanticoke River and Fishing Bay on the Eastern Shore of Maryland, was also rapidly losing land to the intruding marsh and sea. The lighthouse was built in 1832 as a dwelling with a light on top of it. The high land around the structure was rapidly eroding fifty years later. As early as 1828 Congress appropriated $6,500 for improvements, which was almost certainly for shore erosion control measures. Another $5,900 was appropriated in 1831.

In 1886, the board warned that expensive shoreline protection for the light would be needed again unless Congress built a new lighthouse. Congress wisely chose to build offshore, for while the island still exists today, it is marshy with almost no high land. When Sharkfin Shoal Lighthouse in Fishing Bay was completed in 1892, the light on Clay Island was extinguished.

Blakistone Island had been a four-hundred-acre island when the first Europeans to settle the region landed and named it St. Clements in 1632. Two hundred years later, when the lighthouse was built in 1851, there were still at least one hundred acres. By 1893, more land had washed away and the lighthouse was in danger of being undermined, so shore protection was built.

Watts Island Lighthouse survived for over one hundred years, despite its location on a very tiny island: Little Watts Island, which had only seven acres in 1833 when John Donohoo built the tower and separate dwelling. Both structures were undermined during a winter storm in 1944 and collapsed a few weeks later. Today, there is nothing left of the island but a shoal.

Most of the endangered lighthouses were directly on Chesapeake Bay waters, where long fetches produced strong wave action. Bay waves eroded the shorelines more than the lapping waves in creeks and rivers, but even lighthouses upriver were threatened by erosion.

Less than twenty years after Jordan Point Lighthouse was built on the James River in Virginia, the red-roofed dwelling with its lantern room mounted on top was in danger of being undermined. Built in 1855 at the same time that the three screw piles were built in the James River, the lighthouse stood on an eroding bank. In 1874, the beach at Jordan Point was protected with loose stones.

Thirteen years later, however, men gave up the struggle with nature. The Lighthouse Board advertised for bids to remove the old structure and build a new one in 1887. The new lighthouse—a separate dwelling and a wooden tower for the light—was completed for $3,449 in January 1887. But the struggle with the silting land only began again, this time even more rapidly than before. Just five years after the new station was built, Jordan Point was again in danger of being undercut by wave action. "The lower side of the point is being eroded rapidly by the current of the river," the Lighthouse Board report noted in 1892. "The safety of the buildings of the light-station is threatened."

The following year, the board erected a strong wooden wall as shore protection. It ran 279 feet along the channel, or eastern side, of the point and 133 feet along the western side.

In the nineteenth and early twentieth centuries, the spring flooding of the mighty Susquehanna River routinely scoured the shoreline at Concord Point in Havre de Grace. By the time the Conowingo Dam was built in the 1920s to control the flooding and produce electricity, the river waters were lapping at a corner of the foundation of the lighthouse on the point. In the 1940s, a local developer, whose mother lived next to the lighthouse, deposited tons of dirt in front of the tower to protect it from the waves.

Not all erosion was entirely nature's work. Cedar Point Lighthouse was built on a peninsula at the southern entrance to the Patuxent River. The lighthouse is now on a tiny island, one-half mile from shore. Completed in 1896, Cedar Point was one of the later lighthouses built on the Chesapeake Bay, yet one of the earlier to be abandoned in the 1920s by the Bureau of Lighthouses, the body which replaced the Lighthouse Board. Much of the peninsula was already eroded in 1928 when the lighthouse property was sold to the Arundel Corporation. The sand and gravel company proceeded to dredge tons of sand from the area in the 1930s. Today, the dwelling can still be seen, though one wall of the building has caved in. The lighthouse is now completely surrounded by water, with little more than the house on high ground.

Ironically, some of the silt from Cedar Point rode the tide across the mouth of the Patuxent River to Drum Point, where it settled around the base of the offshore lighthouse. Drum Point Light was built in 1883 in ten feet of water and about three hundred feet from shore. By the early 1900s, it was close enough to land that a footbridge was built out to it. By the 1970s, when preservation efforts were under way to move the screw pile, so much shoaling had occurred at that point that the lighthouse was on dry land.

Today, many of the surviving lighthouses stand precariously close to the water's edge, their future resting in the hands of nature. Cove Point Light has only a seawall between it and the mighty Chesapeake; Turkey Point Lighthouse at the head of the Bay stands precariously close to an eighty-foot bluff that is constantly eroding into the sea below. Cedar Point Lighthouse is close to collapse. The preservation of New Point Comfort Light has been helped along by conservation efforts in Mathews County, Virginia, but only riprap stands between the tower and the sea. Point Lookout at the northern approach to the Potomac River has lost most of its front yard. Even many offshore lighthouses have needed stones deposited at their base to prevent the moving water from scouring sand and silt away from their foundations.

Other shore lighthouses are somewhat removed from danger, thanks to shoreline bulkheading and riprap. Land around Old Point Comfort was filled and bulkheaded years ago; Jones Point is protected by riprap; and the beachfront at Piney Point Lighthouse on the Potomac River has shoaled out into the river over the years.

While Cape Charles Light is still safe, it stands on precious little high land on Smith Island. Even at Cape Henry Light, employees of Fort Story, which surrounds the Coast Guard facility, use bulldozers to keep a giant sand dune, towering fifty feet above sea level, in place between the light tower and the Chesapeake Bay.

Cedar Point Lighthouse was built on a peninsula off the mouth of the Patuxent River in 1896. It is now abandoned and completely surrounded by water, due to erosion and dredging in the area.

Man may yet win the battle with nature and the sea, but time has proven beyond a doubt that it will take a continuous flow of money to keep riprap and other shoreline protection standing between the remaining lighthouses and the Chesapeake Bay.

Chapter Seven

Earthquake!

The house shivered, then seemed to be shoved in a horizontal plane....The motion, noise...
were as of riding in a car which had left the rails and was bumping over the ties;...
loose things on all sides were tumbling about, adding no little to the frightful effect.

The keeper of Bloody Point Range Lights on Daufuskie Island,
South Carolina, about the Great Charleston Earthquake of 1886.

A thunder squall had passed through in the afternoon, clearing the skies and sweeping in a gentle breeze that rustled over the Chesapeake during the early evening hours. But as the sun set on the last day of August in 1886, the wind died out suddenly, leaving an oppressive, stagnant layer of air over the Chesapeake and down the eastern seaboard. Despite the uncomfortable heat, or perhaps because of it, lighthouse keepers wandered out on the decks surrounding their lanterns, where some of them noticed that the stars appeared particularly bright in the clear night sky. It was not unusual for keepers standing long, lonely night watches to spot an occasional shooting star, but that night, the sky seemed to be full of them, creating a meteor shower that entertained lighthouse keepers up and down the coast.

In 1886, keepers were a hardy, self-sufficient bunch who could handle any challenge, from machinery failure to rescuing sailors off schooners sinking in high seas. But what happened the night of August 31 shocked and frightened even the toughest among them.

The keeper of Old Point Comfort Lighthouse was standing in the lantern room when he felt the fifty-four-foot tower move beneath his feet. Looking out over Hampton Roads, he could not believe his eyes: out of the hot night, the seas were rising, forming giant waves. Suddenly, a deep rumbling sound pierced the night air. The eighty-four-year-old tower trembled on and on, like no wind or gale had ever made it do before.

To the keeper, the next two minutes felt like an eternity as he clung to the rail to keep from falling. When it was over, the tower was still standing, but he noticed that the two-foot-long pendulum on his wall clock had stopped its perpetual motion, so strong had the rocking of the tower been. The clock face read 9:55.

The Old Point Comfort keeper hardly suspected at the time that what he felt was part of a series of earthquakes that began at 8:58 P.M. that night in distant Cape Canaveral, Florida, were felt in Georgia around 9:30 P.M., and finally rumbled up the seacoast with amazing speed, to shake seven states from South Carolina to New York Harbor about 9:50 P.M., approximately the same time the quake hit the Chesapeake Bay. Named for its epicenter in South Carolina, the Great Charleston Earthquake set off dozens of tremors and vibrations that shook the eastern seaboard for the next several months, sometimes on a daily basis. The August 31 quake caused lighthouse towers to sway, sometimes so violently that keepers at the top clung to the railings for dear life or were thrown back and forth within the lantern rooms. Revolving lenses ran rapidly on their machinery and, in one case, a huge, one-ton first-order Fresnel lens was dismounted. Pipes rattled and clattered, walls cracked, plaster fell, and the earth moved vertically as well as horizontally. A century later, it would still be considered the second worst earthquake in U.S. history.

Added to the fear and chaos was a tremendous rushing sound that filled the air as the fissure split the earth. It was described almost everywhere as a loud rumbling noise, like the sound of cannon fire. Many keepers portrayed it as the sounds of war.

In South Carolina, which took the brunt of the quake, the keeper at Bloody Point Range Lights on Daufuskie Island described the noise in a report to the Lighthouse Board:

It was altogether a beautiful night, silent and calm, so this noise as of a great gust of wind was startling. This was immediately followed by a rattling noise as of a great number of heavy men with big boots on, tramping to and fro on the back piazza....Then a roaring noise came, booming underground as of heavy cannonading....The house shivered, then seemed to be shoved in a horizontal plane....The motion, noise...were as of riding in a car which had left the rails and was bumping over the ties, and this on a bridge or trestle; loose things on all sides were tumbling about, adding no little to the frightful effect.

Up and down the coast, keepers reported unusual auroral displays and meteorite activity during the months that tremors plagued the seacoast. The northern skies lit up with a bright arc of light on August 23, near the Absecon Light in New Jersey, thirteen days after the first tremor of an earthquake had been felt, and just eight days before the big shake-up on August 31. Two days later, on August 25, the Absecon keeper reported seeing unusual flashes of lightning in the eastern sky, followed by brilliant meteors until after midnight. One keeper in New York Harbor, shaken out of his bed by the August 31 shock, reported a beautiful purple night sky after the quake.

The keeper of Cape Romain Light on Raccoon Key, South Carolina, was sick in bed with malaria the night of the Great Charleston Earthquake, but he noticed how unusually clear the sky was and how the stars twinkled brighter than ever. In the early evening, he witnessed a display of meteors, shooting through the dark sky, greater than any he had ever seen before. Then, at 9:50 P.M., he heard a low rumbling noise coming from a west-south-westerly direction. The keeper later wrote in a report to the Lighthouse Board:

The noise grew louder and louder, sounding something like a battery of artillery or a troop of cavalry crossing a long bridge. In less than a minute came the shocks, the first one lasting about two minutes, the next one about as long, with about two minutes intervals.

It is impossible to describe how horrible and unnatural everything was during the first shock. The cranes, about a thousand of them, that nest on Raccoon Key during the summer months, were flying about making a fearful noise, and all the poultry on the island joined in making the noise. The cattle were running about with fright.

One of the chimneys fell off the assistant keeper's dwelling, and plaster was cracked.

Each keeper who felt the earthquakes was directed to make a report to the Lighthouse Board, which then turned the information over to the U.S. Geological Survey for analysis. The report showed that earthquakes shook both the eastern and western seaboards of the United States between August 1886 and January 1887. The August 31 earthquake moved up the eastern seacoast from south to north, affecting barrier islands and ocean-front lands more so than the mainland, at least until it reached the Chesapeake. Surprisingly, there were numerous reports of tremors on this inland body of water.

Keepers of at least eight lighthouses from the mouth of the Bay to the middle Chesapeake reported feeling the shocks of earthquakes on at least two different days. The keeper at Point of Shoals, up the James River, felt three distinct shocks on August 31, beginning at 9:50 P.M. and

On a hot evening in August 1886, the keeper of Cove Point Lighthouse felt the tremors of an earthquake while sitting outdoors.

Old Point Comfort was one of many lighthouses shaken by the Great Charleston Earthquake of 1886. Named for its epicenter, it was one of the worst earthquakes in U.S. history.

continuing about every five minutes. Farther up the Bay, Solomons Lump Light, a screw pile off the Eastern Shore of Maryland, shook twice from quakes fifteen minutes apart.

A short distance away, the Hooper Strait Light keeper also heard a rumbling sound and felt two distinct shocks; the first at 9:55 P.M. and the second about 10 P.M. Both shocks were light, but they caused the weights in the windows to rattle.

At Cove Point Light, on the west side of the Bay, the keeper was sitting outside on the doorsteps of the dwelling when he felt a slight shock, accompanied by a tremor. The motion continued for a minute and a half around 10 P.M., according to the house clock, which the keeper could see.

At Drum Point, just south of Cove Point, the vibration was strong enough to slam doors, rattle the bell machine, and wake the sleeping children.

Earthquake tremors were not limited to August 31, however. They occurred repeatedly along the seaboard, beginning on August 10 when the keeper of the sixty-eight-foot tower at Waackaack Station, New Jersey, felt the earth tremble beneath

him at 2:10 in the afternoon while standing on the beach overlooking New York Bay.

Tremors were felt daily in South Carolina following the main earthquake on August 31 and continuing for the next two weeks. Then the tremors became more infrequent, occurring several times in October and November, with the last ones felt in early January 1887.

On November 5, the keeper of Cape Charles Light on Smith Island was near the top of his 150-foot tower when it began to shake. He reported that the tower rocked perceptibly for fifteen seconds.

At Thimble Shoal Light, the keeper felt the station shake. Though slight, the shock was strong enough to cause the keeper to go looking to see if something had gone adrift and struck the lighthouse.

Perhaps because of its location off the seaboard, the Chesapeake Bay was spared the severity of the August 31 earthquake, which cracked light towers both north and south of the Bay. At the lighthouse offices at Charleston, South Carolina, the quake was so severe it left the engineer's office in a shambles, with cracked, bulging walls and a leaking roof.

At Charleston Lighthouse on Morris Island, South Carolina, the quake split the earth, creating two- to four-inch-wide fissures that ran from ten to one hundred feet. The keeper counted twenty fissures on the island, many of them oozing water and sand. He had left his dwelling at 9:53 P.M. to relieve his assistant and was standing beside the 150-foot tower with his hand on the doorknob, when the earth began to move. The keeper watched in horror as the tower shook violently. After the second shock had subsided, the keeper rushed up the stairs. He could hardly keep his footing when the third shock hit. The lens swung rapidly back and forth, three or four times in a matter of seconds, yet the tower continued to stand. The shocks continued through the night and the next day. By the close of September 1, the keeper had counted eighteen tremors, and they were only in the second day of the disturbance. The Charleston Lighthouse suffered two major cracks in the earthquakes of 1886, including one that ran more than halfway around the tower.

The reports made by the keepers were of great value, since in many instances, the tremors were felt a distance from the epicenter, and the movement was exaggerated in the tall towers along the coast, yet it was hardly felt on the ground.

Such was the case at Absecon Light, a brick tower rising 159 feet above the seashore of Atlantic City, New Jersey. The lighthouse keeper could hardly make his way off the gallery that encircled the tower at the top for the violent up-and-down motion. When he called his wife to find out if she had felt the earthquake, she suggested he was suffering from vertigo. Likewise, when the assistant came to relieve him of his duties just a few minutes after the quake and read what he had written in the logbook, the assistant told him that "such a record might raise a question as to his sanity," for he had felt nothing on the ground.

While most of the keepers recognized the tremors as earthquakes, at least one assistant keeper thought they were the work of a ghost. At the Hilton Head Range Light on the island in South Carolina, the keeper's dwelling "shook and heaved like a small boat in a heavy sea," reported the primary keeper. Three of the stone caps on the brick piers at the base of the sixty-foot main tower were moved out of alignment, although they had been set in cement.

When the keeper checked with his assistant, who tended the front beacon of the range lights, he learned that the man and his wife had blamed the shaking earth on a long-gone keeper. "They thought it was the ghost of a former assistant, who lies buried near the house, and that he was giving them a shaking up," the keeper reported.

The coastal lights were certainly "shaken up" that year, but somehow every light remained standing when the last tremor was felt. Two weeks later, in mid-January 1887, several lighthouses in California were shaken by very light tremors, nothing compared with the Great Charleston Earthquake on the East Coast.

Repairs were made and life went back to normal. In the future, it would be the West Coast, not the East, that would steal the headlines with reports of earthquakes.

A frozen Chesapeake—like the one pictured here around Sandy Point Lighthouse—made life difficult for lighthouse keepers during the severe winter of 1893.

Chapter Eight

Stranded in the Ice

On the night of the storm, my brothers climbed up in a very tall cherry tree in our yard to look for the light. All across the Bay was only blackness. We knew the lighthouse must have been carried away. We were afraid Papa must have been lost, too.

Mrs. Luther George, quoted in the December 4, 1955, *Virginian-Pilot and the Portsmouth Star* about the loss of Wolf Trap Light in 1893.

*T*he rivers of the Chesapeake had already been frozen solid for three weeks when on January 17, 1893, the thermometer dipped to a record-setting seventeen degrees below zero. The great freeze of the nineteenth century had settled in. All over the Chesapeake Bay and the northeast coast, the cold brought commerce to a standstill, forcing many people out of work. Not even the freezes of the 1870s had wreaked so much hardship on the population.

The ice in Tangier Sound off Crisfield was a foot deep, while ice on portions of the Choptank River, heading upriver to Cambridge, was measured at more than twenty inches by the city tug *Baltimore*, sent by the harbor board to cut ice in the isolated harbors of the Eastern Shore.

The freeze wasn't just up north. The entire Chesapeake had taken on an Arctic appearance as far south as the capes. On January 19, the Baltimore *Sun* reported that the southern Bay was "one huge mass of ice, and it is apparently frozen from shore to shore, the like of which has not been equalled here for thirty-five years. The captains of the company steamers report that the ice extends for miles out in the ocean."

Despite the ice, men continued to traverse the rivers and Bay, but on foot. On January 18, nine men walked across the upper Chesapeake Bay, which was

frozen at least a foot thick. It was just one of numerous ice walks, some done evidently just for the challenge, others out of necessity. Around Annapolis, schoolchildren took a shortcut to school across the frozen Severn River. And Maryland's mighty oyster navy, more used to manning rifles on the decks of their schooners and steamers to control the feisty oystermen who fought over who would harvest the oysters bars, now laced up their ice skates to go to work. Deputy Commander E. A. Hartge, in charge of the state police schooner *Daisy Archer*, ice-skated with two of his crew from the West River to the Severn, a distance of about ten miles, to check on dredgers whose vessels were frozen in the ice.

On the many inhabited islands of the Chesapeake, families struggled in the great freeze to survive, yet no one was more isolated and threatened than the men who tended the navigational lights. Out on the Bay and its tributaries, dozens of lighthouse keepers found themselves alone, with a limited amount of food and fuel, and in the precarious position of keeping an open flame going while ice shook and rocked their stations. To add to the misery, four inches of snow fell overnight on January 18.

That week a party of men from Crisfield walked a mile and a half across the ice to check on the keeper. Janes Island Light had been destroyed

The original Wolf Trap Lighthouse, built on piles, was pushed over in 1893 during one of the worst freezes of the nineteenth century. This caisson, topped by a brick dwelling, was constructed to replace the pile lighthouse.

by ice once before, in 1879. The ice was a foot thick, but there were some air holes around the lighthouse, and one of the men fell through. Fortunately, he was pulled to safety and was able to warm up by the lighthouse fire and dry his clothes before the party headed home.

Falling through air pockets in the ice was the greatest problem facing people who ventured out on the seemingly solid Bay. As the tide rose and ebbed, it cracked and splintered the ice, creating unexpected open water.

By that year, 1893, there were thirty-nine lighthouses out in the water on piles. In the four decades since the first screw pile was built on the Chesapeake, seven lighthouses had been knocked over or sheared off their foundations by ice. Many more had been severely damaged. Lighthouse authorities had learned a few things about protecting these vulnerable structures from ice, but they were about to discover that most of their efforts were in vain when faced with a tremendous freeze like the one experienced in 1893.

During the great freeze, a brief thaw created a complete breakup of the ice. Chunks of ice and snow began to move. Pushed by the wind, the ice

rode up on top of other chunks and piled together into huge icebergs, as high as twenty-five to fifty feet. The lighthouses and their keepers were in danger as they had never been before.

No one felt the chill worse than the young children of John William Thomas. Their father was the keeper of Wolf Trap Lighthouse, a screw pile located off Mathews County, Virginia, in the Chesapeake. As the Bay and its rivers became paralyzed with ice, the children worried about their father.

"It was a bad freeze-up way out in the Bay past the lighthouse," Mrs. Luther George, the keeper's daughter, would later recount to a Portsmouth, Virginia, newspaperman. "We lived on Davis Creek then, down at the end of the county. On the night of the storm, my brothers climbed up in a very tall cherry tree in our yard to look for the light. All across the Bay was only blackness. We knew the lighthouse must have been carried away. We were afraid Papa must have been lost, too."

The ice bore down on Wolf Trap Light, stacking up against the foundations, whose legs were hollow iron sleeves over wooden piles. Just before the house gave way on January 22, keeper John William Thomas escaped by walking across the frozen ice to a nearby tugboat, which was also trapped in the frozen Bay.

Several days later, the Wolf Trap Lighthouse was discovered by the revenue cutter *Morrill* about one mile northeast of Thimble Shoal at the entrance to Hampton Roads, drifting out toward the capes. Only its lantern was above water, posing a real danger to navigation. Fearing a vessel would run into it at night, the captain of the cutter ordered his men to tie a thick rope, called a hawser, around the lantern. The lighthouse was towed across the Bay to the south shore, where it was left to drift onto the beach. It was empty, everything having been salvaged, including the lamps. The rest of the Thomas family did not learn about John William's rescue until a week after the light went out and the keeper was able to make shore and contact his family.

All around the Bay, lighthouse keepers feared for their lives as the narrow legs of the pile lighthouses swayed and bent with the pressure of the ice building around them. On January 21, William Gunter, keeper of Old Plantation Flats, sent a hasty telegram to the Fifth District inspector: "Last night, twenty minutes after one, the light fell from the stand and broke, the tanks have started off. I have fastened them best I could. House near wrecked, what shall I do?" The inspector ordered him to abandon the station. Even the captain of the tug that picked up the keeper reported that the lighthouse appeared ready to fall before the ice. Somehow, the lighthouse refused to yield, however. "If it escapes until morning it will have passed the crisis," predicted a newspaper reporter. He was right; it survived.

The news was not as good for Solomons Lump Lighthouse, located midway up the Bay in Kedges Strait above Smith Island. During the first week of February, the lighthouse inspector received a telegram from assistant keeper Gordon Kellen: "Solomons Lump succumbed to the ice on Wednesday, February 1, at about 2 P.M. It is a total wreck. I have saved all in the house except the bell and its machinery, staying by the house until it fell."

The lighthouse was pushed over by the ice and partially submerged. Kellen, a nephew of keeper J. D. Evans, who was not on the station at the time, made his escape via the lighthouse dory and was found adrift in the boat at the mouth of the Great Annemessex River about 1 P.M. the next day. He had spent the entire night out in the cold of Tangier Sound amid dangerous floes of heavy ice.

Janes Island also appeared fated to topple again, but this time, the icebergs failed to knock down the house. It did, however, wrench the fog bell from its fastenings.

At Smith Island Light, a pile house off the southern entrance to the Potomac River, keeper James Bennett Williams and his assistant abandoned the house on January 20 at 10 A.M., believing it was also about to succumb to the ice. When they returned at the end of January, they found that the ice had broken seven of the braces and one sleeve pile and the walkway around the exterior of the dwelling had moved out of alignment. While they could not shine a light because the structure was out of plumb, they did ring the fog bell to warn vessels away from the shoal.

The assistant keeper of Stingray Point Lighthouse at the mouth of the Rappahannock River in Virginia finally gave up and abandoned his station

on January 25, after the running ice continually snuffed out his light. In a letter to the inspector, the assistant explained that he was all alone and could not keep the light going. The running ice knocking against the house put out the light almost every fifteen minutes, so the light required constant attention. The keeper, Larry Marchant, had left the lighthouse before the freeze began and had been unable to return.

Other stations sustained partial damage from the ice floes. Inside Hampton Roads, Bush Bluff Lightship was dragged off its position at the entrance to the Elizabeth River by ice. The ice also tore several braces off the foundation of Windmill Point Light, at the northern entrance to the Rappahannock River.

The winter of 1893 had taken a devastating toll on the lighthouses of the Chesapeake, but the destruction was not over yet. Two years later, another cold winter produced heavy ice floes, which finally carried away Smith Point Light.

On February 13, 1895, writing in his logbook, keeper Williams described the condition of the house and the situation they endured:

> The station shakes very badly. It is supported by only a few iron piles and I have seen it sway back and forth like a rocking chair. The drifting ice was drifting all around the station and the Bay was covered with ice as far as the eye can see. No kinds of vessels were passing and there was nothing to see but fields of ice. Tomorrow, if the station is still holding up, I feel that my brother and I will be forced to abandon this station, even though we do not want to.

On Valentine's Day, Williams and his brother, Ferdinand, loaded the lighthouse boat with everything they could salvage and pushed it two and a half miles over the ice to Northumberland County, Virginia. Local residents who had seen their flight met them on the shore with warm food and beverages.

That evening, the lighthouse was found adrift in the ice by Captain W. H. Porter of the steamer *Gaston*. Porter was able to reach the wreck by sled and salvaged the lens and machin-

A tug pulling a barge cuts through thick ice on the Chesapeake behind Sandy Point Lighthouse during the winter of 1996. In the nineteenth century, few vessels could pass through the ice and many were stranded, along with the keepers.

ery. Meanwhile, the keeper at Old Plantation Flats was forced to extinguish the light twice because of ice during the winter of 1895. The second time the light was threatened, on February 17, rising temperatures caused the ice in the Bay to break up and move toward the ocean, running with the tide. At 10 A.M., so much ice had lodged against the base of the lighthouse that it caused the structure to lean, and the water ran out of the tanks, submerging the floors. On his last night on the lighthouse, assistant keeper Kirwan said the structure shook so much that he was forced to put out the light and remove the valuable lens for fear it would fall and break, as it had in 1893. Kirwan predicted the lighthouse would not survive two more tides.

After the big freeze of 1893, Old Plantation Flats underwent extensive repairs to be strengthened. The Lighthouse Board had believed it could withstand another ice attack. And, in fact, it did. As the weather warmed and the ice thawed, Old Plantation Flats continued to stand. It stood for another seventy years, holding up in the face of numerous additional ice attacks. It stood until the Coast Guard finally dismantled it as part of its modernization program in the 1960s.

The harsh winters of the 1890s proved to be a turning point for the U.S. Lighthouse Board. In the three decades from 1856 through the 1880s, it had lost only seven screw-pile lighthouses to ice. In the 1890s, however, it lost three lighthouses in two years. Only two more pile lighthouses would be built on the Chesapeake after 1893. Pages Rock, up the York River, was already under construction when the winter of 1893 began. The other screw pile, Ragged Point, completed in 1910, was also on a protected river site, up the Potomac.

Improved technology helped the board make its decision about the types of lighthouses to build. The caissons already in use at lighthouse sites in the Chesapeake had proven they could withstand the pressure of the ice. Consequently, all three lighthouses destroyed in the 1890s—Smith Point, Wolf Trap, and Solomons Lump—would be replaced by caisson lighthouses. Although more expensive to build, they withstood the ice, year after year, providing a safe haven for keepers.

But as time would soon reveal, the danger with caisson lighthouses came not after they were built, but while they were under construction.

Chapter Nine

Isolation, Illness, Death, and the Law

The keeper of this light did not show as much nerve as he should. . . .

Fifth District Inspector Yates Stirling, in a letter to the Lighthouse Board about the keeper of
Smith Point Light, who abandoned his station after it was canted by ice.

T wo weeks after Ferdinand Williams, assistant keeper of Smith Point Lighthouse, helped his brother push a skiff across the ice to safety, he was dead. There is no record of whether the many days in a wildly swaying lighthouse or the grueling two-and-a-half-mile journey across the ice contributed to his death, but they probably did, given the difficult circumstances he lived under during the freeze of 1895.

Many lighthouse keepers suffered physically and emotionally—particularly during harsh winters—under a lighthouse system that expected them to put service before personal health and safety. If they wanted to keep their jobs, keepers had to endure the terrible shaking of the houses and the frightening sight of ice piling up around their station. They knew they faced dismissal if they left the house and it failed to fall. It had happened before. During the bad freeze of 1881, for example, a keeper by the name of Price twice abandoned the Choptank River Lighthouse off Oxford when ice cracked some of the wrought-iron pilings and tilted the dwelling. After the ice was gone, the inspector came by, found the house relatively plumb, and determined that the broken pilings were ice-breakers, not supporting piles. He suggested that Price tender his resignation, which he did.

Given the severity of the winters of 1893 and 1895, Fifth District Inspector Yates Stirling could have shown a little concern for human life. In-

stead, he revealed amazing callousness toward the men who had tried and failed to maintain their lights under the worst of conditions. Scrutinizing each case with a cold heart, Stirling asked for the resignations of at least two keepers and reprimanded others who abandoned lighthouses that swayed, leaned, and cracked, but failed to fall before the ice.

After the 1893 thaw, Stirling accused the Smith Point keeper of not showing "as much nerve as he should" when he abandoned the severely damaged lighthouse which could no longer support a light. "I think the keeper had good reason to believe that the structure would go," Stirling conceded in a letter to the Lighthouse Board. "While perhaps the keeper of this light did not show as much nerve as he should, I would not recommend that any unfavorable action be taken in his case."

However, he asked for the resignation of keeper Gunter of Old Plantation Flats, despite the obviously dangerous condition of the lighthouse and despite the fact that he had given the keeper permission to abandon the station. The inspector based much of his decision on how the lighthouse looked after the ice was gone. Not surprisingly, lighthouses that were leaning when tons and tons of ice pressed against their foundations were often perfectly plumb when the ice disappeared. Consequently, Stirling accused Gunter of acting "in a panic" when Gunter claimed in a telegram mes-

A fully eclipsed moon rises over Sandy Point Lighthouse. Keepers in Chesapeake Bay lighthouses had plenty of time to observe such natural phenomena during long periods of isolation.

sage that the "house was near wrecked." In a letter to the Lighthouse Board, Stirling wrote:

The present condition of this station shows that the keeper sent to this office an incorrect and misleading dispatch by stating that the house was near wrecked, thus showing that he acted in a panic. There is I think justification for his leaving the light as he was entirely alone and, his lens being broken, he could not maintain a light. Navigation also was closed by the ice. But instead of remaining at Cape Charles City and returning to his light which he could have done in a few days, he went to his home in Eastville and could not be induced to return to his station until Ensign Maxwell went there and placed him in the house.

Gunter was one of few black men in the lighthouse service at that time. He had served well at nearby Cherrystone Inlet Lighthouse from 1891 to 1892 and had a very good record. Stirling conceded this, yet reported, "His action in this case shows he is unfit for responsibility and I recommend his discharge."

The assistant keeper, William R. Wescott, was so fearful of dismissal that he produced a doctor's certificate proving that he was ill with pneumonia. Nevertheless, Wescott was also fired because he had failed to find a substitute during his illness.

Keepers and assistant keepers were expected to provide substitutes when they were ill. Undoubtedly, they were also expected to pay the substitutes out of their own meager wages. While some lighthouse keepers found regular substitutes among their family or friends, most found it difficult to get a replacement, particularly in the dead of winter. Consequently, many keepers simply overlooked the requirement for a substitute. The keeper and his assistant generally covered for each other, failing to note in the logbook any missed time unless the illness or injury was serious enough to demand a substitute. No doubt, it was a way of saving money as well.

Bad weather posed serious, if not deadly, problems for a sick or an injured lighthouse keeper. If he was alone in the lighthouse, which was often the case, the keeper had to muster up the strength to row or sail himself back to shore.

Before the age of radio, which did not reach the offshore stations until the 1930s, keepers had little means of communicating with the shore, except by flagging down passing boats. This was how one keeper in 1895 notified his superiors that he needed immediate medical assistance.

In February of that year, during the freeze and thaw that destroyed Smith Point Lighthouse, John Reynolds, keeper of Sandy Point Lighthouse, became too ill to continue his duties. He flagged down Captain Collins of the tug *Frances* and asked the captain to take him off the lighthouse. Captain Collins could not get close enough to the light to take the keeper off, so he relayed the message to the superintendent, and the lighthouse tender was sent to the light.

During the ice floes of 1893, the Sharkfin Light did not shine for almost a week. Residents of the Eastern Shore could see that the light was dark but could not reach the keeper to help.

"It is feared that Captain Cole, the keeper, who is alone, has either perished from cold and hunger or is too ill to perform his duties," the Baltimore *Sun* reported on January 20, 1893.

Sharkfin Lighthouse stood in Fishing Bay, between Bishops Head and Deal Island on the lower Eastern Shore of Maryland. While many water stations were within a mile of land, Sharkfin was located five miles from the nearest shore. With one foot of solid ice in the Bay, it was virtually impossible to reach the lighthouse by boat, and residents could only assume that the keeper was too ill to make it out on foot.

By the time the thaw was over, however, the light was shining once again, and Captain Cole, who put in an order for his regular supplies, did not report any serious illness or malfunction of the light. Whether Captain Cole failed to light his lamp because running ice prevented him from keeping the flame or because of a brief illness, such as flu, may forever remain a mystery, for the Lighthouse Board evidently never learned what happened, either.

One keeper spared the ordeal of 1893 was Stingray Point Lighthouse keeper Larry Marchant. He was caught on shore when the ice formed and

The caisson lighthouses, like Point No Point, are picturesque, but lonely, places to live. Most of the last keepers and coastguardsmen who served on the lighthouses were more than happy when the lighthouses were automated.

could not get out to his station. When Marchant retired in 1920 after thirty-two years of service at Stingray Point, he told a Baltimore *Sun* newspaper reporter, "I have not been sick a single day and have not lost a day's pay. The secret of my good health is that I have been where the doctors could not get to me."

Marchant may have gotten along just fine without a doctor, but in numerous cases the isolation of the water stations proved dangerous, if not fatal, to the keepers. The logbooks are dotted with accounts of sickness, injury, and death. In some cases, the keeper simply stuck it out at the light; in more severe cases of illness or injury, he was taken by boat back to shore for medical treat-

ment. Several keepers talked of suffering from appendicitis while out on the lighthouse. (An infection of the appendix can be deadly if the appendix ruptures.) Several early lighthouse keepers suffered or died from the ill effects of not receiving immediate medical attention for the illness. Fortunately, by the time Bloody Point Lighthouse keeper Tom White fell ill with acute appendicitis in 1945, radios had been installed in the lighthouses.

"The boys [assistants] couldn't have gotten me to shore," White recounted in the Baltimore *Sun* article of October 31, 1948. "But with the radio we were able to get in touch with Annapolis and they sent a patrol boat to take me to the hospital at the Naval Academy. Without the radio,

that Wingate became "crazy with his head" just before he passed away. The two men had been together on the lighthouse for four years.

The most common injury on pile lighthouses was falling through the trapdoor in the walkway when it was accidentally left up. The trapdoor opened onto a ladder that led down to the platform beneath the dwelling. At Tangier Sound Lighthouse, the keeper fell through the trapdoor and hurt himself badly enough on December 3, 1913, to require medical attention ashore.

There were also some odd shore-side injuries that prevented keepers from returning to their station. One keeper wrote that he was "detained by being run over by a horse."

Illness in the family obviously created stress and worry for the lighthouse keepers who were forced to spend long periods away from their families. Many serious, deadly, and contagious diseases plagued communities in the 1800s, including tuberculosis, pneumonia, and smallpox.

The years 1896 through 1898 were difficult ones for the keepers of Holland Island Bar. In 1896, the keeper left his station from August 19 through August 25 to see his sick wife. Again in November he was gone for five days to see her. He then reported a death in the family, though it was not his wife. On December 21, 1896, the keeper left again to visit his wife, who was, by now, near death. When he returned on January 7, 1897, he carefully noted in the logbook that his absence "was caused by the death of my wife." But, he added, "I had a substitute in my place."

A year later, it was the assistant keeper who was out to visit ailing family members. Three times in March and April 1898 he wrote in the logbook that he was visiting sick family members. Once he became ill himself, perhaps catching whatever illness his family had. In September, he left again to visit his sick wife and was gone for two weeks. Since there was no note in the logbook about a death in the family, someone reading the account a hundred years later can only wonder if they all survived.

my lighthouse career would have ended then and there."

Many keepers died at their stations, their illnesses never determined or recorded. On Hooper Island Lighthouse, assistant keeper G. B. Wingate died mysteriously on board the station at 5:30 A.M., Wednesday, March 23, 1910. On the seventeenth, Wingate had been well enough to leave the station at 6 A.M. to get the mail. If Wingate fell ill in the ensuing days, it was never logged in the lighthouse book. Keeper C. H. Applegarth, who had been keeper since December 1904, wrote in the logbook

Cape Charles Lighthouse on Smith Island at the mouth of the Chesapeake Bay was very isolated, but three keepers and their families kept each other company.

Chapter Ten

All the Comforts of Home

The scene I remember best is granddaddy cleaning the lens on the lighthouse lamp.

Anna Weems Ewalt, about her early years visiting her grandparents on Drum Point Lighthouse.

When James Loch Weems put in for a transfer in 1891, foremost on his mind was caring for his sick infant daughter, Mary. The thirty-six-year-old Weems was stationed at Cobb Point Bar Light, a screw pile in the Potomac River. But, as he explained to the Lighthouse Board, he wanted a lighthouse position on land so that he could be near his family in case his daughter should need his attention.

Weems had already spent a number of years in the lighthouse service, first as assistant keeper of Cove Point Lighthouse, then keeper of Cobb Point Bar Light on the Potomac River. The Lighthouse Board was sympathetic to his family needs, and on October 1, 1891, Weems took over as keeper of Drum Point Light.

This lighthouse was also a screw pile, but unlike many Chesapeake Bay water stations, which were located from one-half mile to more than ten miles offshore, Drum Point was relatively close to the land. Standing a mere hundred yards off the point at the northern entrance to the Patuxent River, the station guided vessels around a short sandy spit The lighthouse was so close to land that the Lighthouse Board gave Weems permission to have his family live aboard the station with him.

Drum Point Light was a relatively new light station, built in 1883 as commerce on the Patuxent River increased. Efforts to build it as early as the 1850s had failed, but plans for the

lighthouse were resurrected, and in 1882 Congress appropriated twenty-five thousand dollars. Similar to other screw piles, it was built on seven 10-inch-thick wrought-iron pilings screwed into the river bottom. Originally planned as the first of a pair of range lights, its rear light was never built. Evidently, the Lighthouse Board did not see the need for it.

The hexagonal cottage had all the makings of a beautiful home, with the added attraction of a gleaming light on top. It had pine wood floors in the first-story dining room, kitchen, and master bedroom. On the second floor was a small bedroom with dormer windows and a bell room with its clockwork machinery. A narrow spiral staircase extended from the first floor to the octagonal cupola, encased in glass, where the fourth-order Fresnel prism lens showed a fixed red light.

Weems's wife, Alice, immediately set about making a home out of the six-sided wooden cottage on stilts. She furnished the lighthouse with wooden rocking chairs, washstands, wood furniture, and a big oak bed. China chamber pots went under the beds, so that at night family members would not have to go outside to the walkway, which wraps around the exterior of the first floor, to use the outhouse, which hung over the side of the station.

Despite its watery location, the home lacked none of the fineries of life ashore. In fact, Drum Point was the only water station to have its own

Drum Point Lighthouse was so close to land in 1918 that a footbridge connected it to the mainland. Originally, families lived with the keepers in many of the pile lighthouses around the Chesapeake, but eventually the Lighthouse Board banned them from living on the water-based lighthouses, largely because of the danger of ice. Drum Point was an exception to the rule and was home to the family of James L. Weems from 1891 through about 1918.

dining room. Mrs. Weems saw to that because she wanted to have a place to entertain guests properly. And there were many guests, particularly on weekends. Friends and family would row out to the lighthouse, located just a mile and a half from Solomons Island, bringing gifts of food to share with the Weemses.

When they moved into the lighthouse, the Weemses had five children—three boys and two girls—including little, sick Mary. No records indicate what she suffered from, but in the nineteenth century, childhood diseases were common. This one eventually claimed her life; she died in June 1893 at the age of three. Sadly, she was the first of two Weems children to die in the lighthouse. The other daughter, Anne, died in February 1901 at age sixteen, again the cause unknown.

But birth, as well as death, was a part of this lighthouse's history. By 1906, there were three generations housed in the light station. That was the year granddaughter Anna was born. While there were many children born in the land-based lighthouses, Anna Weems Ewalt was one of the few born on a water station on the Chesapeake Bay. (Sevenfoot Knoll was the birthplace of at least two of the thirteen children of Capt. James T. Bolling.)

Before her death in 1995 at the age of eighty-eight, Mrs. Ewalt recalled how on Thursday, July 12, 1906, her father and grandfather went by dory to Solomons to get the doctor before her arrival. The men sailed back with the doctor in plenty of time for him to help with Anna's appearance in the early morning hours of Friday the thirteenth.

"I was born in the big downstairs bedroom, my grandmother's room," Mrs. Ewalt wrote in a 1980 account of her childhood years on the lighthouse, which appeared in the spring issue of the *Mulberry Tree Papers*. Like many newlyweds, Mrs. Ewalt's parents lived with her grandparents briefly in order to save money for their own house. When Anna was a year old, they moved to a house, a few miles from the lighthouse. The family naturally visited the lighthouse often, Mrs. Ewalt recalled.

Saturdays and Sundays we'd row out and spend the day. Sometimes I'd stay longer.

The scene I remember best is granddaddy cleaning the lens on the lighthouse lamp. This was a daily ritual. At dawn he would climb the narrow winding stairs to the cupola and extinguish the light. Then he set to work. It took him a long time because the lamp burned kerosene and if the wick weren't just so, it would smoke up those Fresnel lenses. I can hear him swearing even now. He didn't sit down to breakfast until the job was done.

At night he'd light the lamp again. The big bell also had to be rung whenever we had fog. It worked on weights just like a grandfather's clock and when the weights went down—it took about two hours—the mechanism had to be wound again by hand. People ask me if the booming of the bell didn't bother me. You get accustomed to those things.

Mrs. Ewalt often recalled how on foggy nights, her grandfather seemed to run like clockwork, too, snoring contently for what appeared to young Anna to be exactly one hour and fifty-eight minutes, and waking just in time to quickly rewind the clock with its six-hundred-pound weights, which required a good deal of muscle. It had to be done in about two minutes, or the captains of vessels depending on the bell might think they had missed Drum Point entirely. The job of tending the fog bell was far easier in Weems's day than it had been in the early part of the nineteenth century, when lighthouse keepers rang the bell by hand. Weems, however, still had to wake every two hours throughout the night to perform the tedious job of rewinding the machinery.

"Granddaddy would wipe my hands before I got up from the table, to make sure I didn't get grease on the walls," she wrote. "The walls were an awful gray, . . . but granddaddy kept the place looking spotless."

One of the exciting events for all children, including Anna, was watching for the lighthouse tender to arrive. *Holly* and *Jessamine* were both beautiful iron side-wheel steamboats that served the lighthouses. *Holly* more often handled delivery of supplies, while *Jessamine* was often employed in inspections and construction.

Today, a bedroom inside Drum Point Lighthouse has been furnished with the type of bed, curtains, and accessories that would have been found in the lighthouse at the turn of the century when Anna Weems Ewalt was born here in 1906.

Lighthouse boats would come by every so often, bringing wood, coal, kerosene, and provisions, such as bread, sugar, coffee, and potatoes, to all the lighthouses on the Chesapeake. The fuel was stored on the open platform beneath the cottage. Every bit of space was put to use.

Despite the abundant wood and coal, the cottage, which had no insulation, suffered the full brunt of the winter cold and wind, which often howled around the unprotected point of land and rattled through every crack in the window sashes:

Winters were cold. The parlor was the coldest room because it faced north, and we never used it in winter. People stayed mostly in the kitchen where it was warm and sunny. At night I'd snuggle into a billowy feather bed and bury my head in my down pillow, keeping warm.

Christmas was a cheerful time. There was always a tree, a cedar cut from the slopes on Drum Point. The ornaments were handmade. We'd string cranberries and popcorn and hang cookies from a ribbon. Through the year, grandfather saved his tobacco foil to wrap around walnuts, making other decorations to hang on the tree.

There'd be sprigs of holly, pyracantha and boxwood in all the rooms. Grandmother liked to adorn the pictures and mirrors on the lighthouse walls with holly.

Unlike most lighthouse locations, which lost land as wind and tide eroded the beaches around them, Drum Point continually gained sand, primarily from Cedar Point across the Patuxent River. Before its light would be turned off in 1962, Drum Point Light would become landlocked, while Cedar Point Light, originally built on land, would become an island lighthouse, in danger of falling into the Bay. But when Mrs. Ewalt was a young child, the point was already beginning to stretch out toward the screw-pile light:

The lighthouse, as near as I can remember was…within hallowing distance, as they say here in the county. I couldn't have been more than three or four when I started walking to the lighthouse. Daddy carried me some and I walked some. It must have been a mile or two but people walked farther in those days. We'd go along the sand beach so we'd have to wait until the tide was out.

In 1918, the shore was stretched close enough to the lighthouse that a long boardwalk was built between the screw pile and the shore, where the Weemses kept a garden, some chickens, and a horse and buggy. It was almost like being on land. When another keeper applied for and received permission to put in a telephone in 1923, it further reduced any sense of isolation.

Among the many visitors to the lighthouse were three young girls. One summer, twelve-year-old Rebecca Sedwick Koch, of Calvert County, was visiting the family of William Dorsey at Governors Run, a popular vacation spot. When the Dorsey girls, Mary and Maude, were invited to visit James Loch Weems and his wife at the lighthouse, Rebecca tagged along.

Mary Dorsey drove them to the point in a horse and buggy. The road was very sandy and the trip took quite a while, but finally the girls reached Drum Point. The horse and buggy were tied nearby, and the girls waited for Captain Weems to pick them up in his dory.

"The most exciting time came at night when the steamboats passed with their twinkling lights and blew their horns to signal," Mrs. Koch recalled in an account of the visit. "Most of them Captain Weems knew by name and told interesting tales of their captains and of shipwrecks he had seen.

Mrs. Weems did not want the girls to miss the sunrise, so the next morning they climbed the circular staircase to the cupola, where they found a spectacular view. Captain Weems showed them how he polished the light and refilled the lamps with kerosene. The light was so shiny, it looked like a big, revolving glass eye to Rebecca.

The Weemses collected their wash water from the rain that ran off the tin roof. The rain ran into downspouts, which carried the water in pipes through the ceiling and down into the four wooden, two-hundred-gallon tanks, which stood in the corners of each room. Unlike the keepers at other stations, they did not drink this water.

"My mother, of course, was a city-bred woman and she made my father bring water by the gallons from shore. She wasn't going to drink any of that," Mrs. Ewalt wrote.

James Loch Weems had raised his family at the lighthouse. It had been a place for death and life, for good times and bad. Late in his career, Weems was in need of an assistant, which the board granted him.

Unlike any other water-based lighthouse, Drum Point had a dining room where Mrs. Alice Weems entertained friends and family.

Hardwood furniture, pictures, and old-fashioned oil lamps decorate the interior of Drum Point Lighthouse today at Calvert Marine Museum. Visitors can see how the Weems family lived when the lighthouse served both as a working navigational aid and home to a family.

"I kept going back to the lighthouse until grandmother and granddaddy left in 1919," recalled Mrs. Ewalt. "A few years after that, we moved to Baltimore."

Anna Weems Ewalt was about twelve when she left the lighthouse, but it would not be forever. She never lost her interest in the screw pile, and many years later, she would be called upon to help furnish the hexagonal cottage when it was moved to the Calvert Marine Museum in Calvert County. For years, she revisited those happy childhood memories by guiding hundreds of visitors on tours of her childhood home.

Men nearly died sinking the caisson for Smith Point Lighthouse off the mouth of the Potomac River when they struck a vein of poisonous gas.

Chapter Eleven

Killer Caissons

It was a fight for life. One large wave would fill the cylinder, and it would sink.
A rescue in such a sea would have been almost impossible.

A 1904 *Baltimore American* article about towing Smith Point Light's
caisson to the site of the new lighthouse.

When day broke on September 7, 1897, the waters of the Chesapeake were as smooth as glass, perfect conditions for towing a clumsy caisson to its site in the Bay. Towing caissons and sinking them in place went rather smoothly when the weather cooperated, as it appeared it would when a small fleet of steamers, barges, and tugs left Baltimore Harbor, heading for the site of the new Smith Point Lighthouse. All the materials necessary to build the lighthouse were on the vessels, except the caisson. Because of its size—some thirty-two feet in diameter and weighing one hundred tons—the caisson was to be towed behind one vessel. This was not an easy task, given the unseaworthiness of a round, heavy cylinder. Nevertheless, the towing went well for most of the eighty-mile trip.

The crew was in sight of the Potomac River when the ideal conditions suddenly deteriorated. A squall, packing heavy winds, hit the fleet before they reached the mouth of the river. Big seas quickly developed and waves rolled over the top of the caisson, filling it partially with water. With the caisson foundering and threatening to sink, the workers struggled to lash a canvas top over the cylinder, but water continued to pour through the canvas. A June 28, 1904, article in the *Baltimore American* recounted the horrifying hours that followed:

The crew jumped into the cylinder, where the water was three feet deep and swashing about at a terrific speed, and began bailing.

It was a fight for life. One large wave would fill the cylinder, and it would sink. A rescue in such a sea would have been almost impossible. The [men] began their perilous work at sunset, and the rising sun the next morning saw them still at work. The storm abated and the caisson was saved, but the swells were too high to plant [the caisson], and it was towed to harbor in the Great Wicomico.

A week later, under perfectly calm conditions, the caisson was finally towed to the site and sunk in place. The crew of ninety men worked quickly, mixing tons of concrete and pouring it into the interior of the caisson to weigh it down. It was imperative that the job be done as quickly as possible so that the big caisson would not budge if a storm or heavy seas broke out again. Huge stones were rolled off the barges and positioned around the base to keep the sand and dirt from sifting out from beneath the huge caisson and to prevent it from tipping.

The crew was only several hours into the job of stabilizing the caisson when the skies darkened and a storm once again rolled in on them. The men

Boaters who see the red sector of Smith Point Light know they must change their course or chance hitting a shoal.

break or leak, exposing them to a rush of seawater that could flood the caisson and drown them instantly. If the caisson were sunk very deep, they had to endure pain from increased atmospheric pressure. Such pressure had been known to maim or kill strong men.

The "sand hogs," as caisson workers were nicknamed, had just begun to work that summer day when they hit another danger of caisson work: a vein of hydrogen sulfide gas. The men barely escaped the chamber alive.

Several days later, one of the owners of the company, William H. Flaherty, led fourteen volunteers back down into the working chamber to try to complete the job. The men thought they had beaten the worst of possible disasters when the last shovelful of dirt had been turned. But as they were about to leave the working chamber, the natural vein of hydrogen sulfide gas burst again, filling the chamber with poisonous fumes.

The men scrambled for the one ladder leading up the chamber to safety. In the ensuing struggle, the weaker men fell unconscious from the effects of the gas. Fortunately, the foreman, whose name was Griffin, remained calm and signaled for the men above to drop a rope down into the chamber. Groping to find the unconscious men in the blinding gas, he tied the rope to the nearest workman. One by one Griffin gathered the men under the air shaft leading from the top down into the work chamber and tied them to the rope, so that they could be pulled out of the chamber. Finally, only half-conscious himself, the foreman tied the rope to himself and was pulled out. Griffin was blind for six weeks after the heroic rescue. Many other men took months to recover, but everyone survived.

Despite all their problems, the contractors, Flaherty & Lande, completed Smith Point Lighthouse within a year, the deadline on the contract.

The Smith Point Lighthouse was not the first caisson on the Chesapeake that had given this contractor trouble, and it would not be the last. In 1894, while workers were placing the caisson for Solomons Lump Light, the big cylinder settled out of plumb. The contractors had to sink the opposite side in order to level the foundation. The crew had to add an extra section of cylinder to the top of the structure to give it its correct height.

stuck to their work until the high seas and heavy winds threatened to endanger their lives. Finally, the caisson was abandoned for the evening.

The seas were still rough the next morning when the crew returned to find the caisson tilting five feet from perpendicular. In spite of the stones they had placed around it, the sea had washed the sand out from under one edge.

The crew knew that if the caisson were left in this precarious position until mild weather returned, it could turn onto its side, creating a bigger disaster. To prevent the huge cylinder from tipping further, the men, working in heavy seas, deposited several hundred tons of stone on the side to which the caisson was leaning. Meanwhile, powerful pumps sucked the sand from the other side.

Once level, the caisson had to be sunk another ten feet to bedrock. This was done by thirty-five men who descended into the working chamber with shovels and picks to complete the tedious and dangerous job of lowering the caisson.

Caisson gangs were a tough bunch of men renowned for their courage. They worked in harrowing conditions, in a deep underwater pit where they faced multiple dangers. The caisson could

Flaherty & Lande were but one of a number of companies awarded contracts to sink caissons. And at least half of the twelve caisson lighthouses on the Chesapeake Bay gave the contractors trouble.

Point No Point, one of the last caisson lighthouses built on the Bay, saw several serious accidents before the caisson was firmly in place. In April 1903, a northwest gale caused the temporary pier, built by the contractor as a work platform, to give way. The caisson, no longer supported, turned over, several sections of cylinder plates broke off, and the caisson began drifting down the Bay before the gale. The contractor chased the caisson in his tugboat, but it took two days to retrieve the big cylinder off the Rappahannock River, some forty miles south of the lighthouse site.

In October of that year, the crew tried again to sink the caisson. They positioned the big cylinder and rebuilt the working pier, only to have the pier wrecked by ice that winter before the project was completed. While the caisson suffered little damage this time, it was shifted off its site by the ice field, which also carried away much of the contractor's equipment, four cylinder plates, and the workmen's quarters, besides the pier itself.

In March 1904, the men rebuilt the pier for the third time, and in June they began sinking the caisson, also for the third time. This effort was finally successful, and the lighthouse, located off St. Jerome Creek, north of the mouth of the Potomac River in the Chesapeake Bay, was lighted in April 1905.

A few caisson lighthouses began tilting after they were completed. Bloody Point, off the southern tip of Kent Island on the Eastern Shore, was lighted on October 1, 1882, but a year and a half later it was tilting. On February 29 and March 3, 1884, severe gales scoured the sand from under the northwest corner of the lighthouse, causing it to settle five feet out of plumb. The Lighthouse Board had stone deposited around the northwest side of the lighthouse to prevent further scouring, but all of it disappeared, probably sinking into the mud. In November 1884, sand was dredged from under the high side of the lighthouse until the house began to straighten. However, the workers could never get the house perfectly plumb again. Even today, Bloody Point nods almost indiscernibly about six inches off perpendicular.

It took more than ninety years of exposure to the elements to budge Sharps Island Light. The severe winters of 1976 and 1977 created enough heavy ice on the Chesapeake Bay to push the lighthouse over about twenty degrees.

Given the danger involved in sinking caissons, it is not surprising that men died during the process. There are few accounts of these deaths, but the Thimble Shoal Lighthouse keeper dutifully noted them in his logbook.

In 1914, the third Thimble Shoal Light was the last lighthouse built on the Chesapeake. The second lighthouse at this site, a screw pile, had been destroyed by a collision with a vessel and a subsequent fire in 1909. The keepers occupied a nearby temporary station while the workmen constructed the new lighthouse.

On a gloomy New Year's Day, 1914, the keeper noted that "Mr. Cavell was drowned in the air chamber of the caisson at 10:30 A.M." While the keeper did not elaborate, the caisson quite possibly had suddenly sprung a leak, flooding the working chamber and trapping the man. Another possibility is that heavy seas sloshed down into the underwater work station, drowning him.

On August 14, 1914, less than four months before the new lighthouse was completed and lighted on December 1, another man was killed while working on the new station. The lighthouse keeper recorded even less about this death, but one may assume the man was not killed in the caisson, which certainly was completed by this late date. Given the stormy, windy conditions of the day, he may have slipped and fallen off the structure while working with machinery or materials, or he could have died as a result of any one of several accidents common at construction sites.

The problems encountered at Bloody Point, Point No Point, Solomons Lump, and Smith Point were quite serious, yet they would prove minuscule compared with the events that would unfold in the early 1900s. In those years, Flaherty & Lande began construction of the biggest wooden caisson in history: the Baltimore Lighthouse.

The Craighill Channel Range Lights are still used today to guide ships into the Patapsco River. The front light was the first caisson built on the Chesapeake Bay.

Chapter Twelve

Lighting the Way to Baltimore

No matter how slowly the pressure increases, the men experience severe pains in the head and bleed from the ears, eyes and nose until the pressure is equalized.

A 1904 *Baltimore American* article describing the dangers of working deep underwater in a caisson.

When the giant wooden caisson was finally launched on August 9, 1904, it would go down in history as the biggest ever built. Destined to form the working chamber and the base of Baltimore Light, the wood portion was forty-eight feet in diameter and twenty-three feet high. The caisson would reach a final height of eighty-six feet when completely assembled with rows of cast-iron panels at the site off Gibson Island.

As the fleet of twenty vessels departed Baltimore on September 19, towing the gigantic cylinder on a long hawser behind one of the vessels, the 150 men who constituted the crew for contractors Flaherty & Lande certainly knew the enormity of the task they were about to undertake. Never before had a lighthouse base been sunk so deep; only once before had a caisson of any sort been lowered more than sixty-three feet beneath ground, the depth to which Baltimore Light's base would be sunk. The job would exert tremendous pain and suffering on the sixty men who made up the caisson gang. These sand hogs knew they would be bleeding from the nose, ears, and eyes as the caisson was lowered inch by inch into the mud, and the amount of compressed air was steadily increased. As the caisson neared its base in firm-packed sand, the men would have to endure the pressure of three atmospheres as they worked with picks and shovels to lower the cais-

son. The smallest mistake or miscalculation in operating the air locks when working with such tremendous pressure could cause permanent injury or even death to the men working in the chamber.

From the beginning, Baltimore Light had promised to be trouble. In 1895, five years after the lighthouse was first proposed, engineers conducting borings at the site had found a whopping fifty-five feet of semifluid mud. For the next seven years, construction was delayed as planners and engineers tried to find other means of building the lighthouse, including different sites and new methods of construction. The site, in fact, had been moved three and a half miles south, but the mud problem remained. In 1899, a new method of construction involving an experimental disk pile was tried as a base for the lighthouse, but workers could not get it to penetrate the mud, even when using pumps. Nothing more could be done but to build the world's largest caisson.

So enormous were the problems facing construction of Baltimore Light that had the offshore tower been meant to guide mariners anywhere else but into the channel leading to Baltimore, it certainly would have been abandoned when the first problems arose. But at the turn of the century, Baltimore was the commercial center of the Chesapeake Bay. Tens of millions of dollars rode on the ability of Congress and the Lighthouse Board to light the way to this inland port.

Ever since the first lighthouse was built in Maryland at Bodkin Island in 1823, lighting the way to Baltimore had been of primary concern to lighthouse overseers on the Chesapeake Bay. Early members of the Lighthouse Board envisioned a line of lights leading from the capes to Baltimore.

It would take a half-century to fulfill that dream. Along the way, Baltimore would rack up a number of "firsts" in lighthouse construction, including the first lighthouse in Maryland waters, the first range lights on the Chesapeake Bay, the first offshore lighthouse in Maryland waters, the first caisson lighthouse on the Chesapeake Bay, and now the biggest caisson lighthouse in history. Over the years, four sets of range lights and four individual lighthouses would guide mariners along the channels leading into Baltimore and into the port itself. Great sums of money had been spent on dredging channels and lighting the watery roads, all to make this city, so far off the beaten path, one of the most important ports along the East Coast.

Even many of the lighthouses built on the Chesapeake Bay far from the mouth of the Patapsco River owed their existence almost entirely to Baltimore. Lighthouses were needed to protect the millions of dollars' worth of commerce that was shipped in and out of this harbor each year in the nineteenth and early twentieth centuries. A hundred miles away, Point No Point Light, north of the Potomac River, Hooper Island Light, and Bloody Point Light served little more than to keep vessels that were bound for Baltimore off the unseen shoals and low-lying islands.

When Congress authorized funds for Maryland's first lighthouse at Bodkin Island at the southern entrance to the Patapsco River in 1819, it also approved money for construction of the Chesapeake's first set of range lights leading ships into the mouth of the river. Both projects encountered problems with the contractor. The North Point Range Lights at the northern entrance to the Patapsco were completed in 1824 and were cared for by one keeper. The towers were of different height, one twenty-seven feet from base to lantern, the other, thirty-five feet. When the two lights were lined up, one over the other, a ship captain knew he was heading directly into the mouth of the river. It was the first of five sets of range lights proposed to guide vessels into the port of Baltimore. (The fifth set would never be built.)

Lazaretto Point Lighthouse, across from Fort McHenry in Baltimore Harbor, was completed by John Donohoo in 1831 and became Baltimore's third light system. The name of the lighthouse came from the hospital for contagious diseases, called a lazaretto, that had previously occupied the site.

Lazaretto Point Light would have the distinction of helping to stir the imagination of one of the nation's most celebrated writers. Edgar Allan Poe, who spent part of his life in Baltimore, is believed to have been inspired by Lazaretto Light when he wrote the unfinished story, "The Lighthouse." History also claims that Lazaretto Light figured in a hoax. Poe was visiting Baltimore shortly after the construction of the lighthouse, when word circulated that a man was to fly the two and a half miles from the lighthouse to the Shot Tower in downtown Baltimore. A crowd gathered to witness the historic event. After hours of waiting, it finally occurred to someone that it was April Fool's Day. The joke was thought to be the work of Poe.

Lazaretto Point proved an ideal location for a lighthouse to guide ships up the Patapsco. The point juts out into the middle of the river, providing captains with a clear view of the light at the mouth of the river, ten miles away.

When the Lighthouse Board took over the job of running the lighthouse system in the country from the fifth auditor in 1852, one of its first decisions concerning Maryland waters was to replace the dilapidated Bodkin Island Lighthouse with an offshore screw pile on Sevenfoot Knoll. This light, combined with the North Point Range and Lazaretto, served maritime traffic well as long as vessels remained relatively small and shoal-draft. But as schooners increased in size and draft and as steamboats began to ply the Bay in increasing numbers, many drawing twenty feet of water or more, Baltimore became more difficult to reach. After the Civil War, Baltimore's future as an important East Coast port was in jeopardy unless its channel could be deepened.

Baltimore Light, the biggest caisson ever built, had to be sunk sixty feet through fluid mud. The first attempt to plant the giant caisson was so disastrous that the experienced construction company abandoned the project.

The Craighill Channel Upper Range, originally called the New Cut-Off Channel because it was dredged to cut off a few miles from the Craighill Channel, is still used today. The tiny, octagonal front light, shown here on a concrete parapet, evidently was home for the lighthouse keeper after a storm in August 1893 carried away the bridge connecting the light with the mainland where the original keeper's dwelling was located.

In the mid-1800s, Congress authorized funds for dredging channels up the Patapsco River into the port of Baltimore. The new channels and increased draft of vessels meant that many ships had to travel a straight and narrow path into Baltimore. These narrow channels called for lighthouses and range lights to mark them.

Consequently, on November 1, 1868, the Brewerton Channel Range Lights were completed and lighted. The front light was a screw pile built in six feet of water off Hawkins Point, more than halfway up the river. The rear light was on Leading Point, a bluff of land about a mile west of the front light. Leading Point was a brick dwelling with a lantern mounted on top.

For most of its length, the Chesapeake Bay was deep enough to accommodate the increasing draft of steam vessels and big schooners, but when ships reached the narrow, upper Bay, just above

Sandy Point, the deep channel favored the Eastern Shore, forcing big vessels to head east, rather than hugging the western shore. This increased the trip to Baltimore by miles.

Consequently, within five years after Brewerton Channel was marked, the Craighill Channel was created in the Chesapeake Bay by dredging between the mouth of the Patapsco River and a point several miles north of Sandy Point, just off the western shore. Another set of range lights was built in 1873 to mark this channel. The front light became the first caisson lighthouse on the Chesapeake Bay and was built several miles east of North Point. The rear light was quite an unusual structure for the Chesapeake Bay. Built as an open framework in the shape of a pyramid, it shone 105 feet above the tide. The foundation was set in 2 feet of water off Culkold Point below Hart-Miller Island. The wooden dwelling wrapped

around the base of the foundation and had four big windows overlooking each of the four sides. An enclosed stairway ran up the center of the framework to the enclosed lantern room. Both lights are still in use today. The house, however, was removed from the base of the rear light many years ago.

The North Point Range Lights were discontinued after the Craighill Range Lights were completed. Thirteen years later, however, North Point became the location for the front light of another set of range lights when the port of Baltimore dredged a channel at the mouth of the Patapsco in an effort to cut yet another couple of miles off the watery road to the city.

On January 15, 1886, the New Cut-Off Channel Range (today called the Craighill Channel Upper Range) was lighted to mark this new channel, which followed a path similar to the original

North Point Range. In fact, the Lighthouse Board decided to use the old foundation of the tower and built an octagonal brick tower atop it for the front light. The rear light, located across Old Road Bay on Sparrows Point, was a relatively inexpensive beacon, consisting of an inner wooden shaft, covered with corrugated iron and supported by an iron skeleton frame. Cottage-style dwellings were built for both towers, each having its own keeper.

Earlier, during the Civil War, two events improved yet complicated the future of Lazaretto Light: the first lighthouse depot on the Chesapeake Bay was established here for building, maintenance, and repair of lighthouse buoys, ships, and other property; and iron ore was discovered on the lighthouse grounds.

The excavation of iron ore began during the war in 1864 and continued for several years, netting the Lighthouse Board over five thousand dol-

This replica of Lazaretto Lighthouse was erected at Lazaretto Point east of the Inner Harbor in Baltimore by Rukert Terminals Corporation in the mid-1980s.

lars. The contract with the excavator called for filling the holes as the iron ore was extracted so that the lighthouse would not be undermined. The contract was finally terminated in 1868, after more than three thousand tons of ore had been removed. At that point, it was determined that the only ore left was located under the light keeper's garden, which the Lighthouse Board kindly refused to destroy.

Not surprisingly, iron furnaces began to spring up near Lazaretto Point Light to manufacture the large quantities of ore found not only on the lighthouse grounds, but throughout the region. By 1870, these factories, with their bright lights shining through the night, began to interfere with the function of the lighthouse. Ship captains could not determine which of the lights was Lazaretto, and which were the cupolas of the manufacturing plants. As a result, the lighthouse lantern was altered to show a red light.

Over the next decade, however, the increasing number of factories near Lazaretto Point created a new plague. By 1883, gases from nearby chemical plants were so corrosive that they peeled away the

whitewash on the lighthouse tower as soon as it was put on. In addition to the chemical problem, private buildings were beginning to obscure the light. In 1883, the Lighthouse Board decided to add an additional light on a mast that rose higher than the surrounding buildings. A few years later, the offending buildings must have been removed, for in 1888, the mast light was discontinued and the characteristic of the lighthouse was changed from fixed red to flashing red.

The Lighthouse Board learned something from its continuing troubles at Lazaretto, for in 1886, when a landowner proposed to build structures on Hawkins Point that would have obstructed the Brewerton Channel Range Lights, the board did not sit idly by. The tip of Hawkins Point protruded into the river, between the two range lights. Thomas C. Chappell, the owner of Hawkins Point Farm, initially requested that Hawkins Point Light be removed because it interfered with the improvements he proposed to make on his land. Had Chappell been allowed to build his structures, the Brewerton Channel Range Lights would have been made as ineffective as Lazaretto Light. With the future of Lazaretto Light dimmed by neighboring buildings, the two range lights downriver were more important than ever to navigation on the Patapsco River.

The board tried to resolve the conflict amicably by offering to purchase land on the point from the property owner. Chappell asked an exorbitant price, however, which the board declined.

When the parties were unable to reach an agreement, the case went to the U.S. circuit court for resolution. Judge Morris ruled that private rights are subject to the public right of navigation, and that the federal government had the right to use the soil under the water, just as it had the right to use the water itself to regulate commerce.

With the court case in hand, the board proceeded to initiate condemnation proceedings for the air rights over the strip of land on Hawkins Point where the landowner had proposed to build structures. The courts again ruled in favor of the Lighthouse Board, granting the board an easement to send "unobstructed rays of light over the land."

The Lighthouse Board had learned an important lesson and the problems at Lazaretto would not be repeated. Little could be done, however, about the continuing obstruction of Lazaretto Point Light. By 1906 the light was again obscured by tall buildings, and the Lighthouse Board confirmed that it was practically useless as a navigational aid. (Nevertheless, the lighthouse remained for another twenty years, during which it became, in 1915, the first lighthouse on the Chesapeake Bay to be equipped with incandescent lights.)

The obstruction of Lazaretto Point Light caused a clamor for a new lighthouse to guide vessels into Baltimore Harbor. In 1907, the secretary of commerce and labor wrote a letter to the secretary of the treasury, requesting new range lights for Baltimore Harbor: "Steam vessels going to and from Baltimore have asked, because of the obstruction of the Lazaretto Point light, for the establishment of range lights as a guide for Fort McHenry channel."

He went on to propose the construction of another set of range lights. The front light would be located near the intersection of the Brewerton and Fort McHenry channels and would serve as a turning point for vessels going into or out of the harbor. The rear light would also indicate the shoal near Rock Point, on the west side of the Patapsco River. The eighty-five thousand dollars requested for the front light indicates that it would have been a caisson, while the forty thousand dollars for the rear light was at that time the cost of a screw-pile lighthouse.

In the early 1900s, Baltimore was one of the leading shipping ports on the Atlantic seaboard. Its exports during the fiscal year ending June 30, 1909, topped $77 million; imports were $24 million. Congress had already been generous to Baltimore, providing funds for the widening of the channel to six hundred feet, and dredging to a depth of thirty-five feet. The board argued that it made sense to light the channel properly.

While the lighthouse service argued the merits of the Fort McHenry Range Lights in the Patapsco River, the ambitious construction of the Baltimore Lighthouse began in 1902. Baltimore Light would mark the entrance to Craighill Channel, the long, narrow, recently-widened path through fifteen-foot shoals in the upper Bay below the Patapsco River.

Building the biggest wooden caisson in the country required some of the largest timbers in the world. The caisson contained over one million feet of lumber, much of it in gigantic timbers, twelve to twenty-four inches wide, and as long as forty-eight feet. So big were the timbers that contractors had to search the Georgia woods to find suitable trees for the project. When finished, the caisson weighed 972 tons and drew twenty feet of water as it was towed to the site. Metal cylinder sections would be bolted onto this base to give it its final height of eighty-six feet.

Contractors Flaherty & Lande of New York estimated that they needed just two calm days to anchor the big structure in place. Then the difficult work would begin, with men entering the working chamber to excavate mud and sand from the cutting edge of the caisson.

In a detailed article on June 28, 1904, the *Baltimore American* explained the conditions in which the sand hogs would operate:

At first the work in the working chamber will be light, but as the chamber goes down each two feet, another pound of air is added until, at the final depth, 86 feet, 45 pounds to the square inch will be employed. This is a pressure of more than three atmospheres, and will be the highest ever used in deep sea work, and only two pounds less than has ever been used in any caisson work.

The method of entering the working chamber is tedious. It means instant death to the impatient one who dares make a change too soon. The men enter the air lock and stand on an elevator. The lock, which is a circular chamber of steel, is built to withstand a pressure of seventy-five pounds to the square inch. The lives of the men in the air lock are then in the hands of the lock-tender, who gradually opens the valves and lets the compressed air pour slowly into the lock, gently raising the pressure.

No matter how slowly the pressure increases, the men experience severe pains in the head and bleed from the ears, eyes and nose until the pressure is equalized. When the pressure in the air lock has reached that in the caisson below, the bottom of the lock drops out and the elevator on which the men stand is lowered to the bottom of the working chamber. There they excavate from the cutting edge toward the center. The chamber is brilliantly lighted with electric lights, and a telephone is used to communicate with the contractors, who balance the descent of the structure by having the sand taken from first one cutting edge and then the other.

When the job of excavating is done, the working chamber is filled with concrete and becomes part of the base for the lighthouse.

Unfortunately, the contractors were not to get their two days of calm weather. Just as the weather had failed to cooperate for them at Smith Point Light, now, as they hurried to anchor the Baltimore Light caisson, the weather deteriorated.

On September 21, heavy seas filled the cylinder, causing it to settle to one side, about seven feet out of level. In need of supplies to repair the

The back light for the Upper Craighill Channel Range is a simple structure still in use today, though it is overwhelmed by the tall, smoking towers of Bethlehem Steel.

damage, the contractors were forced to leave the site until October 7. Then, the crew tried to right the huge caisson by filling the high side with concrete, but five days later, a severe storm turned the structure over flat on its side.

Overwhelmed by the enormity of their problems and the onset of winter, the contractors abandoned the project and defaulted on their construction bond. The world's largest wooden caisson had become the Lighthouse Board's biggest headache.

The wrecked caisson lay underwater for almost a year while the insurance company worked out the legal complications of the contractor's default. Finally, at the end of August 1905, the surety company assembled a working party and began to salvage the caisson. It took more than two years to right the caisson by using lifts, cables, pumps, and stone, and another year to finish the octagonal brick dwelling with its mansard roof and octagonal lantern room. On October 1, 1908, Baltimore Light, thirteen years in planning and construction, was finally lighted.

Although Congress agreed to allocate $125,000 for the Fort McHenry Range, it would not be built. By the time the money was appropriated in 1911, the Lighthouse Board had been dismantled, replaced by the new U.S. Bureau of Lighthouses, whose commissioner had other ideas about how to light the channel. By this time, lighted buoys, though they had far less powerful beams, had become dependable aids to navigation. Instead of building two expensive lighthouses that would have to be manned, the commissioner decided instead to use the funds to purchase "a complete system of buoys" for the Patapsco River at a cost of $124,258.04.

The bureau's decision to chose buoys over lighthouses marked the end of the era of lighthouse construction on the Chesapeake Bay. Never again would a new site be laid out for a manned lighthouse. The only lighthouses built on the Bay after the scuttling of the Fort McHenry Range project were Thimble Shoal Light and Ragged Point, which were already on the drawing board. From then on, lighthouses would be automated. Within a decade, the Bureau of Lighthouses would embrace wholeheartedly the concept of the

*Craighill Channel
Range Front Light
originally had two
lights, including this
steamer's light,
mounted on the side
of the dwelling.*

unmanned lighthouse and move rapidly in that direction.

But Lazaretto Point Light, which had survived so many attacks on its worth as a lighthouse, would never survive to see automation. In 1926, a steel skeleton tower was built closer to the water's edge, where it would not be hidden by neighboring buildings. The old Lazaretto tower was dismantled that same year as soon as the new light was blinking in its place.

The rear light for the Craighill Channel Range still exists, but the dwelling that once wrapped around the iron frame was removed when the light was automated.

Chapter Thirteen

The Unlucky Lighthouse

The keeper was awakened one night by a jarring thud and crash.
He bolted out of bed to find the bowsprit of a sailboat poking through his window.

Lewis R. Carman, keeper of Holland Island Bar,
writing in a Baltimore *Sun Magazine* article in 1948 about a former keeper.

*T*he first rays of dawn had yet to light the eastern sky when Capt. W. Irving Pearce guided the four-masted schooner *Malcolm Baxter Jr.* inside Capes Charles and Henry, into the relative safety of the Chesapeake Bay.

It was 6 A.M. on December 27, 1909, and Pearce had just sailed the wooden vessel from Boston on a journey that had been the most harrowing passage of his career. Almost as soon as they had left Boston Harbor, the vessel had been hit by a blinding blizzard, the worst he had ever experienced. The northeaster struck on Christmas day, packing winds of over fifty knots and dumping many inches of snow over New England. Pearce had struggled long hours at the helm to keep the old ship afloat in the huge ocean swells. He would soon learn that many captains had not been as lucky as he. Twelve vessels had been lost at sea off the New England coast during the blizzard, including the magnificent five-masted schooner *Davis Palmer*, which went down with all twelve crewmen, and the three-masted schooner *Nettie Champion*, laden with lumber and bound from Norfolk for New York City. Even on land, scores of people had been injured and thousands more stranded on trains that quickly became locked in snowdrifts. It would be remembered as the worst Christmas blizzard ever.

As he sailed *Malcolm Baxter Jr.* between the capes, Pearce knew little about the magnitude of the damage and destruction of the storm, only that, somehow, he and his crew had survived it. Now, he hailed the tug *John Twohy Jr.* to get a tow into Hampton Roads. The sailboat had no power other than her sails, and it was standard procedure at the turn of the century for sailing vessels to call upon a steam tug to tow them safely past the shoals that make out from the capes, and again past Thimble Shoal at the entrance to the harbor.

A tow line, ninety fathoms long, was quickly secured between the two vessels. Although the ten crewmen aboard *Malcolm Baxter Jr.* continued to maintain full sail, it was now the responsibility of the tug to navigate both vessels safely into harbor.

As the two vessels passed the lightship stationed at the tip of the dangerous shoal, the "Tail of the Horse Shoe," the schooner's crew began to take in sail. Now that they were only an hour out of port, Pearce, feeling secure about the safety of his ship, finally left the deck in the charge of his mate and stepped below for a few moments of much-needed rest.

The mate held the wheel as the schooner trailed in the wake of the tug. It was a clear, cold morning with a brisk southwest wind blowing. As the two vessels approached Thimble Shoal Lighthouse, the mate suddenly realized that the tug was

This caisson is the third Thimble Shoal Lighthouse built off the mouth of Hampton Roads. The first two succumbed to fire, the second after being struck by a schooner.

passing much too close to the light. He turned his wheel to starboard in hopes of giving more room between the vessel and the lighthouse, but with no sail to power her, the big schooner failed to heed the wheel and began to drift in the tide dangerously close to the screw pile. Alarmed, the mate turned the wheel hard to starboard again, swinging it until it locked.

Aboard the tug, Capt. W. S. Williams saw all too late what was happening. "The wind and tide were setting strong toward the light," he would later note in his report on the tragedy. He hauled up from a west-by-southwesterly course to south-southwest, which placed the tug about fifty fathoms off on the starboard side.

His change of course was too late, however. The wind and tide drove the schooner toward the lighthouse so quickly that she could not be pulled clear of the structure. Hoping that the schooner would drop back and pass clear, Captain Williams cast off the hawser that had been connecting the two vessels. Now, the big schooner, her sails all furled, was helpless to battle the tide and the wind that pushed her on a collision course with the lighthouse.

Inside the beacon, the open flame of the light had just been extinguished. It was 8:30 A.M., an hour after sunrise, and assistant keeper Thomas L. Fulcher was in the lantern room at the top of the lighthouse, cleaning the lens. It was a task always performed shortly after sunrise by one of the keepers. Fulcher had the lens in his arms, polishing it, when the flying jibboom of *Baxter* shot through the lantern gallery, shattering glass everywhere and knocking him off his feet.

The schooner's bowsprit rammed into the lighthouse, hitting so hard that it shook the wooden superstructure and upset the coal stove in the living quarters. The stove door flew open and the hot coals rolled onto the wood floor. Lighthouse keeper Joseph B. Thomas and another assistant, Isaac D. Wells, Jr., rushed to douse the flames leaping from the hot coals. But as the wooden floor quickly caught fire, they retreated out the door and lowered the lighthouse skiff to the water. Keeper Fulcher managed somehow to escape from the lantern room down the narrow, winding steps and out the door before the building became engulfed in flames.

After ramming the lighthouse, the stern of *Malcolm Baxter Jr.* swung northwest, allowing the vessel to drift free of the burning structure. The crew immediately set anchor off the lighthouse and lowered a lifeboat with the intent of assisting the keepers. The crew of *John Twohy* reached the keepers first, however, and took them aboard. Everyone had managed to escape unharmed, but the lighthouse was in flames.

It was not the first time tragedy had struck Thimble Shoal Light. The original structure, also a screw pile built in 1872, was destroyed by fire in 1880. Divers managed to recover the lantern and lens. By using a superstructure that had been prefabricated on land for another station, workers had the new house built atop the original pilings in fifty-five days.

Collisions by passing vessels were nothing new to keepers who manned Thimble Shoal before and after the 1909 calamity. In 1891 a steamer ran into the light and caused considerable damage. On April 14, 1898, a coal barge grazed it. In the years after the 1909 fire, both the lightship that replaced the burned structure and the new Thimble Shoal Lighthouse were hit repeatedly.

Keepers who were stationed in a lightship during the five years it took to build a caisson lighthouse beside the old, burnt-out station duly reported the collisions in their logbooks. For example, on November 25, 1911, with a light breeze blowing, an unidentified barge in tow of the tug *Prudence* collided with the remains of the old Thimble Shoal Lighthouse, bending several braces. Just after midnight on April 11, 1913, with a strong southwesterly wind blowing, another unidentified barge in tow of the tug *Kenmore* collided with the station. *B. Mohawk*, in tow of the tug *Virginia*, collided with the station at 8:55 P.M. on May 10, 1914.

Had the Lighthouse Board opted to build another screw-pile lighthouse at Thimble Shoal, the beacon probably would have met the same fate as the two before it. Just three months after the new caisson lighthouse was finally lighted on December 1, 1914, it was struck by an even bigger schooner than the one that had taken down the screw pile. On a rainy, windy morning, March 6, 1915, the six-masted schooner *Addie M. Lawrence* drifted

Thimble Shoal Lighthouse was to be the last lighthouse built on the Chesapeake when it was completed in 1914. At least two men died during its construction.

into the new station at 7:20 A.M., damaging both the lighthouse and the vessel. After the collision, the master of the schooner came aboard the lighthouse to observe the damage and help secure the lighthouse skiff, which was thumping against the station.

The collision was serious enough to draw the personal attention of the superintendent of lighthouses, who arrived on the tender *Orchid* to survey the damage. Repairing the station cost six hundred dollars, which was paid by the owner of the vessel.

A year later, on September 24, 1916, another barge struck the old structure at 8 P.M., breaking one of the iron braces. The keeper hailed the barge, but got no reply.

Occasionally, the keepers were lucky. On February 23, 1912, the schooner *R. T. Runkett* grounded near the station, with enough distance that it did no damage to the lightship that was being used while the lighthouse was being repaired.

With collisions occurring almost yearly, it was no wonder that Thimble Shoal became known as the unlucky lighthouse. But it is understandable why so many collisions occurred there. Thimble Shoal Lighthouse marks one of the busiest ports on the Bay, second only to Baltimore.

Many more vessels pass near this lighthouse than any other lighthouse on the Bay.

Vessels entering Hampton Roads pass by a long shoal, which limits a vessel's ability to maneuver under sail. Historically, therefore, sailing vessels often preferred to be towed by a steam tug. It was quicker and usually safer, but under tow, a sailboat has little or no maneuverability on its own, and tide or wind can easily carry it off course. It was no coincidence that almost every vessel that had struck the Thimble Shoal Lighthouse had been a vessel or barge under tow.

Thimble Shoal is also the most exposed of all lighthouses in the Chesapeake. Located just twenty miles inside Cape Henry, it gets the full brunt of storms blowing off the open ocean, as well as wave action and currents that are considerably stronger than at most other locations on the Bay.

Most Bay lighthouses marked narrow channels, so understandably collisions by passing vessels were a real concern for keepers, particularly in heavy winds, fog, or blinding snow.

Bells Rock Lighthouse, 209 miles up the York River from Yorktown, was one such beacon. In June 1884, a schooner hit the foundation of the light and broke three of its supporting columns. Luckily, the damage was easily repaired within a few weeks.

At Tangier Sound Lighthouse, on February 13, 1905, the sunken vessel *Mary L. Colburn* was thrown against the lighthouse, damaging it.

Colburn had run up on the sandbar, marked by the lighthouse, during heavy ice conditions on the Bay, and sank. When the ice began to thaw and move, the wrecked schooner was literally picked up and thrown against the lighthouse, according to a report by the *Baltimore American*.

> The crash was terrific, and the ship, as though tossed by some giant hand, fetched up broadside to the lighthouse on the southeastern face of the station....Both masts were plucked out of the vessel to the deck. The top of one of the smoke stacks of the lighthouse was carried away by fouling with some of the gear of the schooner as it went by the board. One corner of the roof over the bell suffered a like fate; the head of three

Underwater erosion caused Bloody Point Lighthouse off the southern tip of Kent Island to cant severely shortly after it was constructed in 1882. Workers were able to straighten the tower, but it still nods slightly off perpendicular.

posts around the dome of the light were also wrecked and general damage done.

Keeper John T. Jarvis and his assistant, who narrowly escaped injury, stood by their post, trying as best they could to keep the light burning. As the wrecked vessel repeatedly rammed the lighthouse pilings, it threatened to upset the lantern or even carry away the lighthouse. Jarvis was able to dispatch a letter to the Office of the Fifth District, in which he expressed fear for the security of the lighthouse. The district superintendent immediately sent the tender *Maple* to remove the wreck and repair the structure.

Lewis R. Carman was keeper of Holland Island Bar when the tiny wooden lighthouse barely escaped a deadly ramming by a Japanese merchant ship before World War II. "The fog was as thick and murky as the water of a field stream after a thunderstorm. Our horn was going, but the ship must not have heard us for she plowed against the shoal with a rumble that pumped vibrations up the slender piles that supported our lighthouse," Carman recounted in a Baltimore *Sun Magazine* article. "Fortunately, what could have been a disaster began and ended with that rumble. The ship hadn't hit dead on, so her natural buoyancy somehow enabled her to roll and straighten her course."

Carman found an entry in the logbook by an earlier keeper—one who had not been as lucky as he. "The keeper was awakened one night by a jarring thud and crash. He bolted out of bed to find the bowsprit of a sailboat poking through his window."

*Hooper Island
Lighthouse is located on
a lonely stretch of the
Chesapeake Bay off the
Hooper islands on the
Eastern Shore.*

Chapter Fourteen

Rescues: All in a Day's Work

We started out in a sailboat. . . . Just when we got to the lighthouse, a big storm came up.
My father tried to pass me over to the man climbing down the ladder . . .
but a big wave came along and washed me away.

Loretta Y. Goldsborough, recalling her rescue at Point No Point Light in 1915, in a 1979 interview.

Capt. Filmore Hudgins and his young assistant, Clarence W. Salter, were standing out on the deck of York Spit Light in 1905, watching a bugeye make headway in the choppy waters, when a sudden whirlwind capsized the two-masted sailing vessel. As the wooden boat took on water and rapidly sank, the two keepers rushed to lower the lighthouse dory and rescue Capt. Arthur Hudgins and his companion, Wilbur Diggs, who were floundering in the chilly waters.

"They saw us turn over, got into their boat, and came and saved our lives," Diggs, who became a minister, recounted in a letter written sixty years later to Salter's daughter, Olga Crouch. "We spent the night on the lighthouse and Captain Hudgins brought us back home the next day."

The Reverend Wilbur Diggs obviously never forgot the rescue. Twenty years after the incident, while assisting at the funeral of keeper Salter, who died from an embolism following an appendectomy, the reverend recalled the keeper's bravery. "I owe much to this man," he told those assembled in Mathews County, Virginia, to pay their last respects. "He saved my life many years ago when my boat capsized. I would not be here today, had it not been for him."

While keeping the light was their primary responsibility, lighthouse keepers also played an important role in saving life and property on the unpredictable Chesapeake Bay and its tributaries. Lifesaving was part of their duties and was taken seriously by keepers, many of whom risked their own lives to save others. In the days of manned lighthouses, boaters were assured of help if they could only get near a lighthouse, for keepers seemed to be eternally awake and attentive.

Such was the case near midnight on a stormy night in August 1939. Lewis R. Carman and Hiram White, keepers of Bloody Point Light off the tip of Kent Island, heard a foghorn blowing incessantly. The men rushed out on the walkway of the round iron caisson, nicknamed appropriately the "Coffee Pot," because of its shape. Through the darkness, they could barely make out the outline of a fishing boat bobbing on the rough seas, obviously in a state of distress.

The keepers quickly lowered their eighteen-foot open tender and went after the vessel. The engine of the forty-five-foot fishing boat was out of commission, and the nine people aboard, including four women, had been drifting for six hours and were now near a state of panic, Carman later recalled. The group had left Snug Harbor, just below Galesville across the Bay, early that morning for a fun day of fishing. But when they went to start the engine at 6 P.M. to head home, the motor would not turn over.

"No matter what we did to it, it wouldn't start," Carl J. Hammersla, a member of the fishing

Today's sailboats are designed to survive knock-downs like this one off Sandy Point, but in the nineteenth and early twentieth centuries, lighthouse keepers were often called upon to rescue victims of capsized vessels.

party, recalled. "We just had to try to attract some-body's attention. Three boats came by, and we tried to flag them, but they were too far away and it was too dark for them to see us. We were blowing the foghorn on the boat, and finally the men from Bloody Point Lighthouse heard it and came out in their boat."

"Rescuing folks in trouble near our light was part of our responsibility," Carman recollected. For the keepers, it was a fairly routine rescue, though matters may have gotten much worse for the boaters had the keepers not heard their foghorn and responded.

The keepers did not just tow the boat back to the station; they also helped identify the engine trouble. Carman and White then supplied the boaters with new battery cables to get the engine running again. Meanwhile, they offered their un-expected guests some hot coffee and food and showed them around the lighthouse.

Keepers often offered their mechanical skills and free towing services to stranded boaters. In times of need, the lighthouse was like a parts and food depot in the middle of the Bay. When the U.S.

Bureau of Lighthouses took over jurisdiction of the lighthouses in 1911, the commissioner's report was filled with incidents of keepers towing, feed-ing, and housing stranded boaters. The advent of the powerboat contributed to the increase in res-cues, since a broken-down motorboat was virtu-ally useless.

The tow jobs kept keepers busy. G. G. Johnson, assistant keeper of Old Plantation Flats Light, towed the occupants of one disabled motor-boat to his station, where he furnished them with food, before towing them on to Cape Charles for repairs. G. M. Willis, Sr., keeper of Cedar Point Light, floated the launch *Jane*, which had gone aground near the light, and then let the occupants spend the night at the lighthouse. For keepers, the company of stranded boaters relieved the monot-ony of tending an offshore light.

Not often were the visitors important, but keeper Lewis Carman met two celebrities during his long career aboard lighthouses in the Bay. James Roosevelt, son of the president, came aboard Holland Island Bar Light when the engine of his yacht broke down. The young Roosevelt did not have a radio aboard his vessel and wanted to get word to his father about his engine problems. The keepers did not have a radio, either, but they flashed a message in Morse code to his father, who was on the presidential yacht on the Potomac, directly across the Bay from Holland Island. Carman also met famous radio personality Arthur Godfrey, who was cruising on the Chesapeake Bay and just wanted to have a look around the light.

While many rescues were mundane, in more than a few cases, keepers risked their lives to save people from drowning in storm-driven seas. George M. Wible, keeper of Tangier Sound Light in Virginia, went out in a blizzard during the winter of 1923 to rescue six men adrift in a small boat. The men probably would have drowned had Wible not seen their plight and risked his own life in swelling seas and blinding snow to rescue them.

In 1915, G. M. Willis, Sr., keeper of Point No Point (former keeper of Cedar Point), had to rescue his assistant, William Yeatman, who almost drowned while rescuing a child. The child most likely was his daughter, the late Loretta Yeatman Goldsborough, who often accompanied her father out to the lighthouse to keep him company. In an interview with a historian at the Calvert Marine Museum in 1979, Mrs. Goldsborough recalled an incident at Point No Point when she was washed overboard.

I was five years old, but I remember it. We started out in a sailboat—there were no outboard motors or anything like that at that time—and just when we got to the lighthouse, a big storm came up. There was another man on the lighthouse, and my father got the boat there and tried to pass me over to the man climbing down the ladder...but a big wave came along and washed me away.

At that time, little girls wore those old long dresses, and the air got under my dress and kept me afloat. I thought it was a lot of fun, floating along on top of the water. My father was a good swimmer. He caught me and brought me back.

She doesn't remember fearing for her safety, nor does she remember keeper Willis helping with the rescue. "What I remember most about it was losing my Easter hat. I lost my new straw hat."

Often vessels collided, sank, or caught fire, and when it happened near a lighthouse the keeper was quick to assist. Eugene S. Riley, assistant keeper of Pages Rock Light on the York River in Virginia, rescued the captain of a barge that was sinking as it drifted by his station on January 5, 1912. When a launch caught fire around midnight near Bush Bluff Light Vessel in Virginia in 1913, the lightship's mate, Charles H. Pertner, and seaman John T. Tolson rescued seven men from drowning after they leaped from the burning vessel.

The keepers at Lazaretto Light on the Patapsco River were constantly busy making rescues in Baltimore. In 1914, W. H. Davis, Jr., and his assistant, J. M. Ellis, rescued a man from the river after he fell overboard from the steamship *Charles H. Warner*. In 1917, the steamer *Severn* collided with the bugeye *Mary E. Fouble* just off Lazaretto Point, and Davis went to the rescue of the people on board the vessels. Crew from the tender *Maple* also assisted.

Sometimes there was no hope of help except from the lighthouse keeper. In the bad freeze of 1917, several men were in a skiff caught in the ice near the Janes Island Light Station off Crisfield on the Eastern Shore of Maryland. Keeper H. S. Moore helped them reach the lighthouse, where he offered them food and lodging.

Before the 1920s, airplanes were so new that keepers dutifully reported sightings of them in their logbooks. But in the wake of the Great War and the proliferation of the airplane, they became just another vehicle from which passengers had to be rescued. Rescues from downed aircraft started in 1918, in the midst of war. Not surprisingly, many of the downed planes belonged to the U.S. government and may well reflect the early inexperience of the pilots or the lack of dependability of this new invention.

John E. Morgan, second assistant keeper of Wolf Trap Light in Virginia, rescued three occupants of an "aeroplane" in 1918. That same year, William Yeatman, who had moved on to become keeper of Drum Point Lighthouse, assisted two

Boaters in trouble often aimed for the beam of a lighthouse where they knew keepers would offer them aid. Pictured here is Smith Point Lighthouse.

officers whose plane had become disabled near the mouth of the Patuxent River.

In 1921, the lighthouse tender *Juniper* towed a disabled U.S. naval seaplane from Long Shoal Light in North Carolina to Norfolk, Virginia, furnishing food and lodging to seven occupants along the route.

The following year, Jesse M. W. Shockley, keeper of Sharps Island Light, sighted a hydroplane adrift in the water about one mile from his station. He went to the crew's aid and actually used his little twenty-foot tender to tow the plane, *Lady Baltimore*, with its two occupants to Cooks Point on the Eastern Shore. Then in 1923, York Spit Lighthouse assistant keeper G. C. Hunley assisted two men in a U.S. seaplane that had gone down near his station.

Lighthouse keepers were used to being the rescuers, but occasionally they needed to be rescued. Back in the days before powerboats, keepers often sailed or rowed long distances in small, open boats to get supplies and mail and to visit their families on the mainland. It was not unusual for bad weather to catch up with them as they made their crossings from lighthouse to land. Keepers were usually excellent sailors who could handle their little dories in the worst of weather, but once in a while, Mother Nature pulled a surprise. In 1914, the keepers of Tangier Sound Lighthouse found out just how dangerous the sail home could be.

Chapter Fifteen

The Long Sail Home

Keeper done all within his power to rescue him , but failed.

Capt. Edward L. Thomas, keeper of Tangier Sound Lighthouse, writing in his logbook on February 14, 1912, after the death of his assistant, Capt. William Asbury Crockett.

As he set sail for home on February 7, 1914, Capt. William Asbury Crockett could not have asked for better weather. In winter, unpredictable weather made it difficult for keepers to be certain when they could leave or return to the lighthouse. Severe cold could settle in overnight and create enough ice to force them to postpone family visits ashore. Furthermore, gales, squalls, snowstorms, and heavy fog could force the keeper to sit out the bad weather. So when dawn broke on a clear sky and a relatively warm day, the assistant keeper of Tangier Sound Lighthouse sailed the gaff-rigged sloop to Tangier Island, where he spent a few days visiting his family.

Like most lighthouse keepers, Captain Crockett had grown up on the water and was extremely familiar with sailing vessels. He had been at this station as assistant keeper for about a year, but had spent years in the lighthouse service and was well known among the sailors and watermen who worked the Chesapeake. Just over a year before, in December 1912, while stationed at Smith Point, he had helped rescue two watermen from their wrecked bateau, *Rhoda M. Parker*. He and second assistant keeper Miles Hudgins were later commended by the lighthouse service for rescuing the stranded dredgers, who certainly would have died from exposure in the cold winter waters.

The weather had been moderate in the days preceding his leave, and Captain Crockett held out hope for an early spring. But by the time his short leave was over and the captain was ready to sail back to the lighthouse, winter had begun its miserable return. Early on the morning of February 11, the breeze had freshened, a northwester was blowing, clouds had moved in, and the day had turned bitter cold.

Tangier Sound Lighthouse stood out at the end of a long shoal, about a mile from the southern end of the island. Despite the freshening breeze, Crockett pointed the bow of his little dory toward Tangier Sound Light and set the sail for a long run back to his station. Pushed from behind by a strong northwester, he hoped for a quick sail across the sandbar.

Out on Tangier Sound Lighthouse, keeper Edward L. Thomas watched the progress of his assistant through a window in the square wooden two-story building that sat atop screw piles. The lighthouse was a latecomer, built in 1890 to accommodate the increasing oyster business that had blossomed in Tangier and Pocomoke Sounds in the wake of the legalization of oyster dredging in Maryland in 1865. By the 1880s, towns and island communities such as Crisfield and Deal Island were booming in the oyster trade, and merchants clamored for a light to guide them around the long shoal off Tangier Island. Now, besides the dredging boats, there were also steamboat lines serving Crisfield and other towns.

Like most water stations on the Chesapeake Bay, Tangier Sound Light had two keepers. The

A ketch frames
Baltimore Light
in its sails.

men generally shared the watch, but they were on their own during the eight days a month when the other keeper took his leave to visit his family on Tangier Island. Some keepers took all eight days at once, but most, like the Tangier Sound keepers, took a few days at a time so they could see their families every two weeks.

Keeper Thomas could see that the winds were increasing by the froth blowing off the tops of the waves. By the time his assistant was halfway across the shoal, Crockett was being pushed by well over twenty knots of wind, which was creating big waves in the shallow water. The little boat bobbed up and down, at times disappearing into the deep troughs.

Thomas's gaze was riveted to the window. He knew that Crockett was in the worst of situations, perched in a tiny sailboat on big seas, and pushed from behind by heavy winds. As the boat dipped down into the troughs, it could easily capsize, or the strong winds could jibe the sail. Jibing was a common problem when sailing downwind, particularly in rough seas when a boat could be bounced to one side or the other by the waves. If the boat's relative direction to the wind was altered enough to cause the wind to catch the back side of the sail, it could throw the boom and sail violently across the breadth of the boat.

Captain Crockett was within a half-mile of the station when the jibe occurred. Unable to duck in time, Crockett was hit hard in the head by the heavy, wooden boom and knocked overboard.

As soon as it happened, Captain Thomas rushed to get the second lighthouse boat lowered off the davits and rigged in time to rescue his assistant. Even as he dropped the boat to the water and set sail, however, he knew he would most likely be too late. The water temperature was at freezing this February morning, and that alone could kill a man in minutes. In addition, Thomas, who was coming from the opposite direction, would have to sail into the wind, tacking back and forth to reach the accident scene.

When he finally got there, Captain Thomas found the body of his assistant standing upright on the sandy bottom, the top of his head just above the water. There were no signs of life. With great difficulty, he pulled the dead man out of the water, laid him in the bottom of his little boat, and took the body to Tangier Island. Dr. W. O. Daisy made an examination and determined that the blow to the head, not drowning, had caused his death.

Captain Thomas was naturally troubled by the death of his assistant as he sat down to write in his logbook that night. In barely legible handwriting, he wrote, "Keeper done all within his power to rescue him, but failed. Regretted very much as he was a man that was all right—on everything and he was tidy and clean and one any keeper could rely on. He was a christian man, a gentleman."

A year later, Captain Thomas would be cited for his brave attempt at a rescue, but it would hardly dull the pain of losing a friend and fellow worker.

With the death of Crockett, the Chesapeake Bay seemed suddenly plagued by dangerous weather. Within two days of Crockett's death, it was snowing, followed by gale-force winds for two more days. Amid all this bad weather, Barney Thomas arrived at Tangier Light as acting assistant keeper. Thomas did not know it, but he was about to live through his own nightmare.

On Sunday, March 1, the new assistant keeper headed for Tangier Island in the station's little sailboat. The weather was cloudy and unsettled, and chunks of ice—remnants of the recent freeze—were scattered in the waters. But otherwise, there was no hint of the horrendous storm about to be unleashed on the area.

As Thomas sailed away from the lighthouse, the wind began to increase steadily, whipping at the rising waves and blowing white froth off the tops. An occasional rogue wave rolled over the sides of the dory. With his sail close-hauled, Thomas struggled to guide his little boat upwind as tight into the wind as he could. It was a long, tedious, difficult passage as he rode the big waves that quickly formed in the long fetch between the lighthouse and land. Thomas was almost to shore when the northeaster, now blowing a gale, suddenly cracked the mast, ripping the sail and carrying the entire rig overboard. Thomas was now at the mercy of a savage blizzard.

Even on shore, the storm was causing tremendous damage. In the next forty-eight hours, it

A sailboat beats around Thomas Point Shoal Lighthouse in the Chesapeake Bay.

would rip off roofs, uproot trees, wreck vessels along the harbor in Crisfield, and dump snow on the region.

Thomas had no knowledge of the extent of the storm, but he could see it was blowing him south, away from Tangier and out into the open waters of the Bay, where there would be little chance of rescue. His only hope was to make land at one of the little islands that stood at the southern entrance to Tangier Sound.

As the open boat rolled helplessly south, the breaking waves crashed over the top of the high-sided dory and soaked the new assistant keeper. To make matters worse, chunks of ice pounded against the side of his wooden boat, threatening to smash it.

Using oars, Thomas tried to guide the boat toward Watts Island, but there was little he could do to steer the vessel on the big seas. It did not take long for his body, soaked with freezing water, to become too numb with cold for him to steer any longer. As the island passed behind him, Barney Thomas fell, exhausted, into the bottom of the boat. Suffering from hypothermia, he slipped into

unconsciousness, as the little tender drifted out toward the open Bay.

Fortunately, the distressed boat had been sighted by John and Lewis Cooper, two young men on Tangier Island. They put out in a small motorboat in an effort to rescue the lightkeeper. Eventually, the Cooper boys overtook the disabled sailing boat near California Rock, two miles east of Tangier. They found Thomas in the bottom of the boat, still unconscious. With the storm at its height, the Coopers succeeded in towing the boat to Little Watts Island. There they carried Thomas to the Watts Island Lighthouse. With the assistance of the keeper, they resuscitated Thomas.

Thomas and his two rescuers could have stayed on in safety at Watts Island Lighthouse, but they decided instead to head back to Tangier, wrongfully assuming that the storm was blowing itself out. In the swash between Watts Island and Tangier, they ran out of gasoline. By this time, all three men were wet, cold, and almost exhausted. As the wind swept them away, they nearly gave up hope of reaching land. Then one of the Cooper boys found a small amount of gasoline in a pint

Point No Point stands isolated in the middle Bay off St. Jerome Creek.

bottle. Carefully, he fed it to the carburetor and managed to get the engine started. They had just enough fuel to get the boat into shoal water under Tangier Island. Here they plunged overboard. Leaving both boats to the mercy of the storm, the men waded ashore to safety.

Barney Thomas had survived a difficult initiation into the lighthouse service. A year later,

he would pen his thanks to God in a long quote from the scriptures, which he jotted down in the logbook of Hooper Island Lighthouse, taking half the page. He would go on to perform his own heroics, participating in the rescue of several men from a newfangled invention called a hydroplane, downed off of Cape Henry in 1921, where he would later be stationed as third assistant keeper.

Fog envelopes Thomas Point Shoal Lighthouse in the Chesapeake Bay.

Chapter Sixteen

Imprisoned by Fog

"What in the hell is that thing?" demanded Beatrice Goeshy, while approaching Drum Point Lighthouse in a boat with her new husband. "That's your home," answered keeper William Goeshy. The couple, who had just married, were the only recorded case of honeymooners in a lighthouse. Mrs. Goeshy went on to be named assistant keeper of Piney Point Light.

Drum Point keeper Cale B. Stowe and his wife had taken the outboard motorboat across the Patuxent River to Solomons Island in 1923 to do some shopping at Webster's Store, when the weather suddenly changed for the worse and fog rolled in.

Fog posed one of the biggest headaches for lighthouse keepers. Throughout most of the 1800s, keepers had to ring a fog bell by hand, which was certainly one of their most grueling tasks, particularly when the fog settled in for days. By the late nineteenth century, however, most Chesapeake lighthouses had been equipped with bell machines that rang the bell mechanically. Even these machines, however, were a nuisance, for they had to be wound, like a grandfather clock, every two hours. The keepers were expected to turn on the bell machinery when visibility got below five miles, which meant they had to be constantly vigilant for changes in the weather.

While keepers could always calculate the time of sunset and be back in time to light the lamp, they could only make an educated guess at when fog would roll in. Weather forecasting was still a primitive science in the 1920s. Most lighthouse keepers forecast weather by reading a barometer, observing atmospheric changes, and applying their own personal knowledge gained

from years of living on the water. Like Chesapeake watermen, keepers got to be pretty good at predicting weather conditions. Still, fog could move in silently and very unexpectedly.

Consequently, fog, more than the light itself, bound the keeper to his lonely post, making it almost impossible for him to escape for even a few hours, unless he had a dependable assistant. On many beacons, including Drum Point, the keeper's only assistant was his wife, who generally was not paid for her services. This meant a couple could seldom leave the lighthouse together, for one of them always had to be available to operate the bell machinery—unless, of course, they had children old enough to shoulder this responsibility.

On this particular day, the Stowes had left their teenage daughter, Myrtle, behind at the lighthouse with her good friend, Margaret Carey. Myrtle was a responsible young girl who understood the importance of the bell, but when she went to start the machinery, the fog-bell striker mechanism failed to work. Undaunted, she and her friend dutifully rang by hand the smaller saluting bell, which faced out on the river, until her parents returned.

"It took the two of us to ring it: 'One, two, three, ring!'" recalled Margaret Carey Sponselles, who jotted down the anecdote in a guest book on a visit to the restored Drum Point Lighthouse at Calvert Marine Museum many decades later. "We kept it up until the Stowes returned. They said we could have avoided a very serious boating accident because of the dangerous sandbar."

It is surprising that the two young girls even attempted to start the bell, for they had to wind it up, a job that required a strong arm. The Drum Point bell weighed 1,400 pounds and sat outside the second floor window of the bell room. Directly inside the room was the bell machine, which operated the striker. A small hole in the wall allowed the striker to hit the huge bell, which sat outside. The machine was operated by 600 pounds of weights hanging on chains that passed down into a weight closet on the first floor. When the machine was wound and ready to ring, the weights would be at the top of the ceiling in the closet. It took two hours for them to wind down to the floor. As the weights slipped down under their own weight, the chain moved fly-wheels in the bell machinery, which operated the striker. When the weights finally reached the floor, the machinery stopped working. Drum Point keepers were allowed only two minutes to rewind the weights to the top so that the machinery would again ring the bell.

While the fog-bell machine improved the quality of life for lighthouse keepers, like most machinery, it proved to be a cantankerous device that occasionally broke, forcing keepers to ring bells by hand, sometimes for hours.

Fannie May Salter, the last woman lighthouse keeper in the United States, was alone with her seven-year-old son at Turkey Point Lighthouse at the head of the Chesapeake Bay when she encountered problems with the fog bell.

"It was a cold night and very foggy out," she recalled in an article written for the *U.S. Coast Guard Magazine* during World War II. "Suddenly the whistle of a boat, apparently making for Philadelphia, was heard around our point. I started the bell ringing, but almost immediately a cable connected to the striking mechanism snapped."

The fog bell was located in an unusual bell-house outside the masonry tower. While most bell towers were tall so they could hold twenty feet or

more of clockwork chain, the Turkey Point bell tower was very short with a deep hole underneath into which the chain and weights descended. This was done because Turkey Point was already on a steep, eighty-foot bluff. Engineers wanted to keep the bell, whose sound carried only about four miles, as low as possible so it could be heard by the ships in the Bay below.

It had a thousand-pound bell with a fifty-pound clapper. When the mechanism failed, there was a smaller clapper that could be operated manually. This smaller clapper is what Mrs. Salter used to ring the big bell that night.

"I began to pull the bell, counting to fifteen between each pull," explained Mrs. Salter, who was required to ring the bell four times a minute. "I kept this up for about fifty-five minutes, until the ship was safely around the point and headed for the Chesapeake and Delaware Canal. I was never more exhausted in my whole life. It certainly was one experience I never want to relive."

But she did, not too many years later on a night that her daughter, Olga Crouch, will never forget. It was the night that Mrs. Crouch gave birth to her daughter, Frances Melba, in Perryville, twenty miles away.

When the baby was born, Mrs. Crouch's husband, James, tried to reach Mrs. Salter by telephone to tell her the good news. However, there was no answer at the lighthouse. Although Mr. Crouch called and called all night long, there continued to be no answer.

The couple did not find out until the next morning what had happened to the keeper. It was a foggy night and Mrs. Salter, again alone at the lighthouse with her son, had gone out to wind up the heavy weights that activate the warning bell. She then went back to bed, but a few minutes later, she could hear that the bell had stopped ringing. Bundling up again, she went back out to investigate. She discovered that the cable had broken, leaving the warning bell inoperative. In the distance, she could hear the sound of a tugboat blowing its horn—one long blast and two short ones to denote that it was pulling a barge. Mrs. Salter grabbed the clapper rope and hauled down on it with all her weight at fifteen-second intervals to sound the bell until the tug was safely

The hand-rung fog bell, once used to toll a warning to sailors, hangs over a shed at Cove Point Lighthouse, a reminder of the difficult task once performed by lighthouse keepers. The bell had to be rung by hand several times a minute at regular intervals during fog that might last for hours or even days.

around the point. Then she ran inside to call her daughter and son-in-law, but got no answer. Hearing the horn of another ship in the distance, she hurried back outside to pull the clapper rope on the bell again. Traffic was heavy that night, and the keeper spent most of the night ringing the bell by hand.

Like most fog bells on the Chesapeake, the one at Turkey Point was a clockwork bell. Many styles of bells, horns, whistles, and sirens were invented and used as fog signals from the mid-eighteenth through the early twentieth century. The clockwork bell, however, remained the most popular fog signal in the late 1800s and early 1900s before the advent of electricity. It did not require a lot of space in a lighthouse, an important consideration on the offshore lighthouses, and it was easy and cheap to operate.

The earliest fog signal in North America was a gun used at Boston Harbor Outer Light in 1719 to return the gun signal of a ship in fog. A bell, struck by hand, was first used in 1820, but striking a bell several times a minute for hours, and sometimes for days, was understandably a tedious and tiresome job. A keeper often called upon his wife and children to help with the task.

Alma Gatton of St. Marys County, Maryland, whose grandfather was keeper at Point Lookout at the northern tip of the Potomac River after the Civil War, remembers her parents speaking about the hardships of the hand bell: "The whole family had to take turns ringing that bell. There was no heat [in the bell house]. They had to wrap up."

The 1850s ushered in an age of development and experimentation with fog signals. In 1851, the first weight-driven bell machine was installed, again at Boston Harbor Outer Light. Experiments continued, most of them conducted by clock makers, who were already intimately familiar with the use of weights to drive machinery. George M. Stevens and Company of Boston eventually became the foremost builder of bell machines, but he got his start as a maker of tower clocks.

Over the next few years, inventors experimented with whistles and reed horns operated by compressed air. Most air compressors were powered by steam engines, but one actually used a horse on a treadmill. In 1855, some lighthouses

In the mid-1800s, the clockwork machine, so named because it worked on the same principle as a grandfather clock, was invented to ring fog bells mechanically through a series of pulleys, weights, and chains. This one is on display at Drum Point Lighthouse at the Calvert Marine Museum.

These weights move up and down on a chain in a closet in Drum Point Lighthouse. When the weights reach the bottom of the closet, they must be rewound, just like an old-fashioned clock. On foggy nights, lighthouse keepers had to wake up every two to four hours to rewind the weights.

tried a steam locomotive whistle. After the Civil War, many lighthouses were equipped with this type of whistle. The Chesapeake Bay, however, did not get its first steam-powered siren until 1881, when Cape Henry Lighthouse was finally equipped with a first-class siren (the biggest made) in duplicate.

Despite the new inventions, Chesapeake Bay keepers, for the most part, continued to ring their bells by hand until well after the Civil War. Undoubtedly, the rebellion postponed the introduction of the bell machine to the Bay region. After the war, rebuilding lighthouses and replacing lightships destroyed during the rebellion took priority over updating technology of any sort. Not until the early 1870s did the Lighthouse Board find the money and time to invest in bell machines. By 1870, most new lighthouses on the Chesapeake were equipped with fog signals operated by machinery. Finally, between 1872 and 1874, the Lighthouse Board approved funds to equip most of the existing lighthouses on the Chesapeake with bell machines.

By 1877, improving fog signals had become a priority for the Lighthouse Board, which acknowledged in its report that year that "on parts of the coasts of the United States fog signals are as important as light-houses." The board was so concerned about improving its navigational aids that it actually funded the work of numerous inventors, including several men working on automatic fog signals that sounded as they bobbed up and down in the water.

These early bells and whistles were surprisingly effective. A study conducted in 1894 by the Lighthouse Board revealed that even the less effective clockwork bells carried two to eight miles, while a first-class siren, operated by steam power, could be heard seven to twenty-eight miles out to sea.

By 1926, however, the most popular style of fog signal was still the original clockwork bell. In the Fifth District, which includes the Chesapeake Bay and the waters off North Carolina, fifty-two clockwork bell machines were in use, compared with only three steam whistles, five air sirens, three reed horns, and five submerged bells.

The introduction of the bell machine, more so than any other invention in the nineteenth cen-

On land, the fog bell was housed in a fog-bell tower, like this one found at the Chesapeake Bay Maritime Museum in St. Michaels. The weights moved up and down the tower.

tury, allowed the lighthouse service to save money by reducing the number of keepers stationed at a lighthouse. Stations with three keepers could employ only two, while stations with two keepers might make do with just one.

The fog-bell machine, for all its good, had one very negative impact on its keepers and their families—hearing loss. As the machines improved, the bells, whistles, and sirens became louder. Keepers and their families often said they became used to the ringing; nevertheless, their hearing began to fail. Whether the loss stemmed simply from old age or long years of deafening noise, many family members noticed that their parents who had served as keepers had little or no hearing in their golden years.

The fog bells also took their toll on the structures, particularly when housed on the lighthouse itself, as was the case on water stations. Former keepers and their families often recalled how the house shook as if a minor earthquake had hit the area every time the bell was struck.

In time, yet another invention would augment and, to a great extent, replace the mournful tolling of the keeper's bell. By 1917, the lighthouse service, in conjunction with the Navy Department and the Department of Commerce, was experimenting with a new and exciting way of guiding ships through fog and over tremendous distances, even farther than the eye could see. Radio waves would be the fog signals of the future and, in time, would augment or replace even the light itself.

New Point Comfort Lighthouse became one of the first automated lighthouses on the Chesapeake in 1930. At that time, the dirt road was almost impassable. Today, the lighthouse is no longer in use and stands on an island south of Gwynns Island.

Chapter Seventeen

Automating the Lighthouses

This is a serious time. Looks like the house will go, but we are trusting in God.

W. F. McDorican, assistant keeper of Holland Island Bar Light, writing in his logbook.

As W. F. McDorican, assistant keeper of Holland Island Bar Lighthouse, sat down at the kitchen table to write in his logbook on Tuesday, January 8, 1918, he could barely hold the pen to the paper. Outside the ice ran heavy around the legs of the screw pile, causing the house to bend and sway.

"This is a serious time," McDorican wrote with difficulty. "Looks like the house will go, but we are trusting in God. If it gets much worse, I don't know how it will be. The heavy ice is still here, still plenty of ice."

While the rest of the country went to war in Europe, McDorican and other lighthouse keepers around the Bay fought their own battles with the ice that formed in the wake of one of the worst winters of the twentieth century. The keepers of Choptank River Light off Oxford abandoned their dwelling in mid-January when the ice climbed thirty feet around the pile house and bent it over so far that the coals began to fall out of the stove. Choptank River Lighthouse fell a month later.

But McDorican, who was all alone in Holland Island Bar Lighthouse, stuck out the worst of the winter on the lonely outpost, twelve miles from the mainland, and three miles from the nearest inhabited island, Holland Island.

Bad weather had set in on December 9, and there were three snowstorms before McDorican's boss, keeper C. C. Tyler, departed the house for shore leave on December 28. The next day, it snowed all day and temperatures lingered at only ten degrees above zero. The Bay again froze, preventing the keeper's return. For the next month, McDorican endured snowstorms, freezing temperatures, sleet, fog, and, worst of all, running ice. He could barely work, let alone sleep. As the ice beat up against the narrow legs of the lighthouse, all he could think about was how to survive. Finally, on Wednesday, February 6, McDorican once more wrote in his logbook of the seriousness of the situation, concluding that he would "walk ashore to Holland Island." Almost a month after the ordeal began, McDorican finally reached the safety of land.

If there was a weak link in the lighthouse system it was the pilings on which three dozen or so lighthouses perched over the deadly winter waters of the Chesapeake Bay.

In 1911 and through most of that decade, the Fifth District, comprising Chesapeake Bay and North Carolina, had 181 lighthouse keepers and assistants, which was more personnel than any other lighthouse district in the United States. Yet the district had arguably some of the most vulnerable and dangerous lighthouses in the nation. By the twentieth century, the Lighthouse Board knew how dangerous a situation they had on the Chesapeake with its potential for loss of life and had become more understanding of keepers who abandoned their stations. Perhaps the board and its successor, the U.S. Bureau of Lighthouses, would have continued replacing pile houses destroyed by ice with the stronger caissons. However, new technology was taking the board in a different direction—toward unmanned lights.

Electricity had already begun to replace oil as an illuminant. As early as 1915, Lazaretto Light in Baltimore became the first lighthouse on the Chesapeake Bay to be lighted by electric incandescent lights. The new invention would be slow to catch on, taking another decade or so to replace oil in land-based lighthouses, and another three or four decades to reach the offshore lighthouse. When it did catch on, however, it would revolutionize the lighthouse industry, essentially making keepers obsolete.

Experiments with electricity in the lighthouse service began as early as 1881 when the Lighthouse Board requested an appropriation of fifty thousand dollars for the purpose of introducing electricity in some first-order seacoast lights. "The advances made in the appliances for generating electricity and the great improvements in the efficiency of the burners used in electric lamps, justify the Board in recommending the introduction of electricity in some of the first-order sea-coast lights," the board wrote in its 1881 report.

It was not until 1886, however, that the first electric light was turned on at Hallets Point, New York. Surprisingly, the brilliance of the light generated tremendous opposition and complaints. "The light was so brilliant that it dazzles the eyes of the pilots, and prevents them from seeing objects beyond the light or correctly judging distance within its radius.... The electric light is a nuisance and a hindrance rather than a help to navigation," the Lighthouse Board was informed.

Meanwhile, the Board encountered serious obstacles to installing electric lights at coastal stations where the brilliance would have certainly paid off. The design of the original Fresnel lenses, with their vertical ribs, interrupted the beam of an electric light, diminished the intensity of the light, and shortened the range of visibility.

While engineers worked on the problem of how to adapt electricity to work in Fresnel lenses, the Lighthouse Board continued experimenting with electrically lighted buoys. On November 7, 1888, six electric buoys were placed in the Ged-neys Channel, off Sandy Hook, New Jersey. They were connected to power sources by underwater cables, thereby proving that buoys could be successfully lighted with electricity.

In 1894, the Lighthouse Board was appropriated $150,000 to develop better communications with its coastal lights, lifesaving stations, and offshore lightships. Part of the money went for experiments into the most effective means of maintaining communication between the various isolated stations so that vessels in distress could receive prompt assistance. The Lighthouse Board planned to use part of the money to connect lightships to coastal lights via underwater cables.

Four years later, strained relations with Spain and the subsequent Spanish-American War actually proved a boost to the lighthouse service, which received fifty thousand dollars to improve communications at light stations along the Atlantic and Gulf Coasts. The board rapidly used the funds, building ninety-two miles of land telephone and telegraph lines, laying forty-three miles of submarine cable, and providing communications at seventy-eight light-stations, including the installation of seventy-one telephones. In exchange for the improved equipment, keepers at these seventy-eight coastal lighthouses were expected to assist in identifying and reporting enemy activity off the coast of the United States and were supplied with signal flags, code books, and binoculars to accomplish their additional tasks.

After the war, the lighthouse service funded many experiments with unmanned lights. As early as 1911, it had developed a new type of unmanned post lantern, as well as a new lantern for use on acetylene-gas beacons. By 1916, gasoline engines were rapidly replacing steam engines as power for fog signals when the old boilers broke down and needed to be replaced.

By 1917, with Europe under siege, war again brought about rapid improvements in the U.S. lighthouse system. A committee was formed from members of the Navy Department, Department of Commerce, and the Lighthouse Service "to consider and report on the further use of radio apparatus for fog-signal purposes and to coordinate experimental work along the lines now in progress."

Cedar Point Lighthouse, with its artful sunburst wooden pattern in the gabled roof, was abandoned in the 1920s, some thirty years after it was built, when the peninsula began to erode.

That same year, a thermostat was designed that could ring a bell and warn keepers when undue fluctuations occurred in operating oil-vapor lamps. The device was issued to a number of lighthouses and proved helpful in maintaining a better light.

World War I, for all its misery and death, ushered in a whole new era of efficiency, with improvements in travel and communication that reached out to distant lighthouses. Dedicated more than ever to advancements in technology, the country was working hard to link the lonely lighthouses to the rest of the world via telephone, radio, speedboats, and even airplanes. New technology had developed the radio direction finder, a means of identifying one's position without the aid of light or sound.

Before 1918, only eight lightships and seven lighthouse tenders had any type of radio communication. In 1918, the number of vessels equipped with radio increased to forty lightships and twenty-three tenders. War funds were also used to extend telephone communication to 139 light stations along the coast. The navy also established a number of radio compass stations so that ships could get their bearings before coming into sight of land or a lighthouse. By 1919, the lighthouse service had successfully replaced one lightship with a simple bell buoy that used compressed carbon dioxide gas in storage tanks to sound a bell every fifteen seconds.

By 1918, automation and improved technology were already taking jobs away from the Chesapeake Bay lighthouses and the Fifth District. The district had lost eight keeper positions and was now second, behind the Third District, which includes New York, in the number of keepers and assistants it had on its lighthouses.

Meanwhile, the airplane considerably reduced the isolation of lighthouses. On October 20, 1920, the superintendent of the Fifth District took to the air to do his annual inspection of the distant lighthouses in his district—those in North Carolina waters. He spent two hours in a hydroplane on a trip that normally would have taken four days by boat. It was a first for the district, and a first for the country.

By the 1920s, electricity was becoming a standard in towns and cities, which allowed the

The tall steel skeletal tower beside Fishing Battery Island Lighthouse held the automated light that replaced the lighthouse during the first half of the twentieth century.

lighthouse service to tap into the system to light their lamps. "With the growth of commercial and other electric generating plants and the extension of reliable electric current to the neighborhood of light stations, there has been an increasing use of electricity during the year for lamps in lenses and for fog-signal purposes," the commissioner of lighthouses wrote in his annual report in 1921.

Radio fog signals, or radio direction finders, which transmitted a radio signal to ships, giving them compass bearings, were first introduced at three lighthouses in New York Harbor in 1921. Two years later, Cape Henry Lighthouse became the first lighthouse on the Chesapeake to have radio fog signals installed.

Electricity and other innovations made keeping the light burning and fog bells sounding so much easier than in the age of kerosene. No longer did keepers have to get up in the night to refill the kerosene lamps; no longer did they have to wind fog-bell machinery every two to four hours. In many cases, they did not even have to climb the many steps—hundreds in offshore lighthouses—to start the light burning. It could now be done with the flick of a switch.

Just when things were getting comfortable out on the isolated beacons of the Chesapeake Bay, the lighthouses, one by one, were automated and the keepers dismissed. Some lights even flickered out, made obsolete by tiny lighted buoys.

With each successful invention, lighthouse automation became more and more a reality. By the early 1920s, automation of manned lighthouses was under way. The lighthouse service took pride noting its rapid steps toward automation. In 1923, the service reported that "out of the 4,047 coast and lake lights, 1,665 or 41 percent, were automatic, an increase from 14 percent in 1911." The following year another 75 manned lights were changed to automatic status, and 72 new automatic lights were established around the country. By the end of the fiscal year in 1924, 43 percent of all coast and lake lights were automatically operated. The next year, yet another 74 stations were switched to automatic operation.

Surprisingly, most boaters and the general public did not really notice automation until the 1950s and 1960s, when the program was greatly accelerated. But it all began in the 1920s with the growing use of electricity.

Isolated, land-based lighthouses that were difficult to reach were among the first to be converted. The first to be automated on the Chesapeake Bay was Back River Light in Virginia, an old tower standing on a marshy, eroding peninsula. It was automated in 1915 and decommissioned in 1936. Concord Point in Havre de Grace was automated in 1920, followed by Watts Island in 1923. Lazaretto Light, which had become obscured by buildings, was replaced by a steel tower in 1926, and the 1831 tower was soon demolished. New Point Comfort Light at the entrance to Mobjack Bay in Virginia was automated in 1930. Somers Cove Lighthouse near Crisfield was demolished and replaced by an acetylene gas light in 1930. Hawkins Point, a screw pile that served as the front range for the Brewerton Channel in the Patapsco River, was torn down and replaced with a tower in 1924.

Some lighthouses were decommissioned because they no longer served any useful purpose. Blakistone Island's light was turned off in 1932. The house burned in July 1956, reportedly a victim of lightning, though some people still believe it was arson.

Another victim of fire was Cobb Point Bar Light, a screw pile in the Potomac River which burned in late 1939, reportedly when the keeper, J. Wilson, accidentally dropped a lit cigarette into a cord of wood. The lighthouse was subsequently replaced by a mechanical bell.

Many river lighthouses, which had lost their purpose when traffic patterns changed, were dismantled or automated in the late 1920s and the 1930s. These stations included Craney Island, Nansemond River, Jordan Point, Bells Rock, and Point of Shoals.

Meanwhile, ice continued to take its toll on screw piles during the twentieth century. In 1935, Janes Island Light, near Crisfield, was swept away by ice for the second time. It floated up and down Tangier Sound for three days before it sank. No keepers were on board. The lighthouse was replaced with an automated tower on a caisson base.

Severe ice during the winter of 1918 destroyed not only Choptank River Light (where the Tred Avon River enters the Choptank), but also Bowlers Rock on the Rappahannock River. The latter lighthouse was replaced with an acetylene light and automatic fog bell operated by carbon dioxide gas. The light and bell were placed on a small caisson foundation in 1921, thus ending Bowlers Rock's days as a manned lighthouse.

The Choptank River Lighthouse, however, did not suffer Bowlers Rock's fate. The foundation of the old Choptank Lighthouse was destined to be the only station on the Bay replaced with an existing lighthouse. The Cherrystone Inlet Lighthouse near Cape Charles City had recently been decommissioned. The commissioner of lighthouses decided to use this screw-pile structure to replace the destroyed Choptank River Lighthouse. Consequently, in 1921, the cottage dwelling was taken off its screw piles and barged up the Chesapeake more than one hundred miles to a site near Oxford, where it was reassembled. On June 9, 1921, the light was reestablished, and the old Cherrystone Lighthouse became the new Choptank River Light. The lighthouse was manned once again, and it would continue to be manned until the Coast Guard, which took control of lighthouses in the 1930s, began dismantling the last manned outposts on the Chesapeake in the 1960s.

Concord Point Lighthouse at Havre de Grace was automated in 1920. Land-based lighthouses were the first to be automated, particularly if they were near a source of electricity.

Chapter Eighteen

Death on a Lighthouse: Murder or Madness?

The dead lighthouse keeper was in a nude condition with the exception of an undershirt, a top shirt and a vest. . . and a blood-stained butcher knife was laying a few feet from the body.

The *Crisfield Times*, March 21, 1931, reporting on the mysterious death of the Holland Island Bar Lighthouse keeper.

When Capt. William C. Todd of Deal Island sailed past Holland Island Bar Lighthouse on the morning of Wednesday, March 11, 1931, keeper Ulman Owens was standing on the walkway of the lighthouse, waving, appearing to be his usual happy self. Todd knew Owens and normally would have sailed close enough to exchange a few words, perhaps passing on news to the keeper, who was isolated from the community for several weeks at a time. On this day, however, a stiff breeze was blowing and Todd did not dare bring his vessel too close to the wooden structure for fear of ramming into it. As he waved to the keeper, Captain Todd could not have realized that he would be the last person to see Owens alive.

It was not uncommon for lighthouse keepers to die on the job. A few had drowned; others had suffered fatal heart attacks or other medical emergencies while tending the light. But Ulman Owens would be the only keeper on the Chesapeake Bay whose death would remain shrouded in mystery, tainted with the signs of foul play.

In 1931, Owens was a twenty-year veteran of the lighthouse service. He had been keeping a light on the Bay for mariners since 1911 when he was first stationed at Old Plantation Flats, south of

Cape Charles City on the Eastern Shore of Virginia. The following year he was transferred to Hooper Strait Lighthouse off Dorchester County, Maryland, where he suffered a medical emergency that would plague him for the rest of his life and complicate the facts surrounding his death. Owens developed appendicitis, and since he was unable to get immediate medical attention, his appendix ruptured. Fortunately, Hooper Strait Lighthouse was only a mile offshore, so he was taken off the lighthouse by sailboat and rushed to a surgeon in time to save his life. The surgery was only partially successful, however, and Owens suffered continually from severe digestive problems. Almost everything he ate caused him pain and diarrhea for the remainder of his life. Consequently, Owens grew frail and weak and took strong medicine, including the narcotic opium, to relieve his discomfort.

Fortunately for the keeper, lighthouse duties had eased over the previous twenty years. When he started work at Old Plantation Flats, he had only a sailboat to get back and forth from the lighthouse in the Chesapeake Bay. At Holland Island, Owens was supplied with a motorboat as well as a backup sailboat. The lighthouse was one of the more distant lighthouses on the Chesapeake, standing twelve miles from the mainland of Somerset County so, not surprisingly, the sailboat had not been used for a year.

The light's nonrevolving flash was another modern development. Twenty years before, the lights burned kerosene, which the keeper had to refill halfway through the night. In the old days, when lighthouses had a flashing light, the light burned continually, and the flash was created by revolving the lens, whose beam was partially obscured with a black strip. By 1931, however, Holland Island Bar Light used compressed air and kerosene, fed to the lamp in small amounts by a valve, to create the characteristic flash. To start the light, Owens had only to place the lamp in the pilot light, light its wick, then go down to the kitchen to flip a switch.

The two keepers at Holland Island Bar Light habitually entered weather reports, household chores, and observations in their logbook morning and evening, after tending to their duties in the lantern room. On Thursday morning, March 12, Ulman Owens sat down as usual at the kitchen table to jot down what would be his last entry in the lighthouse logbook. "Thursday, 12 A.M., N.W. fresh and clear. Steamer *Eastern Shore* passed at 6:00." That evening he apparently lit the light, then extinguished it Friday morning, without making any notations in the logbook.

Illness may have interfered with his routine. Besides his stomach ailments, Owens suffered from severe headaches that often disabled him for hours at a time. Once while working in the watch room, everything went black before his eyes, and Owens had to grope his way downstairs to his bedroom. His sixteen-year-old daughter, Ella, who often joined him at the lighthouse for two-week stints of duty during the summer, had been with him on this occasion. Owens asked her to get him his ammonia and a glass of water, which he drank as a home remedy for his headaches. He evidently feared the worst, for he told Ella that if something happened to him, she should pull the cord on the lighthouse whistle three times to attract attention.

Owens survived that attack but would suffer more of them with increasing severity. In January 1931, while ashore, his family noticed that he acted peculiar after suffering a severe headache. Daughter Myrtie noted that he often would not talk to people after a headache, and that he became easily angered, finding fault in everything, which was unusual behavior for a man with a happy-go-lucky personality.

On one occasion in January, while suffering a headache, Owens could hardly talk or catch his breath. His face turned bright red, and he could barely move his limbs. The attack incapacitated him for hours. His girlfriend, Minnie Shores, whom he lived with and planned to marry, was sure he was dying. Afterward, Owens complained that the back of his head hurt and was so sore that he could not touch it.

Despite all his health problems, Owens was generally a happy man who got along well with people and liked his job. He was good friends with his assistant, Ulysses Todd, and the two men evidently covered for each other when they needed to spend time ashore because of family needs or illness. The logbook indicated that neither man had taken more than the allotted eight days of shore leave per month, more than a small stretch of the truth, investigators would later discover.

Yet in the past few months, Owens had given some thought to leaving the lighthouse service. Two bad falls contributed to his desire to change careers. In November 1930, Owens had gone outside on the gallery to look around the lighthouse about 7 P.M. when he fell through the trapdoor, onto the deck landing below. Fortunately, Todd was aboard the lighthouse with him at the time, heard the commotion, and rushed out to help him. Owens was badly scraped and bruised from the fall, but otherwise uninjured.

Then on Christmas day, 1930, Owens was wiping snow off the motorboat, when his foot slipped and he fell overboard. Despite the freezing waters, Owens was able to climb back aboard the lighthouse on his own. He had skinned his ankle, and his hands were bleeding, but again, he escaped serious injury. He later told his family that a third fall would certainly kill him.

Despite his happy disposition, Owens had lately begun to brood about death. He mentioned to Ella that he did not expect to live much longer. He was fifty-two, about the same age his father had been when he died. His headaches undoubtedly contributed to his thoughts of death.

Whether or not he had been ill again on Friday, March 13, Owens evidently was strong enough to climb the narrow circular stairs to the cupola at dusk. The big light was an incandescent oil vapor light of 2,900-candlelight power. Owens put a small alcohol lamp under the vaporizer to heat the big light so that the oil in the light would vaporize. This process took eight to ten minutes, which he usually measured with a stopwatch. When enough time had passed to heat the big lamp, Owens had to go back down the stairs to the kitchen and throw a switch to start the light.

But on this evening, something interrupted Owens's normal pattern. Perhaps he was overcome with one of his severe headaches and rushed downstairs to drink his ammonia water. Or, Owens may have seen a boat approach the lighthouse and gone down to check on it. Whatever caused the interruption, Owens never had the chance to throw the switch and turn on the light that night. The wick in the alcohol lamp was later found burned to a crisp. The kerosene in the big light dripped, unused, onto the lantern floor.

Four miles east of Holland Island Bar Lighthouse, Royce Sterling was working a shift for his father, the keeper of Solomons Lump Lighthouse, which marks Kedges Strait, the narrow channel between the Chesapeake Bay and Tangier Sound just north of Smith Island. As Sterling lighted the lamp that night, he peered through the dense fog that had settled over the region, trying to distinguish the light of Holland Island Bar. He could not see it. Keepers on the Chesapeake routinely checked to see that other lighthouses in their vicinity were operating, but fog often obscured even the powerful beam of the lighthouse. Consequently, as young Sterling settled in for the night, he had no suspicion that Owens might be in trouble.

The next day, his father, Henry Sterling, returned to work and Royce left for home. Shortly after dusk on Saturday, Henry Sterling was lighting his own lantern when he noticed that the light was not yet burning at Holland Island Bar. Unlike the prior foggy night, Saturday evening was clear, and the elder Sterling had no doubt that the light at Holland Island Bar was simply not burning.

Seagulls are the only inhabitants of the lantern room atop Point No Point Lighthouse.

Since it was unusual for Owens to fail to light his lamp, Sterling wondered if something was wrong. For the rest of the night, he continually got up to stare out the window toward Holland Island Bar Light. Every time he looked, the sky was dark.

Sterling was alone at his own lighthouse with no radio contact with the other lighthouse or with shore. While land-based lighthouses had had radio and telephone communications for years, if not decades, keepers on the isolated water stations in the Bay had little means of communicating with the rest of the world, other then to flag down a passing vessel. Since he could not leave his own light unattended, Sterling spent a restless night, wondering what was wrong over at Holland Island.

During the early hours of Sunday morning, Garland Bloodsworth, captain of the powerboat *Marydel* of the W. E. Valliant Fertilizer Company of Baltimore, also became aware that there was a problem at Holland Island Bar Lighthouse. He was on a course from Smith Point Lighthouse to Holland Island Bar Light at 3 A.M. but could not see the Eastern Shore light. The captain had traveled this watery path before and ordinarily could see the light of Holland Island Bar all the way across the Chesapeake Bay at Smith Point, where he made his turn to run toward the Eastern Shore. This night, however, he was forced to use a lead line to check water depth as he approached the shoal waters of the Eastern Shore.

About 4:30 A.M., while checking his bearings with a lead line, Bloodsworth noticed an object in the water heading in his direction. Believing it was a barge adrift, he turned on his searchlights and discovered it to be a big powerboat, about seventy-five feet long. The vessel was running without lights, a violation of navigational laws. As soon as he turned on his searchlight, the mysterious vessel disappeared into the darkness. But Bloodsworth had seen enough to confirm in his own mind that the vessel was a converted submarine chaser named *Whippoorwill*, which was reputed to be running liquor for an owner in Connecticut.

With Prohibition in full swing, the Chesapeake Bay, with its many lonely creeks and long, empty shorelines, had become a perfect backdrop for illegal whisky smuggling. Consequently, the Bay was not always a safe place to be at night. Rumrunners (men in high-speed vessels illegally transporting liquor) and Coast Guard officials often clashed, and gunfire was occasionally exchanged. Honest captains usually minded their own business. Nevertheless, Bloodsworth got in the wake of the mysterious vessel and took a bearing on the course it had been traveling. He calculated that the rumrunner had come directly from the Holland Island Bar Lighthouse, located just a mile and a half north of their location. Bloodsworth continued on his own course, passing the lighthouse fifteen minutes after the sub chaser had sped off into the night. When he got into port, Bloodsworth reported that the light was out.

Meanwhile, about daybreak, a vessel finally passed within hailing distance of Solomons Lump, and Sterling waved frantically to get the captain's attention. On hearing of the concerns Sterling had for the neighboring light keeper, H. J. Garner, first mate on the vessel *Winnie and Estelle*, agreed to check on the keeper at Holland Island Bar Lighthouse. On the way over to the lighthouse, Captain Garner met up with John Tawes Tyler of Crisfield, who was at the helm of an oyster boat. Tyler followed Garner over to the light.

At the lighthouse, the two men lowered the ladder and climbed up to the catwalk that wrapped around the dwelling. As they approached the door into the dwelling, they passed a long, bloody streak along the wall. The men pushed past an overturned chair that had propped the kitchen door wide open to the outside. Inside, Tyler and Garner found a frightening scene.

Owens was lying on the kitchen floor, naked from the waist down. His left arm was outstretched toward a butcher's knife whose blade was spotted with blood. A six-inch pool of blood lay by his side. Garner hurried over to the body and placed his hand over Owens's heart, checking for a heartbeat, but it was obvious that he was dead.

Around them, the kitchen was in a state of chaos, with chairs and a table overturned. It was as if "a wild beast" had plowed through it, assistant keeper Todd would later comment when he returned to the lighthouse that afternoon. A pot of beans, evidently intended as a meal, was burned on the kitchen stove.

A bottle of spirits of ammonia was found beside Owens's body, and his assistant later found that the water spigot had been turned on, both clues supporting the theory that Owens went to get a glass of ammonia water while suffering one of his debilitating headaches.

But to Sterling and Sheriff Luther Daugherty (who both later visited the lighthouse with the local magistrate), and most men who viewed the scene that day, the chaos in the kitchen looked suspiciously like the result of a scuffle, as if Owens had tried to fend off attackers. The kitchen table and the chairs were overturned, the coal from the stove was strewn all about the floor, and papers were everywhere.

Traces of blood were found here and there both inside and outside the dwelling. Aside from the pool of blood on the floor, small streaks of blood, as if made by the back of a bloody finger, were found on several doors. A smear of blood, fourteen inches long and three inches wide, ran along the outside wall of the dwelling, as if someone had dragged a bloody hand casually along the house.

There were other oddities, as well. A calendar had been cut to shreds, apparently with the butcher's knife found on the floor. The most pecu-

On a fateful night in 1931, Holland Island Bar Lighthouse remained dark, clueing the keeper of nearby Solomons Lump Lighthouse that something had gone amiss aboard the screw-pile lighthouse. Holland Island was similar in design to Drum Point Lighthouse, pictured here.

liar fact was that Owens was nude from the waist down at a time when he appeared to have been in the midst of lighting the big light and cooking his meal. Owens's uniform trousers had been hung neatly on a hook at the entrance to the kitchen, but his suspenders were discovered on the floor behind the stove. His boots were found in bizarre places—one in the pantry, the other stuffed down the drain under the water tank faucet in the kitchen. His socks and underwear were never located.

His assistant, who returned to the lighthouse that evening still suffering the lingering effects of influenza, found a cotton sack about the size of a pillowcase on the floor of the pantry. In it someone, apparently Owens, had placed a peculiar assortment of items, including a gallon of cylinder lubricating oil, an old rag sock, a bar of soap, two lamp mantel containers, a tin of boric acid ointment, five lamp wicks, two small blocks of wood, and two bundles of newspapers. Todd could give the Federal Bureau of Investigation (called in to investigate the possibility of murder) no reason why a rational man would stuff all these articles into an old sack.

After the body was moved to shore, Dr. W. H. Coulbourne of Crisfield, acting as coroner, noticed a bruise on the left side of Owens's head, between the temple and the eye, but the bruise did not appear to be serious enough to cause his death, in his opinion. The doctor also found a small cut on the dead man's hand, which he assumed had caused the blood at the scene. There were several other small cuts and scrapes on the body, but no knife or gunshot wounds to indicate a violent end.

Despite the disorder and blood at the scene and the bash on Owens's head, the coroner concluded that Owens had died of natural causes, perhaps suffering a seizure or heart attack. Coulbourne theorized that Owens may have struck his head, suffering a concussion, thrashed around the room, dragging down the chairs and overturning the table, and died, if not immediately, then shortly thereafter.

A coroner's inquest agreed with Coulbourne's theory that no foul play had been involved in the keeper's death. Owens was buried several days later, but his family was dissatisfied with the findings of the inquest. Believing he had been attacked and left to die by rumrunners, they asked

A full moon shines through the cloudy night, competing with the beam of Cove Point Lighthouse.

for a more thorough investigation. On at least one occasion, Owens had told his girlfriend that he had seen a rumrunner. Perhaps Owens had talked too much and the thugs had come to silence him.

On Thursday, March 19, Owens's body was exhumed so that a full autopsy could be performed. Dr. George C. Coulbourne of Marion (not to be confused with Dr. W. H. Coulbourne of Crisfield) removed the stomach, spleen, heart, and pieces of the lungs and intestines so that they could be taken for medical analysis in Baltimore. The tests would determine if Owens was poisoned or died of a drug overdose. Dr. Coulbourne found a blood clot under the bruise on Owens's head and a crack on the outer portion of the skull, which confirmed Owens had suffered a more severe blow than the original coroner had thought. The second Dr. Coulbourne surmised that Owens could have received a blow that caused the concussion, which could have brought about a medical crisis if Owens was suffering from arteriosclerosis, which Dr. Coulbourne believed he was. The doctor had found that the valves of the keeper's heart were very stiff and the heart was enlarged.

Meanwhile, investigators discovered two bottles of laudanum and opium camphor pills in Owens's coat pocket. Laudanum, a medicine containing opium suspended in alcohol, had been brought to the lighthouse with government supplies. The opium and camphor pills were for Owens's stomach trouble. He had been taking them for years, although his personal doctor had not prescribed them and did not know that Owens was taking the narcotic. The discovery led investigators to wonder if Owens had overdosed on the narcotics, accidentally or on purpose.

Some residents of the tight-knit community of Dames Quarter in Somerset County had developed their own theory on what had happened to the lighthouse keeper. It was well known that Owens, twice a widower, had a passion for women. He had had several girlfriends since the death of his second wife, and two of them had left their husbands shortly before moving in with Owens, leading many residents to blame him for the breakup of two marriages. Both women denied that Owens caused them to leave their husbands and insisted their husbands held no thoughts of

violence against Owens. Yet, Owens's involvement with married women raised the question of whether a jealous husband had retaliated. Some residents believed that Owens was the victim of a love triangle and that Minnie Shores's husband had perpetrated the murder. But FBI agents confirmed that her husband was working aboard an oyster boat at the time Owens died.

The theory that Owens died at the hands of rum smugglers gained some credence when Captain Bloodsworth told FBI agents his story of spotting the rumrunner near the lighthouse. The agents followed up the lead and found out that *Whippoorwill* had been in dry dock the week Owens died. The boat was in for repairs after having been shot by machine-gun fire in a confrontation with the Coast Guard in early March. The FBI did find, however, that a similar vessel, *Manohanock*, also reputed to be a rumrunner, was operating in the area.

The investigation into the bizarre death of Ulman Owens came to an abrupt end in early April 1931, when further tests of his vital organs confirmed that he had a greatly enlarged heart, a symptom of heart disease. The FBI decided that he had died of natural causes and closed the case before determining the whereabouts of *Manohanock* on the nights of March 12 through 15.

The book would have closed forever had a man facing charges of illegally transporting liquor kept his mouth shut. While en route to the Baltimore city jail, Guy Parkburst, one of seventeen men arrested when a pair of rumrunning vessels was captured in the Bay on May 12, made a comment overheard by federal agent C. J. Callahan. Later that week, Callahan testified in a court proceeding that Parkburst pointed to two revenue officers and said, "There go the rats that turned us in. Well, the lighthouse keeper got in the headlines. We did that. What these rats get will be worse."

In May, the case of Ulman Owens was reopened, but no one was ever brought to trial. Local law enforcers, doctors, medical analysts, and FBI agents had culled through hundreds of clues, but no one could definitively say whether natural causes or foul play had brought about the death of Owens. Nevertheless, daughter Ella Owens would go to her grave believing her father died at the hands of rumrunners.

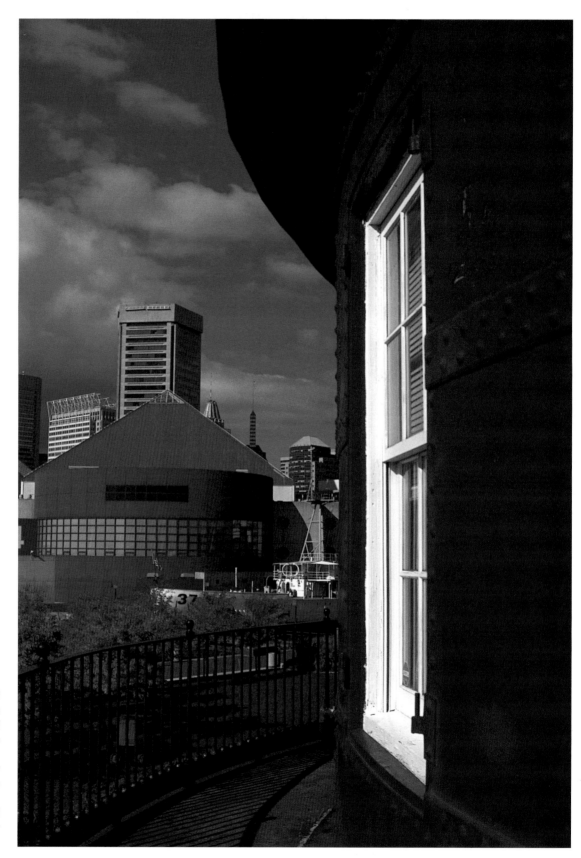

The round design and ironwork construction of Sevenfoot Knoll made it unique in the Chesapeake Bay. Here, with the Inner Harbor in the distance, the bolts that held the structure together are visible.

Chapter Nineteen

Rescue in a Hurricane

I'm going out there to get those poor devils out of the mess they're in.

Thomas J. Steinhise, keeper of Sevenfoot Knoll, who rescued five men
who had abandoned a sinking vessel during the August Storm of 1933.

*T*he storm was already beginning to increase in intensity on the evening of August 20, 1933, when lighthouse keeper Thomas J. Steinhise climbed the circular stairs to the cupola in the round cast-iron lighthouse to trim the wick and fill the lamp with kerosene for the last time that night. The light at Sevenfoot Knoll had guided vessels into the mouth of the Patapsco River, leading to Baltimore Harbor, for almost eighty years. It had weathered horrible winters when the ice piled so high around it that the big metal legs were bent or torn away. Now it would stand up to one of the worst hurricanes in history, though Steinhise hardly suspected this as he settled in on the aging offshore lighthouse to weather what he thought was just another bad northeaster.

Packing winds of up to forty-five knots, this gale was not the typically frightening, but short-lived, Chesapeake squall. It was the tail end of a tropical disturbance off Bermuda, which would hang around for days. The August Storm, as it would later be remembered, hit the Chesapeake Bay with a vengeance that night in 1933, raising the water level of the Bay to the doorsteps of even the shore lighthouses and driving waves right through many offshore pile lighthouses. At Drum Point, keeper John J. Daley described the seas lashing at his station as at least fifteen feet high, with waves flooding the rooms on the lower floor. The high winds and tides washed out a heavy concrete casing and ripped away and sank the station's small boat, forcing Daley to swim to shore with his report on damage.

Years later, the August Storm would go down in history as one of the most destructive, despite its relatively modest hurricane-force winds of ninety miles per hour. For three days it dumped rain on the Chesapeake region, up to eight inches in a day at some locations. Its high tides and driving winds would carve and reshape the shoreline of the Chesapeake and the Atlantic Coast, chiseling out an inlet for Ocean City, Maryland, cutting off New Point Comfort to leave the 1804 Virginia lighthouse permanently stranded on an island, and forcing rescues throughout the region.

Little did Steinhise know that he was in for a three-day binge of rain and wind that would destroy millions of dollars' worth of property and take at least eight lives the first night, including one outside the window of Sevenfoot Knoll.

Fortunately, Steinhise was not alone in the lighthouse. With him was his twenty-year-old son, Earl, who often joined him on the lonely outpost when the assistant keeper was off duty. Despite its iron-clad exterior, the lighthouse was homey and comfortable inside, with a rocking chair in the kitchen by the old pot-bellied stove, where father and son often played card games to wile away the long hours.

The wind was beginning to howl around the iron structure, but the two men were used to it. Keeper Steinhise had spent most of the last sixteen years on lighthouses in the Bay, beginning his career at Tangier Sound Lighthouse in 1919. At age fifty-four, Steinhise was a stocky, two-hundred-pound man of muscle, layered with the kind of leathery skin that was the telltale sign of years spent on the water. When he took his eight-day leave of the lighthouse to go home to a three-story brick row house in Baltimore, which was full of kids, he often brought with him a bucketful of fish caught on a hook and line at the lighthouse. Occasionally, he had a bridled snapping turtle for the family to feast on. Despite the Depression, his ten children and the numerous grandchildren who lived with them never went hungry.

His size alone would have been enough to command respect from the children, but Steinhise also had a personality that called for the greatest admiration. Fifty years later, his grandchildren would remember him as the kind of man who could handle any situation. Certainly, raising so many children and grandchildren had taught him something about being patient and calm in a crisis, virtues he would call upon in the next few hours.

About 11 P.M., as the winds continued to build, Steinhise suggested that his son get some sleep, while he took the first watch. Earl went to bed but was suddenly awakened an hour later.

"It seemed like someone or something had laid a cold, clammy hand on my arm," he later told a reporter. "I didn't see anything.... It was pitch dark, but I could feel there was something wrong, something uncanny, something ghostly."

Outside, the storm had grown in velocity since he had gone to sleep. It was now blowing fifty knots, driving the seas into huge waves that crashed against the lighthouse, shaking the pilings, and vibrating through the entire dwelling.

Terrified, Earl sat bolt upright in his bunk, wondering what had touched him, and feeling certain something was wrong. Straining his ears to hear over the roar of the wind, he finally picked out the sound of a whistle, followed by three more piercing whistles. Recognizing the four blasts as a distress signal from a vessel, young Earl leaped for his oilskins and ran for the lighthouse door. Outside, he spotted his father, leaning against the railing in the howling wind, searching the dark horizon.

"What are you going to do?" Earl shouted at him through the rain and wind.

"Do?" Steinhise huffed. "Why, I'm going out there to get those poor devils out of the mess they're in."

Out on the dark Chesapeake Bay off Sevenfoot Knoll Lighthouse, a tugboat had been swamped by the heavy seas and was sinking fast. The tug, *Point Breeze*, had been outbound from Baltimore at 10:30 that night, heading to dredging operations down the Bay. It was approaching the Sevenfoot Knoll Lighthouse when the northeast squall struck the craft as it wallowed in a choppy sea.

Tons of seawater rolled over the deck and down into the hold, causing the tug to list heavily to port. The next wave lifted the 164-ton vessel right out of the water and flung it back down, submerging its port rail. Oil in the starboard tanks began to pour into the port tanks, increasing the list.

The crew of ten men rushed to pump the oil back to the starboard tank, but the tug was sinking fast from the water it had taken on. The engines were turned to top speed, and the captain pointed the tug's nose toward shore in an effort to beach the ninety-one-foot tugboat before it sank. He was able to reach comparatively shallow water, but when the tug went down, it was still too far from shore for the men to swim for it.

Besides his crew, Capt. Ralph Kirschner had two government inspectors and his seven-year-old son, Ralph, Jr., on board that night. When it was obvious that the men were losing the battle with the sinking tug, Captain Kirschner ordered them to don life preservers.

One crewman, Archie C. Marshall, made three trips below to bring out life preservers before the tug sank. Joseph Blades, who was off watch and asleep when the vessel started to sink, was awakened. He tore loose a wooden grating to serve as a raft.

Fearing they would be sucked under as the big vessel sank, six men leaped into the water. Among them was chief engineer Percy Harrison, who died from exposure despite a heroic attempt by Marshall to rescue him. Marshall later told a newspaper that Harrison, an elderly man, had a life preserver on, "but he seemed to have heavy going

Sevenfoot Knoll Lighthouse stood in the Chesapeake Bay, off the mouth of the Patapsco River, until 1988, when it was moved to the Inner Harbor in Baltimore. It was on the walkway that wraps around the lighthouse that Thomas J. Steinhise spotted a tugboat in trouble during the August Storm of 1933 and launched a tiny dory to save its crew.

and cried out that he was drowning. I got him across my shoulders somehow and swam for what seemed like an hour before we were picked up."

The tug went down more than five miles from shore but, fortunately, was close enough to the lighthouse that the men held out hope of a rescue and began to holler.

Steinhise called for his son to help him lower the lighthouse launch. The twenty-one-foot motorcraft was ample boat for mild to moderate wave conditions, but in the short period since the storm had hit, the waters of the Chesapeake had been churned into monstrous waves, as high as fifteen feet, unlike anything the keeper had ever seen.

"Pop, you'll never make it in this sea," said Earl, fearing for his father's life. "This dinky boat we've got won't weather a blow like this; you'll never make it."

Ignoring his son, Steinhise lowered himself through the trapdoor and got into the wildly rocking motorboat.

"I'll go with you, Pop," Earl shouted after him. "You can't make it alone."

"No, son. You have to stay here with the light. That's an order. I'm captain here," Steinhise responded.

The tide was running fast, forcing the little boat to beat against the pilings. Steinhise tried to get the engine started, but water swashed over the gunwales and drowned the motor.

"Pop, turn back. You can't make it," Earl called to him when he saw the engine choke. But suddenly, the boat shot from his view, carried on a wave. Fortunately the violent northeaster was blowing the little lighthouse tender toward the stranded men, who were clinging to life preservers and anything that would float.

With his engine choked and only the wind, the rudder, and an oar to guide the launch, the keeper strained to maneuver his boat in the rough seas over to the drifting men.

With his eyes stinging from the salt spray blown off the wave tops, he finally made out the outline of the distressed craft, which had foundered in thirteen feet of water, leaving only the superstructure visible above water. Steinhise could make out the figures of men standing on the

Rescue in a Hurricane   121

Sevenfoot Knoll, flanked by the tents of Pier Six Pavilion, was moved to the Inner Harbor in Baltimore, where it can be viewed by the public.

pilothouse, clinging to the stanchions. Knowing they were in less danger than the men in the water, he devoted his effort to picking up the ones who had jumped overboard.

All around him in the blackness he could hear the agonized voices of the sailors, leaving Steinhise with the horrible decision of whom to save first. "Voices seemed to come from all around," he later told a newspaper reporter.

Steinhise described the awful scene in more detail in a letter to the superintendent of lighthouses, which he wrote later that day:

About 12:30 A.M., the tug boat *Point Breeze* went down near this light station with fourteen people on board. I went out to save what I could. The men was scattered in all directions, and it was difficult who to save first as most of them was calling me to come to them. At first I had trouble with the engine as it was rough and the sea was breaking over the boat. One man was dead when I pulled him in the boat. I worked on him but to no avail as others was calling for help then.

Guided only by the shouts of the sailors, he maneuvered his boat until he had picked up several men. They were weak from exposure, but they helped Steinhise get the engine started. Steinhise was about to attempt a return to the lighthouse when alongside the boat appeared the dead white face of a corpse, supported by a nearly exhausted swimmer. Hoping there was a spark of life left in the engineer, one of the crewmen had towed the body to the tender's already overloaded boat. The man and the body were pulled aboard.

Despite the running engine, Steinhise had a bigger battle getting back to the lighthouse than

he had had reaching the men. With the tide and wind both against him and the extra weight of the men, it took nearly an hour for the overloaded launch to reach the lighthouse and safety. The exhausted men crawled up the iron ladder into the lighthouse, where they dropped to the floor and lay panting, while Earl poured hot coffee down their throats.

Meanwhile, the tug *Sarah*, owned by the Arundel Corporation and captained by A. J. Eminizer, hove alongside the foundering *Point Breeze* and took off the remaining crew.

The winds were still horrific when the Coast Guard cutter *Apache* arrived at Sevenfoot Knoll later that day to pick up the stranded men. The Coast Guard had trouble nosing the cutter between the rocks piled at the base of the lighthouse. When the cutter was finally in position, the five

men and the body of the chief engineer were slowly lowered by ropes from the top of the lighthouse onto the bobbing deck.

On January 4, 1936, Steinhise received the Silver Lifesaving Award, a Congressional Medal for heroism that is only awarded in the most daring rescues.

The men rescued that terrible night—Archie Marshall, Joseph Blades, Henry P. Kraske, J. Frank Stephens, and Theodore Malinowski, all of Baltimore—never forgot the lighthouse keeper who launched a little boat in treacherous seas to save them.

Sixteen years later in 1949, when Thomas J. Steinhise died at the age of seventy-one, all the surviving crew showed up at his wake to give their respects and show their gratitude to a brave man who risked his life in the line of duty.

*The whitewashed
lighthouse built by John
Donohoo in 1833 is all
that is left of lighthouse
property at Turkey
Point. The two-story
dwelling was torn down
after vandals damaged
it. A group of interested
citizens in nearby
Northeast, Maryland,
hope to build a
replica of the dwelling.*

Chapter Twenty

Lady Keeper of the Lamp

One boy asked, "How old was the tower?" Mother (Fannie May Salter) answered, "A hundred years old." He said, "Huh, have you been here all that time?" Mother laughed quite a lot about that little episode. She was in her early fifties at the time.

From the writings of Olga Crouch,
daughter of Turkey Point Lighthouse keeper Fannie May Salter.

Clarence W. Salter and his family had spent all day and much of the evening of July 25, 1922, traveling to the lighthouse at the head of the Bay. When they finally arrived, it was dark and they could see little but the bright beam of the light before retiring to the whitewashed dwelling nearby. Now, as morning broke, Salter's wife, Fannie May, and their children, teenagers Mabel and Olga and three-year-old Bradley, got their first glimpse of the gleaming white tower of Turkey Point. They could not help but show their disappointment. The tower was so short.

Unlike the giant towers of Cape Charles and Hog Island—coastal lighthouses that reached 190 feet into the air—Turkey Point Lighthouse was a squat 35 feet. And it sat on a desolate point of land, with no nearby houses. Unlike the coastal lighthouses, which had three keepers and their families living on the grounds, Turkey Point Lighthouse was operated by just one keeper who called upon other family members when he needed help.

As she first gazed up at the little beacon, Fannie May Salter could not have imagined how much she would be called upon to help care for this lighthouse. Fannie May had always loved lighthouses, starting with the one she could see from the window of her parents' estate on Mobjack Bay in Mathews County, Virginia. York Spit Light-

house was a screw pile off the mouth of the York River, just south of Mobjack Bay. When she met Clarence Salter one Sunday after church in 1903, he was the young assistant at the station. As often as possible he sailed over to greet her at the family home. It was on one of these visits that Fannie May vowed, "I will watch your light." The promise would take on new meaning while at this little family lighthouse in the deep woods of Turkey Point.

Her husband had spent twenty-two years in the lighthouse service, but never had Mrs. Salter been expected to share the responsibility of maintaining the light. Always before, Clarence had been stationed at coastal lights with three keepers in attendance, or on screw piles out in the Chesapeake Bay, where families were now forbidden to live because of the danger of ice floes.

Nevertheless, Mrs. Salter and their two daughters had always enjoyed long visits to the water stations and often went out with the keeper, whether or not they had the required written permission from the Lighthouse Board. Once, a lighthouse tender showed up with the inspector on board while Salter's family was with him on one of their many unscheduled visits. Salter hid them away in the cupboards. The inspector conducted his inspection without ever discovering the stowaways.

Turkey Point Lighthouse, just thirty-five feet in height, is dwarfed by the giant cliff it sits atop. The lighthouse at the head of the Bay guides vessels away from the cliffs and toward the Chesapeake and Delaware Canal. Authorities have taken measures to riprap the shoreline, but Turkey Point has lost much of its cliff to erosion over the years and the lighthouse sits much closer to the cliff than it did fifty years ago when Fannie May Salter operated the light.

Keeper Salter was happy with the new appointment, but it took a few days for Mrs. Salter and the children to appreciate the quaint old tower and the quiet surroundings. It stood on a steep bluff at the confluence of the Bay and three rivers and was almost ninety years old when the Salters arrived. Built in 1833, a few years after the construction of the Chesapeake and Delaware Canal, the masonry lighthouse guided ships away from the dangerous bluff at the head of the Bay and safely into the Elk River, which led to the entrance of the C & D Canal.

Inside the tower was a wooden circular staircase of about thirty-five steps. At the top of the stairs was a platform on which rested an iron step ladder that led up to the lantern room. The cupola, or lantern room, housed the Fresnel lens, which was mounted on a pedestal. During the day, the lens was covered with a white linen cloth to keep away the dust. Shades covered the windows of the lantern room during the day, but were removed each night before the lamp was lighted. A portion of the storm panes were red, forming the red sector of the beam that warned mariners away from shoal waters and the steep bluff. If a pilot or sailor saw the red beam, then he knew he was heading for shallow water.

The tower was equipped with large brass kerosene lamps that Salter lighted and placed inside the lens at dusk to illuminate the horizon. During the long winters, the lamp would burn all of its kerosene fuel halfway through the dark night, forcing the keeper to replace it with a second lamp. In a few years, the style of lamp was upgraded to an Aladdin mantle lamp that had a meshwork cap over the flame, which became white-hot, glowing brighter than the old-style lamps.

By the time the Salters arrived, Turkey Point already had a reputation as a "Lady's Lamp." There had been three women keepers, two of

whom were widows who took over the light after the death of their husbands. Elizabeth Lusby became the first lady keeper of Turkey Point, tending the light from 1844 to 1861, after the death of her husband, Robert. Rebecca Sherwood Crouch also took charge of the lighthouse after the death of her husband, John. And when Mrs. Crouch died, one of her daughters, Georgiana Crouch Brumfield, who had married and remained at the lighthouse, was appointed keeper. It was just two years after Mrs. Brumfield's retirement that C. W. Salter was named keeper of Turkey Point.

The new keeper hardly expected history to repeat itself another time, but just two and a half years after his appointment, Salter became increasingly ill. When he was too sick to work, Fannie May substituted. Salter had suffered from stomach trouble for quite some time, but in February 1925, he was diagnosed as having chronic appendicitis and entered the U. S. Public Health Service Hospital in Baltimore for surgery. Three days after the appendectomy, he died of an embolism.

On the way home from the funeral in Mathews County, Fannie May Salter stopped in Baltimore to speak to the superintendent of lighthouses, Capt. Harold King. Mrs. Salter was concerned about how she would support her family (Olga and six-year-old Bradley were still at home) and asked the superintendent about a possible appointment as keeper. Unfortunately, Captain King had to refuse the request because a few years earlier, the Civil Service Commission, concerned that women could not handle the increasingly heavy machinery, had ruled that there could be no more women lighthouse keepers. He gave her thirty days to pack her things and move.

Mrs. Salter left the office with a heavy heart. She had just lost her husband; now she would lose her home. At age forty-two, and with two children still at home to feed, it appeared she would be forced to return to her parents for financial support. But beyond her material concerns, she had grown quite fond of the squat little lighthouse and the beautiful, quiet life on the point during the two and a half years she had lived there. Now she was reluctant to leave it.

Fate works in strange ways, and so it did on her trip home. By the time the family reached Northeast, the nearest major town to the lighthouse, Mrs. Salter's daughter Olga had developed a sore throat, so they stopped by to see the family physician. The physician kindly asked about the family's plans for the future, and young Olga poured out their troubles to the sympathetic doctor. When she finished her story, the doctor offered to help secure the job for her mother by going over the head of the superintendent. As a former state senator, the physician had many friends in the political world, particularly U.S. Senator O. E. Weller. The doctor offered to write the senator on Mrs. Salter's behalf. Delighted, Olga called her mother in to hear the news.

But as the days slipped into weeks and there was no news from the senator, Mrs. Salter began to pack their bags. In a last attempt to get an answer, Mabel, the older daughter who was now employed in Baltimore, wrote Senator Weller, asking if anything had been done about her mother's request to stay on as keeper of the light. He promptly responded, saying he had an appointment with President Calvin Coolidge to discuss the matter. Finally, Mabel received a wire informing her that the president had given his personal permission for Fannie May Salter to become keeper of the Turkey Point Lighthouse.

Seldom in the years since President George Washington handpicked the keeper of Cape Henry Lighthouse had presidents been personally involved in naming a lighthouse keeper. It was an honor that Mrs. Salter would never forget. During more than two decades as keeper, hundreds of articles would be written about Maryland's "Lady of the Lamp," and they would all note her unique appointment by the president.

After the retirement in 1932 of Maggie Norvell, a lighthouse keeper in Louisiana, Mrs. Salter was not only Maryland's only lady lighthouse keeper, but the only one in the United States. Having such a distinction brought her tremendous publicity. She was photographed and featured in many publications, including several times in *National Geographic*. The keeper was even pictured dusting her lens in an edition of *Encyclopaedia Britannica*.

Despite the fanfare, it was a difficult, lonely job for a woman with children. Mrs. Salter often had to brave severe weather—such as thunderstorms, gales, blinding snow, or dense fog—to light the lamp or start the fog bell.

Occasionally wind or drafts in the old tower would snuff out the light, and Mrs. Salter would have to rush out and relight the lamp. Her bedroom faced the lighthouse, and the beam fell directly across her bed. She often said she slept with "one eye open and one eye shut," but whatever it was that woke her, Mrs. Salter never failed to get up to relight the lamp or start the fog bell when it was needed.

Besides tending the light and fog bell, Mrs. Salter raised a flock of turkeys, a herd of sheep, pigs, and other barnyard animals, including a cow. She kept a large garden and put up vegetables for the long winter. Her life was not unlike any farm woman of the era, except she did it alone and had a lighthouse to tend as well.

When the weather was particularly bad, Olga remembers her mother warning them, "Children, I am going down to the bellhouse. If I don't return, you will know I was blown over the bank."

If Mrs. Salter worried about how her children would cope if she were killed or seriously hurt, she never let on. Once, she barely escaped injury when a windstorm tore down a big walnut tree and threw it on the walkway by the tower, moments after she had passed the spot on her nightly task of lighting the lamp.

A year after being named keeper, Mrs. Salter faced another crisis. Olga had fallen in love with James Crouch, the young neighbor who had tended their light while her father was sick. The two eloped in April 1926. On hearing the news, Mrs. Salter—knowing she could not keep the light and raise a seven-year-old son at the same time—insisted that they stay with her at the lighthouse.

And they did, living with the keeper until 1940, when Bradley became old enough to assist his mother with the lighthouse duties.

Mrs. Salter could not have asked for better assistants than her daughter and new son-in-law. Crouch had plenty of keeper blood in him, since his family had operated the light for many years before the Salters arrived.

It was while her daughter and son-in-law were living with her that Mrs. Salter suffered her worst injury on the job. The temperature dipped below freezing one night, turning the porch into a sheet of ice. Some time after midnight, fog engulfed the area and Mrs. Salter got up to start the bell. In the distance, she could hear the blast of a ship's whistle, so she hurriedly donned her bathrobe and slippers and rushed down the steps. As soon as she touched the icy porch steps, her feet slipped out from underneath her, and she fell on her back. In excruciating pain, she dragged herself up the porch and crawled back into the dwelling, crying for help. Eventually Olga, a sound sleeper, was awakened by her calls. She hurried downstairs to find her mother lying on the hallway floor. Olga called to her husband, and they helped her into the living room. Then James went out to start the fog bell for her. Mrs. Salter was soon rushed to the U.S. Public Health Service Hospital in Baltimore, where she was diagnosed as having a fracture of the spine. She spent six weeks in the hospital recovering, but the episode did not daunt her desire to remain the keeper of the light.

During her years at the lighthouse, Olga Crouch assisted her mother with all the lighthouse chores, from scraping and painting the dwelling, a beautiful two-story building, to preparing the lamp at dusk. Among her favorite jobs was saluting ships with three rings of the fog bell as they rounded the bend. Her husband, James, was employed with the Baltimore and Philadelphia Steamboat Company. Because Olga and James were often forced to be apart because of his job, they had worked out a secret signal to express their love for each other. "He would climb up a ladder to a porthole and flash his light three times, signifying I love you," Mrs. Crouch recounted. Even after they moved to their own home, Olga and her husband were not far away, just six miles

Olga Crouch spent years compiling a written history of the lives of her father, Clarence W. Salter, and mother, Fannie May Salter, who both served in the lighthouse service. Mrs. Salter became the last lady lighthouse keeper in America after the death of her husband in 1925. Mrs. Crouch lived with her mother for years, even after marrying, and helped with the daily chores of tending the light at Turkey Point.

down the road, close enough to help out when they were needed.

The family seldom had to deal with rescues. In fact, Mrs. Salter had the lighthouse service remove their boat since they had little use for it and she did not want to have to maintain it. But occasionally, young people vacationing at nearby resorts on the Eastern Shore, across the Bay from the lighthouse, would get in trouble while canoeing off the popular beaches.

In August 1938, two young men who had left Betterton Beach in a rowboat were capsized in a sudden windstorm. The men held onto the sides of the overturned boat and, as night fell, they paddled their way to Turkey Point, guided by the beam of the lighthouse. When they finally reached the point, they were too exhausted to walk up the steep hill. The next morning, they went up to the lighthouse and told Mrs. Salter of their ordeal. She fed them and helped them get home.

On May 31, 1942, Bradley was walking around the bluff when he heard cries for help coming from the shore below. He peered down to see three girls and a man on the shore under the lighthouse. Then he spotted another man hanging onto a stake in the Elk River. The young people had been canoeing when they were caught in a sudden windstorm that capsized one of the two boats. The seas and wind were too dangerous for them to launch a rescue in their little canoe, so they turned to the lighthouse keeper for help. Mrs. Salter called Crystal Beach to send a boat, but since they were a distance away, she also contacted a passing steamboat in the area. Both sent boats, and the man was quickly rescued.

During icy conditions in the winters, Mrs. Salter often received phone calls from shipping companies as far away as New York, asking if she knew the whereabouts and condition of their ships. Mrs. Salter kept an eye on the ships, and if the conditions grew serious enough to warrant aid, she would put in a request for an icebreaker to rescue the stricken vessels. The icebreakers *Latrobe* or *Annapolis* would then be dispatched to cut a path for the ice-bound ships. The icebreakers worked by riding up on the ice and smashing it. The big shipping companies often sent gifts to Mrs. Salter in appreciation of her help. Those gifts included candy, cookies, and binoculars. One company sent a hundred-pound bag of sugar; another offered them free fare on their ferries.

If life in the lighthouse service had one drawback for Mrs. Salter, it was that it interfered with her personal life. During the Great Depression, Mrs. Salter met a man she hoped to marry. However, he, too, worked for the lighthouse service, and at that time, civil service employees could not marry one another. If they did marry, one of them had to give up his or her job. The couple tried to arrange a secret marriage at the office of the Cecil County Clerk of the Court, according to her daughter Olga. However, when the clerk warned them that marriages were published weekly, they changed their minds. Before they could come up with a better plan, the gentleman was reassigned to a lighthouse in North Carolina. With time to think about the marriage proposal, Mrs. Salter opted to stay with her lighthouse and eventually declined the offer.

During World War II, the Coast Guard, which now oversaw lighthouses in the United States, installed a short-wave radio system in the tower, which Mrs. Salter, in her sixties, learned to operate.

Working the short-wave radio for the war effort turned out to be an around-the-clock job. Mrs. Salter had to relay information to the Coast Guard about ship movement in the C & D Canal and the upper Bay, as well as other messages that she received over the radio. For two years, Mrs. Salter hardly left the lighthouse office. When she needed a rest, she catnapped on a sofa next to the radio while her son took over for her. Bradley also made her meals and served her coffee at her desk.

"She was constantly on the radio. We worried that my grandmother wasn't going to make it through, she was so exhausted," remembers her granddaughter, Melba Crouch Barteau, who often visited with her mother Olga.

During the war, lighthouse keepers were required to report any unusual happenings. One of the most unusual things, spotted by Bradley during one of his walks around the property, was an unexploded mine that had washed up on the beach. He reported it, and the mine was quickly removed.

When electricity was finally installed in the old tower in 1943, Mrs. Salter no longer had to mount the steps to the top of the lighthouse, carrying an old-fashioned brass lamp filled with kerosene. She now had only to flip a switch to turn on the light. However, the kerosene lamps remained as a backup system in case the electricity failed.

Mrs. Salter was the only remaining woman lighthouse keeper in a force that had once numbered about 7,500 keepers nationwide when she finally retired in 1948. But she did not move far away—just six miles down the road to live next door to Olga. The lighthouse was immediately fully automated and continues to operate as a working navigational aid today.

The dedicated keeper often said she regretted leaving her lighthouse and talked wistfully about her years there. Mrs. Salter died at the ripe age of eighty-three on March 11, 1966.

Chapter Twenty-One

Bombing the Lighthouses

Three Navy attack bombers on a routine flight last night apparently mistook a Chesapeake Bay lighthouse for a bombing target.

The Baltimore *Morning Sun*, February 20, 1957.

*T*he four coastguardsmen inside Holland Island Bar Lighthouse had lighted the lamp and settled down on a cold February night in 1957 when they suddenly found themselves under siege, attacked by overhead aircraft. Rockets slammed into the waters in front of the lighthouse and ricocheted into the hexagonal dwelling, tearing at least three gaping holes eighteen inches in diameter in the frame siding. Other rockets tore into the metal beams supporting the building, completely severing several of the ten-inch-thick cast-iron legs and bending others. Frightened that enemy aircraft had singled out the lonely outpost in the middle of the Chesapeake for a blatant attack on the United States, the four guardsmen quickly evacuated the lighthouse.

Lighthouses on the Chesapeake had been attacked by enemy fire a century earlier during the Civil War, but this was the first incident of "friendly fire." For years navy officers, fine-tuning their skills, had been strafing an old grounded ship hull known as *Hannibal*, located in the lower Bay off Smith Island, four miles west of Holland Island Bar Light. Somehow, three pilots from the Atlantic City Naval Air Station confused *Hannibal* and Holland, and in the eerie light of misplaced flares, they flew their AD5N Skyraiders in a rocket attack on the lighthouse on the night of February 19.

The three navy attack bombers, part of an all-weather squadron, were supposed to hit the old half-submerged ship, whose superstructure is still a prominent sight on the lower Chesapeake Bay horizon and which is still used for target practice today.

One of the planes dropped flares on the lighthouse. The other two made two passes at what they thought was their target, firing five-inch practice rockets, which fortunately did not contain explosives.

None of the four coastguardsmen, identified as Boatswain's Mate 1/C Arnold W. Doyle, in charge of the station; Engineman 2/C Donald M. Warner; Engineman 3/C William T. Scott; and Seaman David L. Farrell, was injured. Despite the evacuation, the light burned throughout the night.

The second incident of "friendly fire" occurred just a few years later in the early 1960s when pilots from Patuxent Naval Air Station, trying to get in some extra practice, strafed Ragged Point Lighthouse in the Potomac River. They evidently thought that the 1910 screw pile was vacant. In fact, it not only was still a working navigational aid, but was also manned by coastguardsmen, who rushed out on the catwalk of the structure, to the horror of the pilots above. Whether it was originally intended, both screw-pile lighthouses were soon dismantled by the Coast Guard and replaced with simple beacons.

Although the aforementioned attacks were mistakes, several other light stations or their

Pooles Island Lighthouse, built by John Donohoo in 1825, is in remarkably good shape, despite bombing of the island during weapons testing by the U.S. Army at Aberdeen Proving Ground, and a half-century of neglect. Recently, the army restored the old lighthouse.

nearby grounds were routinely used as target practice by the U.S. military. Pooles Island in the upper Chesapeake was taken over by the federal government in 1917 and used for target practice as the United States entered World War I. The island, which was once covered with orchards, was part of the U.S. Army installations at Aberdeen Proving Ground and continued to be bombed for decades after the war. While builder John Donohoo's old masonry lighthouse was never hit, the rest of the island has been off limits to boaters because of the possibility of unexploded ammunition. Even today the waters around the island are often blockaded by army personnel because of firing that continues across the mouth of Bush River.

Pooles Island Lighthouse became one of the earliest automated lights on the Chesapeake in 1917 when the federal government moved out the keeper and other families living on the island. In 1939, the light was decommissioned. Although the light tower remains, the dwelling was soon torn down.

Also used for target practice was Jones Point Lighthouse. The beacon, a little wooden dwelling on land with a lantern mounted on top, was de-commissioned in 1926, and the wooden house fell into disrepair. Despite efforts to save it, the army took over the property, including the old lighthouse, during World War II, and some soldiers used the walls of the lighthouse for target practice.

Both lighthouses are still standing. Jones Point Lighthouse has been totally restored by the Mount Vernon Chapter of the Daughters of the American Revolution, which relighted the lamp. This lighthouse is the only example of a dwelling surmounted with a lantern on the Chesapeake that is available for the public to view. In 1964, the organization agreed to let the National Park Service take over the lighthouse and establish a park on the grounds surrounding it.

Pooles Island Lighthouse is the oldest existing lighthouse in Maryland, built in 1825. The tower is structurally sound and was repaired and painted in 1996. While it stands near the beach, it does not appear threatened by the water. The army long ago stopped bombing the island, but given the real possibility of unexploded ammunition in the vicinity, there is little chance that the public will ever be allowed to tour the Pooles Island Light.

Army personnel erected observation towers around Pooles Island, including this one which shares the landscape with the old stone lighthouse.

The moon rises over Drum Point Lighthouse. At one time, this decommissioned lighthouse was threatened with demolition, but it was saved by the Calvert County Historical Society, which moved it two miles west to its current site on Back Creek in Solomons.

Chapter Twenty-Two

Tearing Down the Screw Piles

Lighthouse keepers fall into about the same classification as pioneers—
with the requirements just about as rough. Good ones are
almost as hard to find these days as Conestoga wagon drivers.

Carl J. Boenning, administrative assistant to the officer in charge of the Coast Guard Depot in Baltimore,
quoted in a 1953 Baltimore *Sun* article.

Celia Atwood and her husband, Dr. Wallace Atwood, glanced out their window one morning during the summer of 1967 to see men working on Windmill Point Lighthouse. It was so unusual to see people on the old light, which had been automated since November 5, 1954, that Dr. Atwood "rowed out and asked what they were doing," Mrs. Atwood recalled.

Stephen M. Pratt, a Scotland, Maryland, contractor, was in the process of demolishing two hexagonal lighthouses off the mouth of the Rappahannock River—Windmill Point Light, at the northern side, and Stingray Point Light, built in 1858, a mile off the southern side of the river. Pratt had contracted with the Coast Guard to replace the lighthouses with skeletal steel towers.

Built in 1869, Windmill Point Light at one time was close enough to shore that old-time residents remembered being able to hear the keepers talking. The point had since eroded, however, leaving the house more than two miles offshore. Stingray Point was named after the strange fish that stung John Smith during his epic exploration of the Chesapeake in 1607. Smith thought he was going to die from the attack, but he recovered and went on to map the Bay.

When Atwood learned that they were tearing down the old lighthouse, he offered the contractor two thousand dollars to buy the structure. "We

thought we would make it into a cottage to rent," Mrs. Atwood recalled of her late husband's deal. At that time, the Atwoods were building a marina at Windmill Point and renting out cottages. It would have been the first and only renovated lighthouse available for rent on the Chesapeake. However, the plan never materialized.

The lighthouse was dumped on their beach in so many pieces that the Atwoods could not find anyone willing or able to piece it together. "They tore it very badly," Mrs. Atwood remembered. In fact, they later learned that one side of the hexagonal structure had fallen into the water and floated away, so they did not even have the entire house.

Meanwhile, Gilbert Purcell, a local boatyard owner who saw Atwood's efforts to save Windmill Point, decided to do the same thing with Stingray Point Lighthouse. He bought the pieces of that building from the contractor.

Two years after being dismantled, the Windmill Point and Stingray Point Lighthouses still had not been rebuilt. Reassembling the lighthouses on shore proved to be too costly in the end, so both sat in pieces until the wood finally rotted away. Even when their lighthouse was too far gone to save, however, the Atwoods dreamed of saving the cupola, the large hexagonal metal and glass dome in which the old Fresnel lens had sat. "We finally

Solomons Lump Light, north of Smith Island in the middle Chesapeake Bay, was stripped of its unique wooden octagonal dwelling after it was automated many years ago. Today, only the brick tower, which supports the lantern and light, remains.

decided to put the cupola up as a lookout station" for the dockmaster, but that never came to be, either, Mrs. Atwood said.

The cupola had a copper roof and was completely surrounded by glass, including one red panel that created the red sector warning sailors away from dangerous shoals. Unfortunately, before the Atwoods got around to mounting the cupola on a slab of cement near the docks, vandals broke all the glass in it. They did salvage the huge

solid brass bell, cast in Baltimore. Measuring more than two feet square, the bell sits on the marina grounds.

Although many land-based lighthouses were automated in the 1920s and 1930s, the Coast Guard, which took over operation of the lighthouses in 1939, did not change many offshore lighthouses to unmanned status until the 1950s. Better energy sources, such as lead acid batteries, made it finally possible to automate these distant lighthouses. Meanwhile, the cutting of new channels across shoals and the reduction of maritime traffic left other pile lighthouses obsolete.

At first, the Coast Guard kept the old wooden cottages as they automated the stations, just as they had done on shore. Stingray Point was automated on November 10, 1950, and Windmill Point was automated on November 5, 1954. Automated in 1951, but left standing, was Pages Rock, a screw pile on the York River. Some caisson lighthouses were also automated, including Newport News Middle Ground in Hampton Roads, Virginia, in October 1954.

After about ten years of unattended operation, the Coast Guard finally decided that the upkeep on the aging wooden cottages, many of which were approaching one hundred years of age, was just too costly. In 1963, conversion to an automatic light cost about $4,900. Without the need to maintain a dwelling, the annual operating cost of the automated station was only $1,300, saving the Coast Guard about $10,000 the first year and $15,000 each following year for every station automated. Once the lighthouse was off manual operation, the beacon was activated by a photoelectric system that turned it on and off according to the intensity of daylight. The new lights even had automatic bulb changers that went into action when a bulb burned out. By taking down the old, bulky dwellings and replacing them with pole beacons, the Coast Guard saved thousands of dollars per year in maintenance.

Contracts for removing the old cottages perched atop piles called for the complete dismantling of the wooden house down to the iron piles. Then a concrete slab 22 feet by 17 feet by 8 inches was poured over the steel beams. On top of that was built a cement block house 8 feet square and 10 feet high. Finally, a steel tower was erected on this to hold the light and fog signal.

The demolition contractors quickly learned that these old houses were not as frail as they appeared. They were extremely well built, with joints mortised and tenoned. The contractor was not allowed to set the houses on fire, because the heat might warp the metal foundation, and fragments of wood would fall overboard and menace small boats.

So the houses were generally removed piece by piece and hauled ashore to be disposed of. One contractor moored a metal scow alongside the lighthouses, covered the scow with a thick layer of sand, and burned the building on top of that.

By 1964, quite a few of the pile lighthouses had been dismantled and destroyed. The Virginia lighthouses destroyed include Tue Marshes in the York River, 1960; York Spit off the mouth of the York River, 1960; Old Plantation Flats, southwest of Cape Charles City, January 1962; and Tangier Sound, south of Tangier Island. In Maryland, the Potomac River lighthouses of Mathias Point, Upper Cedar Point, Ragged Point, and Maryland Point were dismantled in the 1960s. Holland Island Bar Lighthouse, south of Holland Island in the Bay, was destroyed in 1960, and Pages Rock, a screw pile on the York River, in early 1967. Of the three screw piles built in the James River, Virginia, in 1855—White Shoals, Point of Shoals, and Deep Water Shoal—only White Shoals was standing in 1963. It has also since collapsed.

Sometimes candlepower was greatly reduced when the screw piles were taken down and replaced by lights on steel towers. While Windmill Point remained just as bright, York Spit went from an 8,000-candlepower light to a 1,100-candlepower light when the house was torn down and replaced by a beacon.

The twelve caisson lighthouses in the Chesapeake, far sturdier than the cottages, were saved from demolition as the Coast Guard converted them to automatic status. Sandy Point Light was converted to a solar clock device in May 1963; Hooper Island and Point No Point were converted to automated status in the early 1960s. Bloody Point Lighthouse suffered a serious fire in 1960, from which the guardsmen on duty barely escaped with their lives. The caisson was soon converted to automatic status.

In 1964, Baltimore Light became the first—and only—atomic-powered lighthouse in the country. An isotopic power generator developed for the Atomic Energy Commission by Martin Company's Nuclear Division was installed in the lighthouse off Gibson Island. The sixty-watt generator was the size of a trash can, weighed two tons, and was designed to power the light for ten years without refueling. "One hundred and twenty pairs of lead telluride thermo-couples convert heat from radioactive strontium titanate, a safe form of strontium-90, into electricity," a June 1964 Baltimore *Sun* article explained. For some reason, however, the Coast Guard decided to scrap the experiment two years later.

Automation of land-based lighthouses also continued. Cape Charles Light, out on the lonely barrier island of Smith Island, and New Point Comfort Light were automated in July 1963. Point Lookout was replaced by an offshore beacon in 1965 after its civilian keeper, George Gatton, retired.

Amid all the losses of lighthouses to modernization, a rumor developed that the old Cape Henry Light, the first lighthouse built on the Chesapeake, might also be scheduled for demolition. In August 1953, Hurricane Barbara blew across the cape, tearing loose the copper canopy that covered the lantern room. The damage sat unrepaired for almost a year, forcing the closure of the lighthouse to the public. During that time, the rumor of Cape Henry's demolition began to circulate. The Association for the Preservation of Virginia Antiquities, which manages the lighthouse, quickly denied the rumors. The rumor did succeed in spurring people into action, and the canopy was soon repaired.

Improved technology was not the only thing that spurred automation. It was becoming harder and harder to recruit men to stand watch on the lonely outposts. In the nineteenth century, there were thousands of watermen who harvested the Chesapeake under the same harsh, lonely conditions that typified lighthouse keeping. In fact, many oystermen abandoned the middle decks of dredge boats for the relatively easier job of lighthouse keeping. By the 1950s, however, families around the Chesapeake had become spoiled by modern conveniences. The days when men spent long, harsh months on a boat far from home were over, and few men were willing to endure the frugal life of a lighthouse keeper.

Carl J. Boenning, who had helped to supply lighthouses in the Bay for thirty-five years, said in a July 12, 1953, Baltimore *Sun* article that the automation of lighthouses was due more to the approaching extinction of a historic breed of men. Boenning, administrative assistant to the officer in charge of the Coast Guard Depot in Baltimore, began working for the lighthouse service in 1917. In later years, he saw the number of service personnel dwindle steadily.

"Lighthouse keepers fall into about the same classification as pioneers—with the requirements just about as rough. Good ones are almost as hard to find these days as Conestoga wagon drivers," Boenning said. "When a lighthouse keeper retires, the Coast Guard usually finds it more expedient to convert his light to automatic control than to find a satisfactory replacement for him."

Prospective lighthouse keepers, particularly in the old days, had to have a distinctive set of qualifications, Boenning explained. The keeper needed a basic understanding of life on the water, so it was almost essential that he be a waterman or a commercial captain. He had to be satisfied with his own company. Unless he was trying for a mainland station, where he could have family with him, the keeper had to be able to do his own cooking and housekeeping and be willing to be away from his family for weeks at a time.

A lighthouse keeper had to wear several different hats. He would need to doctor his own ills from a chest of medicines and a home remedy book. He had to be something of a machinist to maintain and repair his lights, timing devices, and other equipment. And he alone would act as secretary to keep a detailed log and other records. Beyond these skills, a lighthouse keeper had to be a dependable, all-around waterman in emergencies, for rescue work was an important phase of the operations.

Ironically, automation in the 1950s came when technology had greatly improved living conditions for lighthouse keepers. Radios entertained keepers and kept them in touch with the outside world. Refrigeration made it possible for the lighthouse keepers to have quantities of fresh meat and vegetables aboard the light, so that the food he prepared was tastier and more nutritious, and bottled gas allowed him to prepare it more quickly. The radio-telephone helped to dispel the sense of utter isolation felt on the job. Finally, television offered entertainment and filled the long, lonely hours.

Hooper Strait Lighthouse became the first of only three wooden hexagonal screw piles saved from demolition during the Coast Guard's improvement program in the 1960s. At one time, there were more than forty pile lighthouses in the Chesapeake. Hooper Strait was moved to the Chesapeake Bay Maritime Museum in 1966 and is now part of the museum's exhibits.

In the mid-1950s, there were still about 400 manned stations left in the United States. By 1964, that number had been reduced to 287 out of 10,858 light stations in the country. Of that number, only 36 in the country were still manned by civilian keepers. The rest were run by Coast Guard personnel.

By the 1960s, guardsmen manning the lighthouses worked twenty-four days on and six days off. In addition, they received thirty days' leave annually. Most stations had three or four men, with at least two always on board. By now, tending the light had become so easy that it took only several hours of work per day. Point No Point was entirely self-sufficient, even before the guardsmen left in 1962. The light and foghorn were powered by fifty-four 2½-volt storage batteries, which were kept charged by two gasoline-powered generators. If there ever was a power failure, the guardsmen would put the old kerosene-burning lamp in the lens in place of the electric lightbulb. There was also a backup, mechanically operated bell to take over for the battery-run foghorn. Automation continued with the conversion of the caisson lighthouses at Smith Point and Wolf Trap in November 1971.

In the 1960s, the Coast Guard had managed to dismantle almost every cottage pile house without too much organized opposition, but when it proposed demolishing Thomas Point Shoal Light south of Annapolis in 1975, the public outcry was impossible to ignore. Annapolis had become one of the premier sailing cities in the country. Thousands of boaters routinely sailed the short ten-mile distance from the Severn River or Annapolis Harbor to Thomas Point Light, which marked the confluence of the South, West, and Rhode Rivers, where anchorages were in abundance. These pleasure boaters were quickly joined by state officials in denouncing the scrapping of Thomas Point. The group succeeded in getting the old screw pile placed on the National Register of Historic Places. Faced with such public pressure and forbidden from destroying a national historic treasure, the Coast Guard chose to continue manning the picturesque 1875 lighthouse.

Among the last three lighthouses on the Chesapeake Bay to be automated was Cove Point Lighthouse, which became a computerized light station on August 16, 1986. However, like Cape Henry, which was also automated, it still has coastguardsmen living at the dwelling on the lighthouse grounds.

That left Thomas Point Light as the last manned lighthouse on the Chesapeake Bay. In September 1986, it too was automated, this time without opposition since the Coast Guard planned to keep the structure intact.

Believed to be haunted by ghosts since it was decommissioned in 1965, Point Lookout sits empty at the mouth of the Potomac River. For a while, it was occupied by state employees of the Point Lookout State Park Service, nearby, who spotted a stream of ghostly characters and ghostly occurrences.

Chapter Twenty-Three

Point Lookout:
The Haunted Lighthouse

We were faced with the reality that a ghost had been holding our infant son.

Alan Manuel, who lived in Point Lookout Lighthouse in 1971–72.

Sue Winter Manuel was giving her infant son, Keith, a bath upstairs in Point Lookout Lighthouse in 1971 when she heard footsteps in the hallway. Someone knocked on the bathroom door three times, then continued down the hall. Thinking it was her husband, Alan Manuel, she started talking to him. From downstairs, Alan heard his wife and went to the bottom of the stairs to ask her what she wanted. "Weren't you just up here?" she called down to him. When he responded, "No," she hollered for him to hurry up the stairs.

Manuel looked everywhere, but he could not find anyone or any sign of entry. But his wife was emphatic; she had distinctly heard the footsteps on the hardwood floors and the knock on the bathroom door.

The young couple may have passed off the incident as weird, but a short while later came the clincher.

"We were both down in the living room and my son had been put to bed about a half hour before. We had one of those perfect babies. He was absolutely a peach. He slept all night. He was all you could ask for in a baby. All of a sudden, he lets out this scream...a terrifying scream. We had never heard that sound out of him. Not a thing of discomfort...a blood-curdling scream. We went racing up," Alan Manuel said.

If the Manuels had found disorder in the baby's room it might have been less frightening, but what they found was perfect order...only everything was reversed, including the baby.

"We put him to bed in the same end of the crib every night and since it was cold, he had a blanket, with clips that looped around the crib sides to hold the blanket," recalled Alan Manuel, who now works at the Calvert Marine Museum in Solomons, Maryland.

"Here he is at the other end of the crib. His head is at the bottom of the crib and the sheet, topsheet and blanket had been completely redone. It was like somebody had picked him up and moved him to the other end and remade the bed. He had been physically moved to the other end. By the time we got to him, he was sound asleep."

"[Sue] was completely freaked out. She was beside herself," said Manuel who was also frightened by the incident. "It was horrible. It's one thing to have a ghost walk down the hall and knock on the door, but we were faced with the reality that a ghost had been holding our infant son."

Manuel consoled himself and his wife by telling her, "Of all the ghost stories I've ever heard, I've never heard of a ghost harming anyone. Even though our son was picked up by a ghost, he's unharmed. Everything seemed okay." As soon as they had the opportunity, the Manuels moved from the haunted lighthouse.

They were not the first to experience odd occurrences at the lonely lighthouse that has stood at the mouth of the Potomac River for over 160 years. Since it was decommissioned in 1965, the lighthouse had gained a reputation for housing harmless spirits that seemed to come and go as they wished, leaving in their wake the sounds of footsteps, odd smells, an occasional name spoken aloud, or a deep sigh. Rangers at the nearby Point Lookout State Park have seen strange people at the lighthouse vanish before their eyes, and one woman says she was awakened by a circle of lights she believed were the entities, warning her of a fire.

Mike Humphries, director of the St. Clement's Island–Potomac River Museum in St. Marys County, discovered odd voices on his tape recordings when he visited haunted Point Lookout.

"There was a sweet old man singing, 'Living in the lighthouse, living in the lighthouse,'" recalled Humphries, who has often taken tape recorders to historic sites in hopes of catching the fleeting words of the dead. In another trip, he caught the sounds of a spirit, apparently talking to other spirits, stating in old-fashioned language, "Let us take no offense as to what they are doing." Humphries was baffled at the sounds of a cussing, laughing female voice until he learned about Pamela Edwards, a Civil War keeper who had to be tough to endure life in the midst of a prisoner-of-war camp on the lighthouse grounds.

Most of the voices are nonthreatening, but at least one voice upset Humphries and other listeners. It repeated, "Help me, help me," on the tape. Humphries believes the voice may be that of a man who committed grave sins during the Civil War and who feared eternal punishment.

While many people have written ghost stories about lighthouses on the Chesapeake Bay, only Point Lookout has seriously been considered haunted. In fact, so many strange events had been witnessed by so many different people, that in 1980 Park Manager Gerald Sword contacted the Maryland Committee for Psychic Research and asked them to investigate the paranormal activity at the old square lighthouse. Famed parapsychologist Dr. Hans Holzer visited the lighthouse and recorded voices on tape.

For all the peculiar events that took place after the light was snuffed out, most peculiar of all is that no one who lived at the lighthouse while it operated remembers a single haunted episode.

"I saw strange-looking people, too, but they were all human," said Alma Gatton, when asked about her experiences with the paranormal at the lighthouse. Mrs. Gatton is the granddaughter of a former keeper and the wife of the last keeper. She spent ten years at the lighthouse between 1955 and 1965 with her husband, George, and their two children, George, Jr., and Maria.

"I heard all this screeching, too, but did you ever hear the wind whistling around a door?" she asked. "I never heard a sound, never saw a thing that I couldn't account for. I never heard my grandparents talk about ghosts. I knew a lot of the keepers, but I never heard any of them speak about ghosts until the state took it over. And then it was full of ghosts."

The Point Lookout Lighthouse that Mrs. Gatton remembers is not the frightful, mysterious place of recent years, but a quiet, pleasant waterfront home where she raised her children in peace and tranquility. She and her children often spent time fishing and crabbing along the shore. While she did not swim off the point, her children did.

"At one time, the fish were so plentiful, you didn't have to throw a line, just take a crab net and dip the fish right out. Great big rockfish...you could dip 'em right out," she said.

While it may have been pleasant in her time, Point Lookout has had more than its share of tragedies. Several lighthouse keepers died during their tenure, leaving the wives to tend the light. The first wife was Ann Davis, who served from 1830 to 1847 and who reportedly has been seen still tending the light in recent years. One of the rangers saw "a lady dressed in blue at the top of the lighthouse stairs" one day. The woman looked exactly as Ann Davis has been described, wearing a long blue skirt and a white top. "I blinked, looked again, and she was gone," the ranger reported.

One of the more famous women keepers was Pamela Edwards, who kept the light throughout the Civil War. That was not an easy time to live at Point Lookout. The federal government established a Union hospital on the grounds and later turned part of the area into a Confederate prison. Conditions at the prison were extremely harsh; four thousand prisoners died and were buried there.

These tragic deaths have been blamed for at least some of the ghostly characters that walk the beach and the grounds around the lighthouse. Several rangers at the state park swear they have seen strange, old-fashioned men and women, some dressed in Confederate garb, walking in the park, often vanishing into thin air.

While the keeper generally was not involved in holding prisoners during the rebellion, it is believed that Pamela Edwards may have been forced to house several women prisoners briefly in a room at the lighthouse before they were moved to a federal prison. Laura Berg, a state employee who lived at the lighthouse with her husband, Erik, recalled in a newspaper interview that one room upstairs smelled every night as if something had died and decomposed in it. She scrubbed the room over and over again, trying to get rid of the smell, but at night the smell returned. Finally, parapsychologists supposedly identified feelings of pain and suffering flowing from the room. They finally identified the feelings as coming from persons who had been imprisoned in the room. After this discovery, the smell vanished. "It was as if they wanted us to know what had happened to them," Berg told a reporter.

Berg was involved in another paranormal experience in which she credits the spirits for saving her and the old lighthouse. One night she was awakened by "a circle of six small revolving lights on the bedroom ceiling." She immediately smelled smoke and rushed downstairs to find her space heater on fire.

A nineteenth-century shipwreck off the point has also given rise to a lonely spirit. Ranger Gerry Sword, who lived in the lighthouse and chronicled his experiences with the paranormal for the local historical society, wrote that once, while he was preparing for the onset of a violent electrical storm, he saw "a young, clean-shaven, white male peering through the window" of the lighthouse. When Sword opened the door, the man "simply

A former lady keeper, long dead, has been seen cleaning the lens inside the Point Lookout cupola. She is one of several ghosts who reportedly haunt the premises.

disappeared through the screening of the enclosed porch." Sword, who liked to research history, later discovered that a man very similar in appearance to his "visitor" was a victim of the 1878 shipwreck of *Express*, a steamer that got caught in a violent storm, similar to the storm that Sword experienced that day.

Despite the many tales of supernatural experiences, for the people who actually ran the Point Lookout Lighthouse, life there was far from supernatural. Their memories are of a simple, but hard, life made pleasurable by the family's sharing the work and by living on the beautiful Bay.

Shortly after the Civil War, William M. Yeatman, Alma Gatton's grandfather, took over as keeper of the Point Lookout Lighthouse. He remained there for over thirty years, until his death in 1908. Yeatman was familiar with the war camp, "having been a constant visitor at the prison, where he sold eatables to the soldiers," one early reporter noted in an article that was reprinted in the April 1980 *Chronicles of St. Marys*, a monthly bulletin of the St. Marys County Historical Society. Yeatman was described as "a man below the medium stature, nearly seventy years of age, wrinkled, with an old-fashioned beard of snowy white about his chin and neck."

Mrs. Gatton, who visited her grandparents as a child, remembers that they kept cows and chickens and had a big garden on the grounds around the lighthouse. Her grandparents had twelve children, some of whom continued to live at the lighthouse after they were married. Her father, Percy, was one of the sons who remained for a few years, so Alma's brother was actually born at the old lighthouse.

Tending a lighthouse was very demanding back then. All the children, particularly the boys, took turns ringing the hand bell during inclement weather, Mrs. Gatton said.

Mrs. Gatton remembers when the dwelling was enlarged. "The kitchen was taken off and moved out further in the yard. The new house was built around the old. Some people lived in tents while it was being rebuilt."

Her father was briefly in the lighthouse service, stationed at Love Point off Kent Island, but her mother did not like having him away so often. One of Percy's brothers, however, William, Jr., would go on to spend a life in the lighthouse service, much of it stationed at Point Lookout. His son, Harry Yeatman, remembers life at Point Lookout Lighthouse as "a good life, really."

"The whole family had to work," said Harry. "We all had our chores. We didn't do any playing until the chores were over. Every day you had to clean those kerosene lamps...they get smoked up. We had an old pot-bellied stove and I remember bringing coal from the store."

Harry remembers that the Fresnel lens was particularly hard to clean because of all the angles in the glass. The lens was enclosed in brass, which had to be polished, along with other brass items, such as lanterns. Once a week the whole family worked together polishing the metal.

William, Jr., had tended at least three other lighthouses before returning to Point Lookout. While at Point No Point, he went through a difficult winter when he was forced to build a sleigh and push it across the ice to safety. "He thought the ice was going to knock [the caisson lighthouse] down," said Harry, who was not born until his father was transferred to Piney Point, a land station farther up the Potomac River. His mother died of tuberculosis, and Harry was raised by his older siblings.

The children fished and crabbed and sold some of their catch. Crabs brought fifteen cents a dozen. The boys all learned to shoot a gun, and even at ten years of age were expected to bring home game for the supper table.

"Father would give us three shells. If you wasted them, you didn't get any more for a week. Those three shells should supply you with a meal," Yeatman said.

One of his uncles, Herbert Yeatman, worked tending buoys for the lighthouse service and was often at the lighthouse, which also served as a buoy depot. During the August Storm of 1933, Harry Yeatman remembers the tide rising so high that there was three feet of water in the front yard, and the keeper and his children were isolated for a short period of time. The children thought it was great fun, but the eight-foot tides and sixty-knot winds carried away hundreds of buoys that they had lashed down in the side yard. The buoys were scattered all over the Potomac River, and the family was able to retrieve only some of them.

The biggest problem at the light was swimmers who often got in trouble in the strong currents that developed where river meets Bay.

"One of my brothers [Bill Yeatman] saved two people," remembers Harry, who at the time was about twelve years old. Harry went out in the boat with his older brother to help the swimmers who got caught in the undertow at the point.

"My brother took the skiff and rowed down there. They were hollering. At Point Lookout, the water drops right off. One was down under the water and Bill found him." Both were pulled into the boat and taken safely to shore.

Point Lookout Lighthouse was first powered by electricity in 1935. For a few years, a windmill charged the batteries that supplied power to the navigational light and the rest of the house. The windmill was used for about six years before the lighthouse was equipped with a modern generator.

One of the big benefits of electricity was that the old fog bell that operated on clockwork machinery was no longer needed. The bell had to be wound every two hours. With the advent of electricity, the family was supplied with a modern fog horn, which required only a flip of the switch.

Owned by the U.S.Navy, Point Lookout Lighthouse is surrounded by a heavy, chain-link fence to keep out curious visitors. The structure has been greatly enlarged since John Donohoo built it in 1830.

Harry Yeatman and his brothers and sisters spent many hours walking the shores and the property around the lighthouse. The old Civil War forts were still intact, and the children played in the three trenchlike fortifications surrounded by moats that filled with salt water.

Throughout his childhood at Point Lookout, Harry Yeatman found little to frighten him. "I've walked that shore and around the light all hours of the night, and haven't heard a thing. I've heard a lot of strange noises, but if you go look at it, most of the time you find it's the wind that fools you."

Alma Gatton returned to Point Lookout as the wife of the keeper in 1955, just in time to weather the most frightening events of her tenure: two hurricanes.

Hurricane Connie struck first, washing out the narrow causeway between the Bay and the creek that allowed them to get to the point by car. "I was the last one to go across to the lighthouse before the road was washed away," Mrs. Gatton remembers. It took road crews about a month to haul in stone and dirt to fill the gaping hole that had once been blacktopped road. The keeper and his family went back and forth by boat while the work was under way. Before the road crews could

blacktop the road, however, another hurricane, Diane, struck, washing out the road once again.

By the time she returned to Point Lookout almost forty years after her grandfather had tended the light, there was no room for a big garden. Erosion had eaten away much of the point, and what was left was often washed by high tides that left the soil poisoned with salt.

Electricity had relieved the keeper of maintaining a kerosene lamp all night, and there was no need to ring a bell or rewind the clockwork machinery. There were now three keepers at the lighthouse, which meant there was plenty of manpower to scrape and paint the buildings, without the need of family members. However, Mrs. Gatton often found herself sleeping lightly, waking to find that fog had rolled in and the fog horn had not been turned on by the keeper manning the night watch.

The years she spent at Point Lookout are recalled with great fondness. Mrs. Gatton's husband retired in 1965. Three months later, the light was turned off forever, replaced by a pole beacon off the point.

And the lighthouse itself has come to be home to a new cast of characters: laughing, cussing, sometimes sad, sometimes sentimental ghosts.

*Piney Point
Lighthouse before its
recent restoration.*

Chapter Twenty-Four

The Forgotten Lighthouses

You couldn't breathe. The mold was four inches thick.

Milton Hartwig, Coast Guard maintenance employee, speaking about Point No Point in the 1970s.

Of all times for the light at Sevenfoot Knoll Lighthouse to go out, it had to happen in the middle of the winter of 1976–77 when ice blanketed the upper Bay in a crust so thick that even big ships found it hard to smash their way through the barrier. A few decades earlier, the Coast Guard could have counted on a lighthouse keeper—locked in the lighthouse—to get the light shining again. But automation had replaced the keeper in 1948, and now in the 1970s there was nobody aboard Sevenfoot Knoll to attend to the problem.

The easiest solution was to drop a man in by helicopter, and since Milton Hartwig ran the maintenance division at the Coast Guard facility in Baltimore, which operates out of Curtis Bay, he was asked to do the job. While standing on solid ground, Hartwig had no problem with the idea of being dropped aboard the lighthouse. But as the big aircraft hovered in the Bay over Sevenfoot Knoll, the catwalk of the round cast-iron screw pile looked like a tiny target to hit. Hartwig was already in his harness and rigged to go down, when one of the Coast Guard personnel reminded him, "Now, you don't have to do this if you don't want to."

Hartwig hesitated. He had been a guardsman before becoming a civilian worker, but he had never before been dropped out of a helicopter. The helicopter shook, its engines roaring so loudly that the men could barely hear each other as they positioned Hartwig for the drop. "I think I don't want to do this," Hartwig said suddenly, but it was too late. They were already lowering him toward the little target below. The drop took long enough for Hartwig to imagine all the possible scenarios. He could be bashed into the side of the lighthouse or dragged against the structure after he touched down. The harness could get caught in the lighthouse superstructure. He could miss the lighthouse altogether and land on the cracked ice below. But in a matter of moments he was standing on the deck, loosening the harness, and breathing a sigh of relief.

As soon as he climbed into the cupola, he could see the problem. There was no mechanical or electrical failure; it was just a case of poor housekeeping. The windows were dirty. The windows were so dirty, in fact, that the powerful beam could no longer penetrate the filth.

When Hartwig finished cleaning, not only could ships see the light again, but they could also see a red sector, which no one had known existed.

The 1970s were a dark time in lighthouse history not only for Sevenfoot Knoll, but for most lighthouses on the Chesapeake. In the wake of automation, those left standing were either abandoned and left at the mercy of the elements, or closed up and left to mold and rot.

Hartwig remembers stepping inside Point No Point after it had been locked up for years. "You couldn't breathe. The mold was four inches thick." The Coast Guard had boarded up the lighthouses, hoping to thwart vandals from breaking

Big cracks have formed in some of the caissons, including this one in the base of Bloody Point Lighthouse. Here a coastguardsman opens the steel door to the tower for a regular inspection.

into the empty dwellings and destroying the interiors. Windows were bricked in and doors heavily secured. Unfortunately, the effort to save the buildings by sealing them had caused them to be airtight, which created its own kind of damage from fungus and rot.

Meanwhile, vandals still found ways to cause serious damage to the lighthouses. Graffiti was the least of the problems. Thoughtless intruders started fires and ripped out the interiors. Drum Point Lighthouse was an easy victim, since by the seventies, silting had carried the shore out to the screw pile, which was now standing on dry ground where anyone could get to it. When this lighthouse was finally salvaged by the Calvert Marine Museum, there was evidence that several fires had been set inside the wooden structure. Likewise, fires had been set inside Sevenfoot Knoll Lighthouse, and much of the interior wood frame had been torn out.

Even when they did not break in, vandals managed to do considerable damage from their boats, shooting at the lighthouses, using them as target practice. On June 18, 1979, vandals used a

different tool of destruction—a baseball bat. The thugs smashed to pieces the antique Fresnel lens that was still in use at Sandy Point Lighthouse. The three-foot-high lens had been in the lighthouse since it was first lighted in 1883. The lens was used to focus and direct the light from kerosene lamps originally and, in recent years, electricity. Located just a half-mile off the shore of Sandy Point north of Annapolis, the light had been automated since 1963.

Since the Fresnel lens was handmade of crystal a century ago, it could not be duplicated by modern craftsmen and was considered a priceless antique. It was replaced with an acrylic lens. The Coast Guard offered a $1,250 reward for information leading to the arrest of the culprits, but no one was ever convicted.

That same year, Fort Washington on the Potomac River and Turkey Point were vandalized, both easy victims because of their isolated locations in parks that close at night. At Turkey Point, gunshot blasts twice smashed the light's acrylic lens, and its batteries were broken and lead wires stolen. In each case, the light was out for a day, endangering passing ships. It was not the first time vandals had hit Turkey Point, which is still a working light. Years ago, the old Fresnel lens was stolen by two men. The priceless lens was recovered, but it was not reinstalled. Vandalism was such a big problem at remote Turkey Point that the Coast Guard tore down the dwelling and removed the interior stairs in the tower to prevent culprits from damaging the lighting apparatus.

Even Concord Point Lighthouse, which stands in the midst of the town of Havre de Grace, had a problem with young people shinning up a metal pole outside the tower and knocking out a window well above the ground.

By the end of the seventies, the Coast Guard conceded that the problem of vandalism had grown "substantially worse" in recent years. In the summer of 1979 alone, sixty acts of vandalism and theft were reported at lighthouses, buoys, day beacons, and light towers on the Chesapeake. The replacement cost of destroyed or stolen items totaled nearly fifty thousand dollars, not including the Fresnel lens, which was irreplaceable.

Meanwhile, the Coast Guard did little to maintain even the exterior of the lighthouses, and many began to look weathered and unkempt. Caissons, which had stood one hundred years with little more maintenance than a coat of paint and basic repairs, were now showing wide cracks in their bases. As roofs leaked and waves swashed in, the cracks got worse. Something had to be done if the last of the lighthouses on the Chesapeake Bay were to survive.

By the late seventies, Milton Hartwig had also seen the decay and decline of the lighthouses, but there was little he could do about it, since orders for repairs came from over his head and he and his crew were normally kept busy. The day finally came, however, when the maintenance crew found themselves without work.

"We were standing around with nothing to do. I knew if I didn't find work, we'd be laid off," Hartwig said of a few weeks during the late seventies. The maintenance man, who had become a big fan of the lighthouses, had been out on the old structures often enough to know what needed repairing. For one thing, Craighill Channel Range Front Light, a little caisson off the mouth of the Patapsco River, needed a new roof. The old one was leaking, causing interior damage. Hartwig took his men to the light, and they started to work. It was one of the first efforts to do major renovations to a lighthouse since the structures had been automated.

Over the years, Hartwig eventually took his crews to all the lighthouses to replace boarded windows with a strong plastic called lexan, which resisted penetration by bullets. Ventilators were installed in the windows so that air could flow through the old dwellings, stemming the growth of mold and fungus.

The interior of Baltimore Light reveals a beautiful wooden circular staircase, still in mint condition. The lighthouse recently underwent repairs by the Coast Guard.

Meanwhile, the Coast Guard was changing its attitude toward the last existing lighthouses. By the 1980s, money was being allocated to repair and restore some of the old structures. Consequently, Coast Guard tenders were sent to do major renovations on almost every lighthouse in the Chesapeake under Coast Guard authority. One by one, the old houses were scrubbed, painted, and repaired.

In the early 1990s, Hartwig and his men went to work on Baltimore Light. Before starting the work, however, Hartwig researched the history of the lighthouse and found that it originally had dormers. Consequently, he restored the dormers when he repaired the roof, and today the lighthouse off Gibson Island looks exactly as it did when it went into operation in 1908.

Hooper Strait Lighthouse is open to the public at the Chesapeake Bay Maritime Museum in St. Michaels, Maryland.

Chapter Twenty-Five

The Renaissance

*An almost unbelievable saga of frustrations and disappointments over
a nine-year period has finally come to a conclusion. On Tuesday, December 10,
the Calvert County Commissioners voted unanimously to transfer
the Drum Point Lighthouse to the Calvert County Historical Society.*

Unidentified 1974 newspaper clipping, from the files of the Calvert Marine Museum Library.

The decision by the Coast Guard to raze the decommissioned lighthouses in the 1960s ignited a flurry of activity to save the old structures. All around Maryland and Virginia, public and private groups were organizing to save what was left of the Chesapeake's beacons. For most screw piles in the Bay, the efforts would come too late. A few were saved, nonetheless, and many nonprofit groups quickly formed to save and maintain the land-based lighthouses that were still salvageable.

Chesapeake Bay Maritime Museum in St. Michaels, Maryland, was the first organization to successfully move a screw pile and open it to the public. In 1966, the museum learned that Hooper Strait Lighthouse, in lower Dorchester County, was scheduled to be torn down and replaced by a simple beacon. The museum contacted the contractor, Stephen M. Pratt, of Scotland, Maryland, who agreed to sell the building to them for one thousand dollars.

The museum immediately went to work bulkheading Navy Point, where the lighthouse would be relocated. Numerous companies donated material and work to the job, greatly reducing the museum's cost. The Arundel Corporation of Baltimore agreed to move the old lighthouse at cost. On Friday, November 4, 1966, the lighthouse

ceased operating as a navigational aid. High winds and rough seas the next day, however, delayed the scheduled move. Finally, on Sunday, November 6, under almost ideal weather conditions, the hexagonal structure was cut in half and placed on a barge. By 6:30 P.M. the tug and barge, loaded with its odd cargo, were chugging out of Hooper Strait, headed for the Miles River and a new home for the old lighthouse. The trip was "smooth and uneventful," according to the tug's crew, and the barge was docked at the maritime museum at 10:30 A.M. the next day.

Then the job of putting together the pieces began. Fortunately, the maritime museum had been involved in the dismantling, so they had only two pieces to reassemble. Monday afternoon, the bottom floor of the lighthouse was moved off the barge and onto its new foundation. The following day the top of the lighthouse was hoisted onto the bottom half and the two pieces were secured. Everything went smoothly, and the job was complete by noon.

Hooper Strait Lighthouse was carefully restored to reflect the authentic colors of the lighthouse and the original living conditions of the keepers. The cupola was painted black, the roof red, and the sides and rails white. The top railing on the first floor was painted red. The louvered

The Hooper Strait Lighthouse and Point Lookout Bell Tower are among the favorite exhibits on the grounds of the Chesapeake Bay Maritime Museum in St. Michaels.

shutters were painted dark green, while the underpinning of the building was painted red—all the traditional Bay lighthouse colors.

While the Chesapeake Bay Maritime Museum was the first to move a lighthouse successfully, it was not the first group to try to save a screw pile. Even before Hooper Strait found a new home, another group across the Bay had already begun efforts to acquire a lighthouse. From nearby Solomons, the Calvert County Historical Society could almost spot Drum Point Lighthouse at the mouth of the Patuxent River. But it would take nine years to cut through the red tape necessary to acquire and move the lighthouse.

A hexagonal cottage on screw piles, Drum Point was built in 1883 just off the northern entrance to the Patuxent River. Over time, the land has shifted, silting in, instead of eroding like most sites around the Chesapeake. Consequently, Drum Point Light had become a land-based lighthouse. As such, it should have been easy to acquire and renovate, but things did not turn out to be so easy. Land near the lighthouse was difficult to buy, and for three years a congressional subcommittee

balked at deeding the lighthouse over to the society because Congress did not want it moved off the point. The state's efforts failed because the land surrounding the lighthouse was privately owned and the state was unable to acquire it.

Seven years after the society began its effort in 1965, it still had not obtained ownership of the lighthouse. In order to protect the structure from demolition, the society successfully applied to have it placed on the National Register of Historic Places on April 11, 1973.

In 1974, the museum finally learned that it could have the lighthouse, but not the land it sat upon. With the help of the local county government, Drum Point Lighthouse became the property of the Calvert County Historical Society on December 10, 1974.

By this time, the lighthouse was virtually in ruins. G. Walther Ewalt, then president of the society, described the structure's condition: "Vandals have already set the lighthouse on fire, attempted to steal the large bell, stolen the brass lens stand and ripped all doors from their hinges, even knocked out the railing. It looks terrible."

With a twenty-five-thousand-dollar grant from the state of Maryland, the society contracted to have the lighthouse moved two miles upriver to the Calvert Marine Museum. Work on the new lighthouse foundation began in February 1975.

When it came time to move the lighthouse in March 1975, the area around it had to be "backwashed" by a tugboat. The boat's powerful screws churned a channel in the sand to allow the crane to reach the landlocked lighthouse.

Workers used cutting torches to sever the ten-inch-diameter iron screw pilings, but the pilings turned out to be solid, forcing the crew to spend two days at the task. The lighthouse was lifted intact and placed on a barge. It took two tugs to pull the barge and its forty-one-ton lighthouse to her new home.

The restoration took several years. On June 24, 1978, the Drum Point Lighthouse was officially dedicated and opened to the public. Inside the lighthouse are numerous authentic pieces, including the original china used by the Weems family, donated by their granddaughter, Anna Weems Ewalt, who also helped oversee furnishing the lighthouse. Former light keeper John Hansen also made a contribution: the chair he used while serving at the station.

Not too far from the Drum Point Lighthouse is Piney Point Light, fourteen miles up the Potomac River. A conical brick structure with a detached two-story dwelling, Piney Point was decommissioned in 1964 and acquired by St. Marys County in 1980.

Of the eleven lighthouses built to guide vessels up the Potomac in the nineteenth and twentieth centuries, Piney Point is the oldest, and one of only four surviving lighthouses along the river. (The others are Point Lookout, Fort Washington Bell Tower, and Jones Point.) Today, the six-acre site is owned by the Museum of St. Marys County Department of Parks and Recreation.

The lighthouse keeper's quarters at Piney Point were renovated and rented out to provide income for restoration of the site. Built in 1836 by John Donohoo as part of the original contract for construction of a lighthouse, it was once a one-story building with an A-frame roof, measuring thirty by twenty feet, consisting of a central fireplace, parlor, dining room, and cellar. Like many dwellings, this one was later enlarged. A fog-bell

Piney Point Lighthouse recently received a new coat of paint. Owned by the St. Marys County Department of Parks and Recreation Museum, the grounds are open to the public.

The Fort Washington Bell Tower, which also houses the light, still guides traffic on the Potomac River. The grounds surrounding the tower and the old fort are now open to the public.

tower, built near the lighthouse, was destroyed in 1954 by Hurricane Hazel.

New Point Comfort Lighthouse, decommissioned in 1963, was in sad repair when the Mathews County Historical Society asked the county Board of Supervisors to acquire the structure from the federal government. The tower was deeded to the county two years later. Residents of Mathews County and nearby Gloucester County formed a committee and raised eighty thousand dollars for the lighthouse restoration. Not only did the committee face the problem of saving the structure, but it also had to deal with the issue of saving the island on which the lighthouse stood. During the next five years, the committee placed riprap around the lighthouse, resurfaced the ma-

sonry walls, repaired the railing around the lantern room, cleaned and painted the light cage, and repaired the brick wall. Window shutters were installed, a dock constructed, and a walkway built.

All of this was done for the sake of preserving history, for New Point Comfort is so remote, there is little hope of making it a tourist attraction. The lighthouse was once located on a peninsula, but the August Storm of 1933 cut a channel behind it, making it an island.

When Concord Point Lighthouse in Havre de Grace was decommissioned in 1975, the Coast Guard gave it to the city with the proviso that the city maintain the tower and keep the beacon, which is still magnified by an authentic Fresnel lens, lighted at night. A group of volunteers called

Harbor. Unlike the Hooper Strait Lighthouse, Sevenfoot Knoll was not easy to move. The 220-ton lighthouse—the only round, iron screw pile in the Chesapeake—was so heavy that it bent the loading frame when crews from the Empire Construction Company and the Marine Division of Tidewater Construction Corporation tried to move it. Winds gusting up to thirty knots became a serious problem as the crews began welding support braces to the loading beam. When the lighthouse was finally lifted out of the water with its iron legs intact, the crew still faced one more difficult moment. The seven-mile ride to Baltimore required that they pass under the Francis Scott Key Bridge, not an easy task since the lighthouse was hanging from a 185-foot derrick, which steadied the structure on the barge. The workers had to lower the height of the derrick by thirty feet to pass safely under the bridge. To make matters worse, the tug and barge were hit with heavy winds as they reached the bridge. Fortunately, the lighthouse rode out the heavy seas without damage.

Descendants of Sevenfoot Knoll keeper Thomas J. Steinhise, who saved the lives of five men in a dramatic rescue during the August Storm of 1933, organized an all-out campaign to clean up and restore the lighthouse and to preserve the keeper's memory. The restoration project brought together the big family, many of whom had not seen each other for decades. On some weekends there were fifty family members busily scraping paint and cleaning the interior of the lighthouse.

While the lighthouse itself was saved and preserved, only a small portion of it—the front room—is open to the public. The rest of the structure is used by the Living Classrooms Foundation as offices.

Meanwhile, the only reproduction of a Chesapeake Bay lighthouse was completed on private property in Baltimore in 1985. The original Lazaretto Lighthouse, built by John Donohoo in 1831, was torn down in 1926 after it was obscured by neighboring buildings and replaced by a skeleton tower. The new lighthouse stands fifty feet from the original site and was built by Norman G. Rukert, Jr., president of Rukert Terminals Corporation, which owns the property at Lazaretto

the Friends of Concord Point Lighthouse, Incorporated, maintains and preserves the lighthouse and opens it to the public. The tower was in excellent shape when the group took it over. Even most of the original mortar was intact.

For many years, Sevenfoot Knoll Lighthouse, automated in 1948, was destined to be moved down the Chesapeake Bay to the Mariners' Museum in Portsmouth, Virginia. That never happened, however, and the light remained at its post south of the mouth of the Patapsco River until 1988, when it was finally acquired by the city of Baltimore. The forty-foot tall, round, cast-iron lighthouse was cut loose on October 11, 1988, hoisted onto a barge by a massive crane, and moved up the Patapsco River to Pier 5 at the Inner

Point. The lighthouse was erected in the memory of Rukert's father, Norman ("Cap") Rukert, Sr., who died in June 1984. The elder Rukert had written a series of books on Baltimore and had planned to make the re-creation of the lighthouse his next project.

"It's just a nice thing we wanted to do for the community and for Dad's memory," the younger Rukert said.

At Turkey Point Lighthouse, the Lions Club from Northeast, Maryland, helped the Coast Guard paint the lighthouse. A local group has hopes of rebuilding the old dwelling, which was torn down.

Cedar Point Lighthouse is on the edge of collapse. It stands on a tiny island at the mouth of the Patuxent River, and parts of it may be saved for posterity. In December 1981, the lighthouse cupola was removed from the dilapidated structure and moved ashore to the Naval Air Test and Evaluation Museum. A nonprofit group, Friends of Cedar Point, helped bring about this move. There is some interest in the community in moving the cupola

again, this time to the center of Lexington Park, where it could be better enjoyed by the public.

The U.S. Navy, which owns the Cedar Point Lighthouse site, located offshore from the Patuxent River Naval Air Station, has asked for suggestions on what to do with the remaining structure. The lighthouse has partially collapsed—one whole side has fallen into the water. Two museums, St. Clement's–Potomac River Museum in St. Marys County and Calvert Marine Museum in Calvert County, have expressed interest in acquiring the intricate wooden gables shaped in a decorative sunrise pattern. The remainder of the lighthouse will likely be razed.

Cove Point Lighthouse, which is still a working navigational aid, may someday be accessible to the public. Currently, the Coast Guard maintains a residence for an employee in the old keeper's quarters, but in May 1996, talks were held with Calvert County officials about turning the automated lighthouse and grounds over to the county. If this should happen, the lighthouse would remain a working light, but the Calvert Marine

In June 1988, Bloody Point Lighthouse got a much needed restoration by the Coast Guard. For years after automation, the lighthouses were closed up and left to fall into disrepair, until the Coast Guard began an aggressive program in the 1980s to repair and maintain them.

Cedar Point Lighthouse, which once stood on a peninsula jutting into the Bay below the mouth of the Patuxent River, now stands on an island and is close to collapse.

Museum would probably arrange tours of the grounds and maintain the structures.

Today's Coast Guard is far more sensitive to the historic value of the remaining lighthouses under its jurisdiction than it was thirty years ago when it supervised the demolition of so many of the Chesapeake's beautiful pile lighthouses. Regular inspections of the lighthouses are made and money has been allocated for major renovations. Consequently, almost every lighthouse under Coast Guard jurisdiction has received life-extending maintenance over the past decade or so.

Thanks to the many people who care about the old beacons and who have worked to save them, the future of Chesapeake Bay lighthouses appears bright.

Newport News Middle Ground Lighthouse, located in Hampton Roads, is still a working navigational aid.

List of Lighthouses, Lightships, and Tenders

*I*n the course of researching this book, I compiled several helpful lists, including lighthouses built on the Chesapeake Bay, lightships (or light-vessels, as they were originally known) that served the Bay, and lighthouse tenders—the vessels used to build, supply, and tend to the needs of the lighthouses during the nineteenth and early twentieth centuries.

It would seem to be an easy task to count the lighthouses built on the Bay, but the job is complicated by the fact that so many were rebuilt, sometimes several times. Then, there are range lights, which have often been miscounted as a single entity when, in fact, there are two separate lighthouses in most ranges. I also found at least one questionable lighthouse—a light that was operated at the Naval Hospital in Norfolk for fifty years. This light appears to be more of a beacon, originally built atop a bathhouse, though it was rebuilt and enlarged in 1868. There is no reference to a keeper's house accompanying the beacon and, mostly likely, it was tended by a caretaker on the hospital grounds or, perhaps, this keeper provided his own quarters in the nearby city. Nevertheless, I have left this light in the list since it was obviously an important early beacon.

In all, there were eighty manned lighthouse sites on the Chesapeake Bay and its tributaries, counting range lights with separate dwellings as separate lighthouses. (North Point Range was tended by one keeper, so I counted it as one site, while Brewerton Channel, Craighill Channel, and the Craighill Upper Ranges all had two separate lighthouses in each range, so are counted as separate lighthouses.)

How many lighthouses were actually built is even more difficult to pin down. I counted at least 106 lighthouses built on the Bay and its tributaries. Most of the additional 26 lighthouses represent entirely new structures on new foundations and in new locations to replace existing lighthouses threatened by erosion or destroyed by ice. A few were rebuilt on existing foundations, particularly in the case of pile lighthouses built over water and destroyed by ice. These numbers do not include wooden structures that were rebuilt due to rot and age, lack of height, or other problems. (For example, Fort Carroll Lighthouse was moved and rebuilt every time the fort was improved, at least six times.)

All three lists were drawn primarily from the *Report of the United States Lighthouse Board*, which was issued annually from 1853 to 1910, and from the annual reports of the United States Bureau of Lighthouses, which took over jurisdiction of the lighthouses in 1911. Later information was gathered from the Coast Guard, which took jurisdiction in 1939. Early facts were gleaned from the records of the National Archives in Washington, D.C.; from the *U.S. Light-House Board Compilation of Public Documents and Extracts from Reports and Papers Relating to Light-Houses, Light-Vessels, and Illuminating Apparatus, and to Beacons, Buoys, and Fog Signals, 1789-1871*, a compilation of important early letters relating to lighthouses, found in the Nimitz Library at the U.S. Naval Academy in Annapolis, Maryland; and from the *Report of the Officers Constituting the Light-House Board, 1852*, found in the Mariners' Museum in Newport News, Virginia. Information on when lighthouses were automated was also found in many newspaper clippings, listed separately under "Sources."

Lighthouses are listed chronologically by the year in which the *first* lighthouse was built on that site. A map of Chesapeake lighthouses is located on page viii.

Lighthouses

OLD CAPE HENRY

Old Cape Henry, a ninety-foot, octagonal sandstone block tower, was constructed in 1791–92 at the southern entrance to the Chesapeake Bay. It was the Chesapeake's first lighthouse and the first lighthouse built by the new federal government, at a cost of $17,500. The lighthouse, which has a copper dome covering the lantern room at the top, was designed by architect John McComb, Jr. (who also designed the old City Hall in New York). President George Washington took a personal interest in construction of the lighthouse and appointed the first keeper.

The lighthouse actually began as a joint venture of the colonies of Maryland and Virginia in 1774, but the Revolutionary War intervened shortly after the stones were moved to the site and before construction got under way. When the beacon was built, McComb was able to recover some of the stone from the venture sixteen years earlier, but sandstone from quarries on the Potomac River had to be brought in to complete the tower. The original lighting apparatus was a common spider lamp, which burned numerous fuels, including fish oil, sperm oil, colza oil, lard oil, and kerosene.

The light was damaged in 1861 and temporarily put out of service by Confederates during the Civil War, but the Union soon repaired the damage and lighted the lamp, which was given a military guard from Fort Monroe for protection.

An inner brick wall was added in 1857 and wooden steps were replaced by iron steps in 1867. Cracks were found in six of the eight faces of the tower in the early 1870s. Two of the cracks extended from the top of the tower to the bottom; consequently, the tower was determined to be unsafe and construction of a new tower was recommended. The old tower was deeded over to the Association for the Preservation of Virginia Antiquities in 1932. In August 1954, Hurricane Barbara tore loose the bronze canopy at the top of the tower, but it was eventually repaired. The lighthouse now stands as a monument to the landing of John Smith's party at Cape Henry in 1607 and is open to the public.

NEW CAPE HENRY

An appropriation of $75,000 was granted by Congress in 1878 for a new Cape Henry Lighthouse. The cost eventually rose to $225,000. The new lighthouse is a 150-foot iron tower with a spiral staircase containing 227 steps. On December 14, 1881, the new tower, complete with a first-order Fresnel lens, was turned over to the keeper. It was equipped with two first-class steam-powered fog sirens—the first on the Chesapeake.

In July 1887, "a system of magneto-electric call-bells, for the use of the keepers, was installed, connecting the tower and fog-signal building with the keepers' dwellings. This system, which is arranged with a code of signals specially devised for the purpose, affords a convenient means of communication between the keepers." In 1923, Cape Henry became the first lighthouse on the Bay to be equipped with a radio fog-signal device.

The light today can be seen nineteen miles out to sea. It has a red sector, framed by a ruby-glass arc in the tower, which marks the shoals of Middle Ground and the Tail of the Horse Shoe. The lighthouse was automated in 1984 and is still used as a navigational aid.

OLD POINT COMFORT

Construction of Old Point Comfort Light began in 1802 and was completed the following year. The fifty-four-foot tower marks the northern entrance to Hampton Roads, Virginia, and is surrounded by Fort Monroe. In the 1700s, a fire was kept lighted here to guide vessels into the harbor. An eighteen-foot beacon was built in 1855 to guide vessels to anchorage inside Hampton Bar; it was tended by the Old Point Comfort keeper.

In 1891, the dwelling, which was very old and beyond repair, was rebuilt. In 1892, fifty cartloads of earth were deposited around the front of the dwelling to grade the premise, and about three hundred feet of galvanized-iron pipe were laid to connect the station with the water supply at Fort Monroe. The station is now automated and is still used as a navigational aid.

SMITH POINT

1885

Between 1802 and 1803, a tower and detached dwelling were built at Smith Point, at the southern entrance to the Potomac River. The tower was rebuilt twice because of damage caused by hurricanes and severe erosion, first in 1807, just five years after construction, and again in 1828. The tower was so ineffective that a lightship was placed offshore in 1831 and, for a number of years, both the tower and the lightship marked the point. A screw-pile lighthouse was erected to replace lightship and lighthouse. It was first lighted on September 9, 1868.

During the winter of 1893, the lighthouse was damaged by ice. The keepers abandoned the station when the dwelling became canted by ice and was no longer able to show a light.

The lighthouse was carried away by ice on February 14, 1895. The illuminating and fog-bell apparatus and a few small supplies were recovered from the wreck. On March 2, 1895, Congress quickly appropriated $25,000 of the necessary $80,000 to reestablish the light at Smith Point, this time with a caisson lighthouse. The point was temporarily marked by a lightship.

The cast-iron caisson was thirty feet in diameter and forty-five feet high, supporting an octagonal two-story brick dwelling with a square tower rising thirty feet above the top of the cylinder.

This fifth Smith Point Lighthouse was lighted on October 15, 1897, and the light-vessel was withdrawn. It showed a fourth-order lens which flashed white every thirty seconds; a red sector covered the shoals off Smith Point. The fog bell was operated by clockwork installed in December 1897, sounding a double and a single blow alternately at twenty seconds.

The lighthouse was automated in November 1971 and is still in operation today.

NEW POINT COMFORT

The tower and detached dwelling of New Point Comfort Light were built in 1804 on the north shore of Mobjack Bay. In 1930, the lighthouse was automated. The peninsula on which it stood became an island during the August Storm of 1933, which cut a small creek behind the lighthouse. The light was decommissioned in 1963 and is currently owned by Mathews County, Virginia, which had it repaired and repainted.

BODKIN ISLAND

Bodkin Island Light, built between 1822 and 1823, consisted of a tower and detached dwelling and was situated on an island south of the Patapsco River to mark the route that leads to Baltimore. Construction of this first lighthouse in Maryland waters was begun by Evans and Coppuck, who built the foundation before being fired for incompetence. John Donohoo completed the job, his first of many lighthouses.

Bodkin Island Light was always plagued with a poor foundation and, in 1856, after completion of Sevenfoot Knoll, was decommissioned. Both the island and lighthouse are long gone.

NORTH POINT RANGE LIGHTS

In 1823 two towers were built at North Point on the northern entrance to the Patapsco River. One keeper tended both lights in the range. The range lights were decommissioned after construction of the Craighill Channel Range Lights in 1873.

THOMAS POINT

The first Thomas Point Lighthouse was constructed in 1825 on the northern point at the entrance to the South River by John Donohoo, at a cost of $5,676. However, the tower was built too close to the water.

In a letter to the Honorable John P. Kennedy, chairman of the House of Representatives Committee on Commerce, Stephen Pleasonton, the fifth auditor of the U.S. Treasury, who oversaw lighthouse matters, explained the problem: "This light was placed upon a clay bank at least 30 feet high, and about 500 feet from the water. Such was the action of the water upon the bank that in a few years it was washed away to within 50 feet of the light; upon being informed of which, I directed a quantity of rubble stone to be placed at the base of the

bank. This arrested the water but in a slight degree, and in 1838 it had approached within 15 feet of the lighthouse when I contracted with Winslow Lewis to take down the tower and rebuild it in a secure place for $2,000."

The lighthouse was equipped with a fifth-order Fresnel lens on May 15, 1855.

On November 20, 1875, a new lighthouse, resting on ten-inch wrought-iron screw piles one mile off Thomas Point, was completed. The new water station was equipped with a 3½-order Fresnel lens, flashing a red light every twenty seconds. The old house on land was decommissioned, but it was temporarily called back into service two years later in 1877 when ice shook the screw-pile house and damaged the lens.

When the Coast Guard proposed to tear down Thomas Point Shoal Light in 1975, it was met with public opposition. The lighthouse was placed on the National Register of Historic Places and was thus spared. In September 1986, it was the last manned lighthouse on the Chesapeake to be converted to automated status. It is still in service as a navigational aid.

POOLES ISLAND

Pooles Island Lighthouse was built by John Donohoo in 1825 on an island off Bush River to mark the main shipping channel to the east and a shallower channel to the west of the island. The station was "severely damaged by a storm in June, 1881, rendering repairs necessary to the roof, the dormer window, chimney, and plastering. In 1883, the brick-work was built up on the masonry dwelling and another story of three rooms, was added," according to an annual report of the Lighthouse Board.

In 1917, as the country entered World War I, the U.S. Army acquired the entire island as a site for weapons testing and a number of Pooles Island residents, including the keeper and his family, were moved off the island. The lighthouse was automated that same year; it was decommissioned in 1939. The dwelling has long since been torn down but the forty-foot tower remains.

CONCORD POINT

Concord Point Lighthouse was built by John Donohoo in 1827 at Concord Point in Havre de Grace, Maryland, on the Susquehanna River. The thirty-nine-foot conical tower is built of Port Deposit granite, which was cut on site.

This lighthouse has the distinction of being the only lighthouse on the Chesapeake that was tended throughout its manned career by a single family. John O'Neill was awarded the position of first keeper of the light after single-handedly defending Havre de Grace against a British invasion during the War of 1812. His descendants tended the light until it was automated in 1920.

The lighthouse was equipped with a steamer's lens on May 10, 1855. Later, this was replaced by a small sixth-order Fresnel lens and, on October 28, 1891, by a larger, fifth-order lens.

The lighthouse was decommissioned in 1975 and the lens was stolen the following year, but it was replaced by another authentic Fresnel lens. A group called the Friends of Concord Point Lighthouse was formed to maintain the structure and began restoration in 1979. Despite decommissioning of the lighthouse, the Friends have continued to show the light every night at dusk and have opened the lighthouse to the public. The nonprofit group is currently involved in restoring the original keeper's dwelling, located across the street.

Concord Point Light is the oldest lighthouse in Maryland to be continously lighted.

FOG POINT

Fog Point Lighthouse was built by John Donohoo in 1827 on Smith Island in the middle of Chesapeake Bay off Crisfield, on Maryland's Eastern Shore. It marked the narrow passage north of Smith Island through Kedges Strait. The lighthouse was a white house with a lantern placed on top of the dwelling. The original lamps and parabolic reflectors were replaced with a fifth-order Fresnel lens on August 18, 1855. The 1872 annual report of the Lighthouse Board notes that Fog Point, located one and one-quarter miles from the channel, "affords no security to vessels from going ashore on the reef off Solomon's Lump." Fog Point Light, which "has served to mark the entrance to Kedges Strait for a long time, is of little value as compared with other positions that could have been selected for a screw-pile structure."

The light was decommissioned on September 10, 1875, when Solomons Lump Lighthouse was lighted. It fell into ruin and has since disappeared.

CAPE CHARLES

The first of three Cape Charles lighthouses was built in 1827 on Smith Island (a different island from the one on which Fog Point Lighthouse was built) to mark the northern shore of the mouth of the Chesapeake Bay. The lighthouse, however, was always considered too short to be seen by offshore vessels. In 1856, $35,000 was allocated for a new lighthouse. A new site was selected and construction began in 1857. The 150-foot tower was still under construction near New Inlet on the northeast end of Smith Island, when the Civil War broke out in 1861. Rebels removed the illuminating apparatus in April of that year and plundered much of the materials needed to complete the new tower, which was finally lighted in 1864.

1914

By 1878, the sea was encroaching on the site of the lighthouse. By 1883, the water-line was within 300 hundred feet of the tower—and even closer to the keeper's dwelling. It was recommended that one or more large jetties be built, at a cost of $15,000. By 1885 the sea had come within 125 feet of the keeper's dwelling, and 225 feet of the tower. A jetty was built in 1886, but it was washed "somewhat at the sea extremity." The Lighthouse Board suggested more jetties.

On August 30, 1890, $150,000 was appropriated for a new station. In 1891, while building jetties to protect the old tower until the new one was finished, work was slowed by mosquitoes "so numerous and troublesome as to practically cause a suspension of operations."

Contractors faced a hostile environment during construction of the third lighthouse. The wharf built for landing materials was washed away three times during heavy storms. One vessel chartered to carry stone was wrecked and another badly damaged.

In June 1892, a red band, 25 feet wide, was painted around the old tower about 60 feet above its base so that mariners could easily distinguish the tower from other coastal lighthouses. Plans called for the new tower to be erected three-quarters of a mile inland from the second Cape Charles Lighthouse.

Title to a ten-acre tract of land was secured in 1892 through condemnation, and a temporary wharf and tramway were designed for landing materials. When completed, the tower, built of iron cylinders supported by a spider web frame of ironwork, was 192 feet 7 inches in height, including the lantern. The light of the first-order Fresnel lens was first shown on August 15, 1895. The lens, about 12 feet high and 6 feet in diameter, represented the first adoption of the Mahan system in a first-order light. It flashed 9 times during its 30-second revolution. The flashes in the new light, however, were too quick to be distinct, so the intervals between the flashes were lengthened. In 1899, telephones were installed.

The light was automated in July 1963 and solar panels were added to power the light in 1996. It is still maintained as a navigational aid. The main dwelling remains in good shape but has been boarded up. For a while, it was used by a hunting club.

COVE POINT

Cove Point Lighthouse was built in 1828 by John Donohoo. The light consisted of a conical tower, constructed of locally manufactured brick, with a detached dwelling on the shore. Its light shone forty-five feet above sea level and marked the shoal that extends offshore near Calvert Cliffs, Maryland.

On June 12, 1855, the lighthouse was equipped with a fifth-order Fresnel lens, which exhibited a fixed light, varied by flashes. In 1897, a fourth-order Fresnel lens was installed with a weight-driven rotation mechanism.

In May 1883, the roof of the dwelling was removed, the walls were raised to create a second story, and a new roof, covered with tin, was added.

"A substantial wooden shore protection was built in November, 1891, to arrest the advancing water-line. The foundation of the fogbell tower, which the water had already reached, was moved back sixteen feet." The brick tower was covered in concrete in 1953.

Cove Point was automated with a computerized system on August 16, 1986. The lighthouse is still a navigational aid and the fourth-order Fresnel lens is visable for twelve miles. The lighthouse was occasionally open to the public before automation, and plans are in the works to open it again.

BACK RIVER

Back River Lighthouse was built in 1829 by Winslow Lewis. Located six miles north of Old Point Comfort in Virginia, it stood on marshy land near the southern entrance to Back River. The conical tower and separate dwelling were built of brick and connected with an elevated walkway. The station was damaged by rebels during the Civil War and finally restored in 1863. By 1878, the tower was dilapidated. "A portion in front having been undermined and thrown down by the action of wind and waves, was thoroughly repaired in August and September. Stones were carefully packed around the foundation," the Lighthouse Board's annual report noted that year. In 1881, "As an experiment to prevent the drifting of the sands from about the tower, movable screens were made and placed; this was but partially successful; experience in placing them may render them more efficient."

In September 1888, "450 cubic yards of riprap stone were deposited around the lighthouse to protect it from the advance of the sea," the annual report stated.

In 1903, "The concrete protection wall around the keeper's dwelling was completely wrecked on the sea front. A bulkhead was built about 459 feet long along the front and sides of the dwelling. Then, during a very severe storm in October, 1903, two weeks after the construction of the bulkhead had commenced, the dwelling and the elevated walk leading to the tower narrowly escape destruction. The repair party, by working day and night for three days, succeeded in saving the dwelling and supporting the walkway so that the light might be maintained. Seas dashed to a height of 14 feet against the porch of the dwelling and moved from their places large stones near the tower. The tin roof was

partly torn from the dwelling, and the gutters and down spouts were carried away."

The lighthouse was automated in 1915 and decommissioned in 1936. The land around the tower had washed away by the time Hurricane Flossy demolished the lighthouse on September 27, 1956.

POINT LOOKOUT

Point Lookout Light was constructed on the north shore of the Potomac River in 1830. Built by John Donohoo, it was intended to be a conical tower and separate dwelling, but so much of the funding was spent purchasing the land that a cheaper house with a lantern on top was finally built. In May 1883, the old roof was removed and the dwelling raised one story to accommodate the keeper's growing family. A new tin roof was added and porches were built on the front and back of the dwelling. The building was expanded again after 1900.

Point Lookout became a depot for the lighthouse service in later years. It was decommissioned in 1965, after the last civilian keeper retired, and was replaced by a light on a pole in the water. For a while, the lighthouse was rented to state employees, some of whom claimed it was haunted. The house still stands unused and is owned by the U.S. Navy.

LAZARETTO POINT

The beacon at Lazaretto Point marked the eastern boundary of Baltimore Harbor. Built in 1831 by John Donohoo at a cost of $2,100, the thirty-nine-foot tower was constructed of stone. Its original parabolic reflector lighting system was replaced with a fourth-order Fresnel lens on June 14, 1855.

In 1883, "The gases from the numerous chemical works in the immediate vicinity destroyed the paint, and even the whitewash, soon after it was put on; otherwise, the station is in good order," the annual report noted. "The present light is inefficient, and is obscured by buildings in the neighborhood belonging to private parties. A mast was erected from which a light is displayed above the existing obstructions, in addition to the light in the lighthouse."

In 1885, a plan was developed for moving the light to another location, about seventy-eight feet closer to the channel so that it would not be hidden by neighboring buildings.

In 1888, the light was changed from fixed red to flashing red and the mast light was discontinued. In 1906, the annual report noted that "Lazaretto Point light was recently obstructed by the erection of high buildings, which now practically destroys its value." In 1915, it became the first lighthouse on the Chesapeake Bay to be lighted by an electric incandescent light.

The lighthouse was decommissioned in 1926 after a steel tower was built to replace it. It was torn down shortly thereafter.

In 1985, Norman Rukert, Jr., president of Rukert Terminals, a waterfront warehousing company that owns Lazaretto Point, built a replica lighthouse, based on the original plans, in memory of his father, Norman ("Cap") Rukert, Sr., who had hoped to make construction of the lighthouse his next project before he died in June 1984.

CLAY ISLAND

Clay Island was constructed in 1832 on a marshy island at the confluence of Nanticoke River, Fishing Bay, and Tangier Sound. The light was exhibited from a cupola on the keeper's dwelling. The 1886 annual report of the Lighthouse Board stated, "The land near this site is being rapidly washed away, and, unless a new lighthouse is to be erected in the near future, it should be protected by an additional quantity of riprap stone."

The lighthouse was decommissioned after completion of the screw-pile Sharkfin Shoal Lighthouse in August 1892.

WATTS ISLAND

1944

Watts Island Lighthouse was built in 1833 by John Donohoo on Little Watts Island, a seven-acre island in Pocomoke Sound, south of Watts Island. It was located on the Eastern Shore of the Chesapeake Bay in Accomac County, Virginia, northeast of the southern entrance to Tangier Sound. The light was a 48-foot tower with a nearby residence, 20 by 34 feet, built at a cost of $4,775.

The kerosene lantern was converted to gas in 1913. By this time, erosion had already claimed four acres of the island. The lighthouse was automated in 1923 and continued to stand until undermined by a severe winter storm in 1944. A few weeks later, the lighthouse collapsed. Today, only a shoal exists where the lighthouse and island once stood.

TURKEY POINT

1928

Turkey Point Lighthouse, built in 1833 at the head of the Chesapeake Bay, was designed by John Donohoo to guide maritime traffic to the newly constructed Chesapeake and Delaware Canal. The station consisted of a thirty-five-foot, conical stone tower with a separate dwelling. It still stands on a steep, eighty-foot bluff at Turkey Point, at the confluence of the Susquehanna, Northeast, and Elk Rivers and the Chesapeake Bay. A red sector guided vessels away from the bluff.

In 1888, an unusual fog-bell room was constructed. As the Lighthouse Board annual report notes, "Owing to the height of the bluff and the advisability of having the bell placed as low as practicable, the weights were run in a well excavated under the room for the purpose." In 1889, the dwelling was raised one story, adding four rooms. A new front porch was also built.

This lighthouse was distinguished as being tended by Fannie May Salter, the last woman lighthouse keeper in the country. Electricity did not reach the light until 1943. When Mrs. Salter retired in 1948, the tower was automated. The dwelling, vandalized and neglected, was torn down and the stairs inside the tower were removed to thwart efforts by vandals to damage the light. The Fresnel lens was stolen and recovered, then replaced with a plastic lens. The lighthouse is still a working navigational aid. Visitors must hike along a grassy path to reach the structure, which is in Elk Neck State Park.

PINEY POINT

1912

Piney Point was constructed in 1836, fourteen miles up the Potomac River, on the northern bank. John Donohoo built a brick tower with a separate one-story dwelling, twenty by thirty feet. The original parabolic lighting system was replaced with a fifth-order Fresnel lens, first lighted on June 5, 1855.

The house was enlarged to a two-story dwelling. A wooden fog-bell tower built near the lighthouse was destroyed by Hurricane Hazel in 1954.

The lighthouse was decommissioned in 1964. It is currently owned by St. Marys County Department of Parks and Recreation, which has restored the tower and dwelling. The grounds are open to tourists, and a small museum is open during the season, but the tower and dwelling are not open to the public.

SHARPS ISLAND

The first Sharps Island Light was built in 1838 on Sharps Island, which at one time was a large island in the middle of the Chesapeake Bay off Tilghman Island. Erosion has claimed the island, which is now marked only by a shoal. Not surprisingly, erosion plagued this first house. The lantern was on top of the keeper's dwelling, and the lighthouse was located on the north end of the island to mark the entrance into the Choptank River.

The second lighthouse was a screw pile, built in 1866–67. Ice threatened to carry it away the first year, but it survived. The screw pile suffered, however, in the heavy drift ice of 1877–79. "Two of the diagonal cast-iron braces were carried away; one tension-brace was broken and one of the horizontal beams bent." Screw-pile ice-breakers and two hundred cubic yards of riprap stone were put in place to protect the water station. Nevertheless, the lighthouse was carried away in 1881 with the keepers aboard. "The keepers remained on the wreck until it grounded. Their conduct is highly commended," the annual report stated.

A caisson lighthouse was immediately built to replace it. "The structure is an iron tower, 37 feet in height, resting on an iron caisson, 30 feet in diameter and 30 feet in height, filled with concrete. It shows a fixed white light of the fourth order, 55 feet above mean low water."

The lighthouse was pushed about twenty degrees out of plum by severe ice during the winter of 1976–77. It is still canted today, though it remains a navigational aid. In 1996, after taking public comment regarding the leaning tower, the Coast Guard decided to secure and continue using it.

GREENBURY POINT

Greenbury Point Lighthouse was built in 1849 on the northern point of land at the mouth of the Severn River in Annapolis, Maryland. It was equipped with a steamer's lens on May 14, 1855. The lighthouse was a picturesque one-and-a-half-story dwelling with a tall octagonal tower rising from its center.

The annual reports of the Lighthouse Board stated that by 1878, the land around Greenbury Point was washing away, and eventually the lighthouse would be in danger. "The light, in its present position, is of little use, and is so small that it can hardly be distinghuished from the lights of the Naval Academy and the harbor of Annapolis."

In 1889, Congress made an appropriation of $25,000 for a light on the shoal to replace the one on the point. Greenbury Pont Shoal Light was lighted on November 15, 1891. The structure was a hexagonal wooden dwelling on seven screw piles, which supported a lantern, showing a fixed white fourth-order light. While driving the piles for the lighthouse foundation, builders noticed that the pilings failed to give the resistance needed for a safe support for the stucture. Consequently, the engineers designed "cast-iron disks, of as great a diameter as the spaces between the parts of the ironwork would allow, to which cast-iron sleeves were fastened securely. The sleeves and disks were then slipped on over the piles, and forced down until the disks had obtained a solid bearing on the shoal. The sleeves

were then firmly bolted to the piles. In this way the bearing surface was largely increased. This method of strengthening the foundation was successfully used at Gull Shoal, N. C.," the annual report said.

The shore station was discontinued, but the old lighthouse was retained as a day mark until it finally collapsed. The cottage lighthouse in the Bay was dismantled and replaced with an automated beacon in 1934.

BLAKISTONE ISLAND

Blakistone Island Light was built in 1851 on St. Clements Island (once known as Blakistone or Blackistone Island) at the mouth of St. Marys River at the Potomac River. Built by John Donohoo, it was a brick building with a lantern mounted on top. In May 1864, it was attacked by rebels who destroyed the lantern but spared the structure. The lens was soon replaced.

In 1893, the Lighthouse Board noted that erosion of the waterfront continued to be a problem and called for some kind of erosion control.

The lighthouse was decommissioned in 1932. The house burned in July 1956, apparently the victim of lightning.

FISHING BATTERY ISLAND

Fishing Battery Light, built in 1853 on Fishing Battery Island (also known as Donohoo's Battery after John Donohoo, the owner), was Donohoo's last lighthouse before his death in 1854. The two-story brick dwelling supports a lantern thirty-two feet above the ground. The island is located near the mouth of the Susquehanna River and the light guided vessels through a narrow channel in the Susquehanna Flats.

In 1881, the annual report noted, "Extensive improvements made by the U.S. Fish Commission [which used the island] include filling around the property owned by the government for lighthouse purposes, and the raising of the grade of the island. To conform to the new grade and for sanitary reasons, it was found necessary to remove the lower floor of the lighthouse, fill the enclosure with clean soil and lay a concrete floor.

"In August, 1889, a suit of ejectment was brought in the U.S. circuit court to test the right of the government to occupy the site of this light station. The case was decided in favor of the U.S."

The lighthouse was replaced by a steel skeleton tower, but the house remained intact. Despite lack of maintenance, the dwelling is in excellent shape, though the island has eroded and little is left of it, but a small parcel around the lighthouse. A channel leads into the island, and interested boaters cut the grass, repair the pier, and picnic on the island during the summer.

NAVAL HOSPITAL BEACON

The Naval Hospital at Norfolk served as the site of an important early beacon. Created in 1854 at a cost of only five hundred dollars, the light sat atop the bathhouse at the wharf of the Naval Hospital. The structure was rebuilt and enlarged in 1868, and the lantern was raised nine feet. In 1882, "Complaints having been made that this light was inefficient, gas from the city works of Portsmouth, Va., was substituted for oil as an illuminant, making a decided improvement," the Lighthouse Board report notes. There is no indication in the board reports that a dwelling ever accompanied this light.

The light remained operational for fifty years, until April 30, 1904, when it was decommissioned after dredg-ing operations in the harbor of Norfolk reached the area of Hospital Point, making the light unnecessary.

FORT CARROLL

Fort Carroll was built in 1854 on a manmade fortress in the Patapsco River to guide vessels clear of the fortification. This lighthouse was moved more often than any other on the Bay, either because of age, decay, or repairs and improvements under way at the fort. Given the small size of the fort, however, the move was never more than one hundred feet or so.

The lantern was originally mounted on top of the keeper's dwelling, but by 1875 the skeleton frame had become so decayed that it endangered the safety of the keeper. A new beacon was erected on the southwest salient, over the second tier of casemates on the fort. The lens and fog-bell machine were moved into the new structure, and the light was operational as of May 5, 1875. The old lantern cupola was removed from the keeper's house, which was retained as a dwelling, and the roof was repaired.

In 1888, a new dwelling was built for the keeper at a cost of a little over one thousand dollars. The two-story building measured twenty by twenty-five feet and had a porch.

Ten years later, the light and fog-bell tower interfered with improvements being made at the fort. Consequently, the tower was torn down on October 17, 1898, and the lens and fog-signal apparatus were removed. A lens-lantern was placed on the parapet of the fort in front of the former position of the light until December 30, 1898, when the former light was reestablished on a new wooden tower erected about one hundred feet north of the site of the old structure. The fog bell, which had meanwhile been rung by hand from a position on the parapet, was placed on the new tower and operated by machinery. The focal plane of the light was forty-five feet above mean high water instead of seventy-four feet, as before. A new model fifth-order lamp was installed.

In 1900, the light tower was moved about one hundred feet to the south in order to make room for more improvements to the fort. In April it was restored to its former site, and the light was changed to show a fixed white light with a red sector. The tower supporting the light and fog bell had been built in one of the old casemates of the fort. In 1901, this casemate was demolished as a part of a series of improvements to the harbor defenses, leaving the lower story of the tower open. It was repaired. Today, the tower can still be seen by passing boaters. Both lighthouse and fort have long since been abandoned.

PUNGOTEAGUE CREEK

Pungoteague Creek was lighted on November 1, 1854. This was the first lighthouse built on piles over water in the Chesapeake Bay and the first of many to be overturned and destroyed by ice. It was built on seven pneumatic piles and was equipped with a fifth-order lens. In its first year of operation, the keeper was reprimanded for burning too hot a fire in the lighthouse and endangering the structure.

The light was "overturned by a large mass of floating ice" in 1856. The lantern, illuminating apparatus, and other fixtures were recovered from the wreck. For many years after the destruction of the Pungoteague Creek Light, the board planned to build a second lighthouse, but never did.

WHITE SHOALS

White Shoals Light was one of three screw-pile lighthouses lighted on February 6, 1855, on the James River. Located below Sandy Point on the lower end of the shoal and on the starboard side of the main channel heading upriver, the little screw pile was painted white with a red roof. The light consisted of a large, pressed-glass masthead lens, suspended in the lantern of the house. In 1867 ice pushed the house out of alignment. It was rebuilt in 1869 and the delapidated structure was still standing in the river in the 1970s, but has since collapsed.

POINT OF SHOALS

Point of Shoals was lighted on February 6, 1855, and, like its two sisters on the river, had a pressed-glass masthead lens. It was located on the James River, near the center of the bend in the river which forms Burwell's Bay, a little below Mulberry Island Point on the starboard side of the main channel, heading upriver.

The lighthouse was damaged by ice in the mid-1860s, declared unsafe in 1869, and rebuilt. It was torn down in the 1960s.

DEEP WATER SHOAL

Deep Water Shoal was also first lighted on February 6, 1855. It was located on the James River, on the shoal on the starboard side of the channel, above Mulberry Island Point and below Lyon's Creek. The screw pile was white with a red roof; its lighting apparatus consisted of a masthead lens. The board annual report stated the lighthouse suffered "considerable damage from the ice and storms of the past winter, in 1857. . . . An entire new structure will be erected before the close of the season." The screw pile was destroyed a second time by ice on January 20, 1867. A "more substantial" lighthouse was completed on January 15, 1868. It was torn down in the 1960s.

JORDAN POINT

Jordan Point was lighted on February 7, 1855. Built on a point of land on the port side of the James River heading upriver, it was a white house with a light on top of its red roof. A large, pressed-glass masthead lens was suspended in the lantern room. By 1874, the beach on the upper side of the point was rapidly washing away, endangering the structure. Loose stones were deposited on the beach as shore protection, but in 1887 the Lighthouse Board opened bids for the construction of a new dwelling. A house and separate tower were completed in January 1887, at a cost of $3,449.

In 1892, erosion again threatened the lighthouse. The following year, major shore protection was erected along the waterfront. The house was later sold and the wooden tower was replaced by a steel tower in 1941.

JONES POINT

Jones Point Light, a house with a lantern mounted on top, was lighted on March 3, 1855. It was built on the upper Potomac River near Alexandria, Virginia, at a cost of five thousand dollars.

The light was decommissioned in 1926, and the old wooden house fell into disrepair. The Mount Vernon Chapter of the Daughters of the American Revolution restored the lighthouse, and in 1964 the nonprofit group entered into an agreement with the National Park Service, which established a park around the site.

SEVENFOOT KNOLL

Sevenfoot Knoll was first lighted in 1856, two years after construction began. It marked the southern approach to the Patapsco River and was the first water station in Maryland waters. This lighthouse was unique in that it was the only round screw pile and the only cast-iron screw pile on the Bay. In its early years, Sevenfoot Knoll was painted black with white shutters.

More recently, it was painted dark red. One iron pile was broken by ice in January 1884.

The lighthouse was automated in 1948. For a period in the 1970s, it appeared that the lighthouse would go to the Mariners' Museum in Newport News, Virginia. The museum hoped to turn it into an exhibit, but the arrangement was never made and the lighthouse remained a navigational aid until the late 1980s, when it was replaced by a beacon and donated to the city of Baltimore. The old lighthouse was moved to its new home on Pier 5 in Baltimore in October 1988. Today, it is used primarily as offices for the Living Classroom Foundation. A small exhibit is open to the public during visiting hours.

FORT WASHINGTON

In November 1856, a beacon was constructed on the Potomac River, at a cost of five hundred dollars. A sixth-order Fresnel lens was moved into a tower in 1870.

"The erection of the keeper's dwelling was begun on October 16, 1884, and on January 14, 1885, it was finished. Structure is frame," the annual report noted. Evidently, this was the first keeper's dwelling at the site. The 1900 annual report complained that "the lantern of the tower is small and poorly ventilated." The Lighthouse Board recommended that a larger lantern and a tower built six or eight feet higher than the existing one be constructed so that the light would show above a structure which had been erected at the military post by the War Department.

"To increase the range of visibility of this light by placing it at a greater elevation, and as a temporary expedient, four new caps were put on the sills of the fog bell tower in November, 1901, and a platform was built on them to support a lens lantern. On January 25, 1902, the lens-lantern light was exhibited from the fog bell tower for the first time, and the sixth-order light in the light tower was extinguished. The new light is about 28 feet above mean high water."

The move proved to be permanent. The light is still exhibited from the old fog-bell tower today and remains a working navigational aid on the Potomac River.

CHERRYSTONE INLET

Cherrystone Inlet was first lighted on January 1, 1858. The screw-pile lighthouse in the lower Chesapeake Bay marked the channel into the Eastern Shore port of Cape Charles. The light was attacked by rebels during the Civil War and was reestablished in 1862 by Union forces. In 1888, a red sector of about 210 degrees of arc was placed in the light to guide vessels away from shoal water and to mark the turning point after the shoal was crossed. "This sector will show red from the bay and preclude the possibility of mistaking it for the one on Old Plantation Flats," the Lighthouse Board noted.

The lighthouse had been decommissioned by 1921 and that same year became the only lighthouse ever moved to another site to be used as a working navigational aid. It was barged to the site of the Choptank River Light, which had been destroyed by ice, and set up on the existing pilings.

STINGRAY POINT

1885

Stingray Point was first lighted on January 1, 1858. This screw pile was a hexagonal wooden cottage located south of the Rappahannock River. It was automated on November 10, 1950, and torn down the summer of 1967. Sections of the lighthouse were sold to Gilbert Purcell, a boatyard owner who hoped to rebuild the lighthouse on land, but never did.

SANDY POINT

1885

Built in 1858, the first Sandy Point Light was located north of Annapolis, Maryland, where Sandy Point State Park is today. Because it was built on land, it was too far from the channel to serve mariners well.

The second light was built offshore and lighted on October 30, 1883. It was first proposed as a screw pile, but after the harsh winter of 1881 in which Sharps Island Light was carried away by ice, the design was upgraded to a caisson. The Lighthouse Board evidently had grand plans for this lighthouse, but in 1883 it failed to get full appropriations for the structure. "Rather than delay the work longer, it was decided to erect a less expensive tower than was first suggested, but upon the foundation originally proposed. This is a cylindrical iron caisson, 35 feet in diameter, and 32 feet and 6 inches high, filled with concrete and resting on the shoal." The first two sections of caisson were sunk into the sand three feet and leveled by means of a water jet and force pump. The lamp was lighted on October 30, 1883.

In 1890, the Board reported, "The walls of the house are faced with pressed brick, with molded brick ornamentation. Owing, probably, to the fact that it has not been painted for some years, the salt moisture has caused considerable disintegration of the bricks, which have scaled off in many places." The structure was painted to prevent further corrosion.

In 1890, the old lighthouse was recommissioned as part of a set of range lights guiding ships into the deepwater channel. "In order to assist mariners to more readily find the entrance to the Craighill Channel in the daytime, a beacon-range was established in December, 1889, consisting of a mast 25 feet high surmounted by a cage painted white, erected in front of the old lighthouse, which serves as the rear beacon. The range is a line passing through the center of the lantern on the old house and red buoy No. 4 of the Craighill Channel. This line runs to the west of the entrance buoy No. 2 and guides vessels into the mouth of the channel."

The lighthouse, which was automated in May 1963 and converted to a solar clock, is still in use as a navigational aid. On June 18, 1979, vandals destroyed the priceless Fresnel lens with a baseball bat.

CRANEY ISLAND

In 1820, Craney Island became the site of the first permanent light-vessel in the country. In 1859, Craney Island Light was constructed on screw piles in Hampton Roads at the mouth of the Elizabeth River. The lightship was removed when the square wooden lighthouse was completed.

In 1862, the lighthouse lay in ruins, the victim of a rebel attack. A temporary light was established and a new lighthouse was completed in 1863.

In 1883, it was reported, "The superstructure of this lighthouse is decayed. During every rain it leaks. The necessary lumber and mill-work for a new building were purchased, and its construction will soon be undertaken." On April 22, 1884, the new structure was completed. It was built at Lazaretto Depot and placed on the iron substructure in March and April.

In 1891, "A new main gallery post was put up to replace one broken by a passing vessel." The lighthouse was decommissioned and the hexagonal house torn down in the 1930s.

UPPER CEDAR POINT

1925

Upper Cedar Point Light on the Potomac River was built on screw piles and lighted on July 20, 1867. It was decommissioned on December 20, 1876, when Mathias Point Lighthouse was completed. The structure remained as a fog signal and day beacon. Six years later, it was relighted. It was dismantled in the early 1960s.

LOWER CEDAR POINT

1912

Lower Cedar Point, first lighted on August 6, 1867, was one of numerous screw piles built in the Potomac River in the nineteenth century. The wooden superstructure of the lighthouse was entirely destroyed by fire on Christmas day, 1893. The cause of the fire was never determined. A lens lantern was immediately placed on the substructure to mark this important turning point in the Potomac River. Originally, it was proposed that a caisson lighthouse be built at a cost of $75,000, but the request was soon reduced to $25,000 to cover only another wooden cottage.

A new lighthouse was erected on top of the existing iron foundation and was lighted on September 5, 1896. In October the red sector was removed, and the fourth-order light showed a fixed white light. A fog bell operated by clockwork struck a single blow at intervals of twelve seconds. The house has long since been dismantled and replaced by a skeleton tower.

HOOPER STRAIT

Hooper Strait Light was built on sleeve-piles and lighted on September 14, 1867. Located at the entrance to the Honga River in Hooper Strait, this first lighthouse was destroyed by ice in January 1877. A new hexagonal house mounted on a new foundation of screw piles was completed on October 15, 1879. Unlike its predecessor, its foundation was very strong, consisting of seven piles of solid wrought iron, ten inches in diameter, and penetrating twenty-five feet into the shoal. The new light showed a fixed white light of the fifth order.

In 1966, when the Coast Guard contracted to have it torn down, the Chesapeake Bay Maritime Museum in St. Michaels purchased the hexagonal cottage lighthouse from the demolition contractor for one thousand dollars and had it barged in two pieces to its museum grounds at Navy Point, St. Michaels, where it is now restored and is the centerpiece of the museum. This was the first successful move and conversion of a working lighthouse to a museum on the Chesapeake Bay.

JANES ISLAND

1928

Janes Island Light, which began service in October 1867, was built on screw piles at the entrance to the Little Annemessex River in Tangier Sound near Crisfield. It was destroyed by ice on January 20, 1879. A second lighthouse was built exactly like the second Hooper Strait Light. It was completed on December 20, 1879, and showed a fixed white light of the fourth order.

In January 1893, the fog bell was wrenched from its fastenings by floating ice. The bell toppled over onto the boat hoister, causing damage to bell, hoister, and boat. Replacements were obtained from the wreck of Solomons Lump Light.

The second Janes Island Lighthouse was carried away by ice in 1935 and floated up and down Tangier Sound for three days before it sank. It was replaced with an automated tower on a caisson base.

SOMERS COVE

1915

Somers Cove became operational in 1867 and was equipped with a sixth-order Fresnel lens. Located in the Little Annemessex River, it marked the entrance to Crisfield Harbor, a busy seafood port in the late 1800s. The little house was demolished in 1930 and replaced with an acetylene gas light.

BOWLERS ROCK

1885

Bowlers Rock, a dangerous rock in the Rappahannock River, was first marked by a lightship in 1835. The ship was destroyed by rebels during the Civil War, and on June 10, 1868, a wooden lighthouse on screw piles was completed.

The 1895 annual report of the Lighthouse Board noted that the iron foundation had "suffered from the impact of the ice during the past winter. Its age and position render doubtful its ability to withstand without protection another similar experience." The board requested that heavy riprap stone be placed on the axis of the current to act as icebreakers.

Bowlers Rock was finally destroyed by ice around 1918, and in 1921 an acetylene light and automatic fog bell operated by carbon dioxide gas were built on a caisson structure to replace the iron-pile lighthouse.

BREWERTON CHANNEL RANGE LIGHTS

The two Brewerton Channel Range Lights were lighted on November 1, 1868. The structures— one near Hawkins Point, the other on Leading Point—marked the Brewerton Channel in the Patapsco River, leading to Baltimore. The front light, Hawkins Point, was a unique rectangular

1928

wooden house on screw piles, accommodating two lights. The rear light, Leading Point, was built on the bluff and was a brick dwelling surmounted by a lantern, with an elevation of forty feet above the ground and seventy feet above the tides. By 1878, the timbers in Hawkins Point were decaying, and the board considered discontinuing the light. But it still stood in 1881, when a new tin roof was put on the lighthouse and other repairs were made.

In 1886, the board ran into its first legal problem regarding lights already in existence in the Fifth District, when a property owner tried to have Hawkins Point Light removed on the grounds that it interfered with a system of improvements he proposed to make. The federal government went to court to stop the property owner from putting up buildings that would interfere with the range lights—and won.

In 1924, Hawkins Point and Leading Point were finally torn down and replaced with automated towers. The range is still in use today.

WINDMILL POINT

Windmill Point in the Chesapeake Bay, off the north shore of the Rappahannock River, was originally marked by a lightship in 1834. The lightship was removed by rebels in 1861, and another vessel marked the shoal from 1868 to 1869, when a lighthouse on screw piles was completed.

By 1905, this was one of the oldest screw-pile lighthouses in the district and structurally weak. One thousand tons of riprap stones were deposited around its base. In the winter of 1917–18, piles and braces were damaged by ice. The lighthouse was repaired in 1921.

Windmill Point was automated on November 5, 1954, and the house was torn down in 1967. The wooden sections of the lighthouse were sold to Dr. Wallace Atwood, owner of Windmill Point Marina. Atwood's dream to rebuild the lighthouse on shore and rent it out to visitors never materialized. Today, an automated light on a metal tower stands on the old lighthouse foundation.

YORK SPIT

York Spit, off the mouth of the York River, was first marked by a lightship in 1855. Like all the other lightships in the southern Bay, it was removed by rebels in 1861. The lightship was temporarily reestablished in 1867 until a new hexagonal lighthouse built on wooden piles encased in cast-iron sleeves was completed in 1870.

The shoal on which the water station stood evidently suffered from erosion, for in 1900 the Lighthouse Board noted that soundings and measurements were made from time to time during the years to ascertain the extent of scour under the house and around the piles. In 1901, the soundings were made again. "The erosion of the shoal has been considerable since the structure was built in 1870," the Board reported.

In 1903, 1,150 tons of riprap stone were placed around the piles to protect the foundation from further scour, and in June, 1,200 additional tons were placed around the lighthouse.

York Spit was demolished in 1960 by the Coast Guard, and an automated tower light now marks the shoal.

WOLF TRAP

Wolf Trap Shoal was first marked by a lightship in 1821. In 1870 a house on screw piles replaced the lightship.

Wolf Trap was carried away by ice on January 22, 1893. The illuminating apparatus and most of the other portable property were recovered from the floating wreck. Congress appropriated $70,000 to replace the light. Meanwhile, a gas-lighted buoy was placed temporarily at the former site of the lighthouse in March 1893. The buoy was replaced on June 30, 1893, by the tender *Holly*, which served as a light-vessel for a month before light-vessel No. 46 was assigned to duty on July 31, 1893. This ship showed two fixed white reflector lights, one at each masthead.

A caisson lighthouse with a brick superstructure was lighted September 20, 1894. The lighthouse showed a fixed white light, varied by a white flash every ten seconds. In February 1895, there were complaints that the light was not strong enough, so the lens machinery was adjusted to produce flashes every twenty-five seconds. A second-class Daboll Trumpet, operated by a Grob petroleum engine, sounded during fog.

The lighthouse was automated in November 1971 and is still in use today, although big cracks in the caisson have caused water leakage into the interior basement.

CHOPTANK RIVER

A lightship marked this site, off Benoni Point near the mouth of the Tred Avon River, from 1870 to 1871, when the Choptank River Light was completed. The lighthouse stood on ten wooden piles encased in cast iron. Six of the piles formed the foundation; the other four were fender-piles, or icebreakers. The hexagonal lighthouse showed a sixth-order light. It was "somewhat damaged" by ice in 1881. "Three of the spur-piles were broken though little injury to the house." In 1881, a fifth-order lens replaced the sixth-order lens to increase the effectiveness of the light.

In 1918, the lighthouse was knocked off its foundation by ice. In 1921, the decommissioned Cherrystone Inlet Lighthouse was moved to the Choptank River site, where it took the place of the former structure. The light was reestablished on June 9, 1921, and operated until the 1960s, when the lighthouse was torn down.

LAMBERTS POINT

Lamberts Point, lighted in May 1872, was a square house on five screw piles, showing a red light of the fifth order. It was located on the Elizabeth River, off Hampton Roads, Virginia. A few months after it was completed, the lighthouse settled about fourteen inches on the west side, "on account of an unequal distribution of supplies left at the station, and the soft character of the soil on which the screw-flanges rested," the Lighthouse Board reported. "It was leveled without difficulty and at little expense," by lowering with water jets those piles that had not settled. Extra piles were driven.

Unfortunately, that did not end the lighthouse's problems. In 1885, the board reported, "The Norfolk and Western Railroad Company built a large coal wharf, with elevated tracks extending from the shore to the lighthouse. The wharf covers a large portion of the lighthouse site, and the company's works come close up to the lighthouse on its eastern side. The dredging alongside the wharf to make a new channel has caused the lighthouse to settle six inches or more on one side. The danger to the station from fire is largely increased, and injuries have occurred to the dwelling from accidents."

In 1886, it was reported: "Further settlement of the house has taken place. The structure should be abandoned when the Bush's Bluff light-station is completed." However, no such station was ever built.

In 1887, the board reported the following: "The settlement of this house continues. It is now very unsightly, and should be abandoned. The Norfolk and Western Railroad, which has run its coal-pier entirely up to and around the structure, thereby weakening its foundation, should, however, be required to maintain a light there."

By 1892, another storage shed had been built by the company, "which entirely deprives vessels approaching the lighthouse from up the river of the benefit of its light. Considering the limited extent of its utility it seems inadvisable to incur longer the expense of its maintenance. It has been decided to discontinue this light."

The light was decommissioned on December 31, 1892, the same year that nearby Bush Bluff, located just north of Lamberts Point on the Elizabeth River, was marked with a lightship.

The fog signal was reestablished on the old lighthouse structure on April 1, 1901. Today, the building no longer exists.

LOVE POINT

Love Point was lighted August 15, 1872, off the mouth of the Chester River, at a cost of $15,000. It was a duplicate of the original Choptank River Light. In its first winter, the lighthouse sustained "considerable injury from fields of heavy ice. Two of the main columns of the light-house were broken, so the light was discontinued for awhile." In January 1879, ice banked up around the platform of the house but this time did no damage. Riprap had been deposited previously and may have prevented damage.

Love Point was demolished during the 1960s, and an automated light now sits on the old iron foundation.

THIMBLE SHOAL

Thimble Shoal was lighted on October 15, 1872. The screw pile, located on the shallowest portion of Horseshoe Bar near Hampton Roads, was known as "The Bug," because the iron-work foundation resembled the bent legs of a bug. It was equipped with a fourth-order

lens. The lighthouse replaced the lightship at nearby Willoughby Spit. It was destroyed by fire of an unknown origin on October 30, 1880. "Owing to the importance of the light, it was determined to rebuild it at once from funds available in the general appropriation for repairs," the board reported. "The iron-work. . . was found to be intact; the water-tanks, boat-davits, and part of the lantern and lens were recovered by a diver." A superstructure already made for Bells Rock, which was similar in

plan, was put on Thimble Shoal. On December 6, the tender *Tulip* went to the site with a working party and by December 24, 1880, the beacon had been relighted, after only fifty-five days.

On the night of March 15, 1891, the lighthouse was considerably damaged when an unidentified steamer ran into it. One end of the main gallery was badly damaged and one of the iron girders was broken. It was promptly repaired.

On April 14, 1898, the lighthouse was struck by a coal barge forming part of a tow. The entire lower gallery on the southeast side was carried away and the two adjoining sides were damaged. All the joists in the southeast section were broken and pushed out of position. The lower socket casting on the southeast corner was badly cracked, and the five-inch horizontal brace on the southeast side was bent about five inches out of line. Other parts of the ironwork suffered, and the house was lifted about one-half inch off the radial beams. The shock also broke the pinion of the revolving machinery of the lens.

On December 27, 1909, the screw pile was completely destroyed by fire, following the partial demolition of the station when the schooner *Malcolm Baxter, Jr.*, in tow of the tug *John Twohy, Jr.*, collided with it. This time, it took five years to rebuild the lighthouse. On June 25, 1910, $68,000 was appropriated to reestablish the light on a caisson base. Bids were too high, so operations were suspended until an additional $39,000 was secured, which was appropriated August 26, 1912. In 1913–14, the caisson was sunk by the compressed air process, and on December 1, 1914, the new lighthouse was operational. This was the last lighthouse built on the Chesapeake Bay.

On March 6, 1915, the schooner *Addie M. Lawrence* collided with Thimble Shoal Light and repairs in the amount of six hundred dollars were made by the owners of the schooner. The lighthouse was automated in 1964 and is still in operation today.

CRAIGHILL CHANNEL RANGE LIGHTS

Construction of the Craighill Channel Range Lights, marking the channel leading to the Patapsco River in the upper Chesapeake Bay, was begun in 1873. On November 20, 1874, a temporary light was placed on the rear, or upper, light "to give commerce the benefit of this important light," the board noted. Accommodations on shore were made for the keeper until the lighthouse was completed in March 1875. The lighthouse is an open iron frame in the shape of a pyramid, rising 105 feet above the tide. The keeper's dwelling was located at the base of the framework.

The front, or lower, light was the first caisson lighthouse on the Chesapeake and one of the earliest built in the country. A temporary square-frame house was placed on top of the caisson and a light exibited from it in 1874 until the structure was completed with a round iron dwelling mounted on the caisson in 1875.

"The cyclone of August 21, 1888, carried away the roof of the [rear] dwelling, the copper smoke stack, and portions of the galvanized iron covering of the shaft, and caused injury to doors, windows, and gallery. The damages were repaired in September and October," the board noted.

In 1889, "During the year a suit was brought against the United States for damages by the owner of the land on Miller's Island near the lighthouse, for alleged unauthorized occupation of the [rear lighthouse] site, which he claimed was on his property, under the laws of riparian rights. The United States district court before whom the case was tried, decided against him, holding that the government had the absolute right to erect and maintain a light-house wherever it was necessary, on any submerged land in navigable waters."

Both lights are still in use today, though they have long been automated. The keeper's house on the rear channel range light was eventually torn down, leaving only the skeleton frame.

DUTCH GAP CANAL

Dutch Gap Canal, a set of lights marking the entrance to this canal near Richmond on the upper James River, was first lighted on June 10, 1875. The keeper's residence was a plain frame dwelling located midway between the two small frame structures, which were each planked and arranged with a supply room. "The buildings are of substantial character," the board noted in 1875. Both lights were twenty-seven feet high and located at either side of the entrance to the canal on the port side. The lights were originally to be a sixth order, but it was decided to use small lanterns, burning mineral oil. Evidently, one of the towers was destroyed within a few years, for in 1878, "The remaining one of the small wooden towers was washed away during the high water in December," the Lighthouse Board reported. Two masts, or poles, for supporting the lanterns were subsequently constructed.

In 1887, an appropriation was made for the purchase of additional land so that the keeper's dwelling, which was endangered by the caving in of the bank, could be moved. After a disagreement with the landowner over price, the purchase was finally made and, in 1890, the keeper's dwelling was moved on rollers about 130 feet without the need of much repair.

TUE MARSHES

Originally called "Too's Marshes," this square screw-pile lighthouse on the south side of the entrance to the York River in Virginia was first lighted on August 15, 1875. It was built at a cost of $15,000. In the late 1890s, the spelling of the name was changed to "Tue's Marshes." The screw pile was demolished in 1960.

SOLOMONS LUMP

The original Solomons Lump was lighted on September 10, 1875, in Kedges Strait, between Tangier Sound and the Chesapeake Bay. It was a square structure, resting on five wrought-iron screw piles.

In January 1893, the lighthouse was wrecked by moving ice. Though not carried from its site, the house was pushed over and partially submerged. In June a lens-lantern light was established on the wreck to mark its position at night. An appropriation of $30,000 was made in March to reestablish the light.

A new caisson lighthouse was completed on September 30, 1895. The caisson was not level when sunk and had to be dropped another 2½ feet to level it. The new lighthouse consisted of a cast-iron cylindrical foundation, 25 feet in diameter, resting on a steel caisson. The 37-foot caisson and cylinder plates were partially filled with concrete. A unique hexagonal wooden superstructure, with a brick tower which housed the lantern, was built upon the caisson. This lighthouse was the only caisson on the Chesapeake to have a wooden dwelling. The focal plane was 46 feet 6 inches above mean high-water line. The light was a fixed white of the fifth order. The fog bell was struck by machinery ever ten seconds.

The wooden dwelling was torn down, but the tower remains, housing an automated light.

MATHIAS POINT SHOAL

Mathias Point Shoal was lighted on December 20, 1876. It was a hexagonal dwelling on screw piles, housing a fifth-order lens with a fixed white light. Located halfway up the Potomac River, it was meant to replace Upper Cedar Point Lighthouse, which was two miles upriver. Upper Cedar Point was relighted six years later, due to continued requests from ship captains. Mathias Point was demolished in the early 1960s.

NANSEMOND RIVER

Nansemond River Light, at the mouth of the Nansemond, which branches off the James River in Virginia, was first lighted on November 1, 1878. The hexagonal sleeve-pile structure showed a fixed red light of the sixth order. It was demolished in the 1930s.

BELLS ROCK

Bells Rock was built at West Point on the York River in Virginia and first lighted on May 30, 1881. The hexagonal lighthouse sat on iron piles and showed a fourth-order fixed white light. The house originally built for this site was used to replace Thimble Shoal, which burned in 1880. In June 1883, "three other columns were broken by a colliding schooner." A fourth column had been broken previously, but the reports do not mention how it happened. In 1928 the house was demolished and replaced by an automated light.

BLOODY POINT

Signed petitions were collected in 1868 requesting a lighthouse off Bloody Point, at the tip of Kent Island on the Eastern Shore of Maryland. A caisson, topped by a round iron dwelling, was first lighted on October 1, 1882. It marks the entrance into Eastern Bay but was also meant as a guiding light on the Chesapeake.

"A straight run can be made from it to Sandy Point buoy, thus avoiding Thomas's Point Shoal, should that light be destroyed by the ice," the Lighthouse Board noted. "The structure. . . consists of an iron caisson 30 feet in diameter and 30 feet high, surmounted by an iron tower 37 feet high."

In 1884, the board reported, "Severe gales occurred on February 29 and March 3, scouring the sand from under the northwest side of the lighthouse and causing a settling of the structure toward that direction. The inclination is about 5 feet from the perpendicular at the focal plane. It was decided to fill in at once about the northwest side of the caisson with riprap stone to pre-

vent further washing of the sand." Later, however, the board noted, "From recent soundings it is evident that this stone filling has disappeared or sunk, and the depth of water is slightly greater than at the time the settling was first noticed."

In November 1884, the board made efforts to straighten the tower. "The sand was dredged from under a part of the structure until the tower moved in the proper direction. The structure could not be kept in a vertical position, although much care was used, but the inclination is less than one-half as great as before."

Today, the tower, known as the "Coffee Pot" because of its shape, still tilts slightly. An electrical fire broke out on April 30, 1960, and completely gutted the lighthouse. Two coastguardsmen tried to extinguish it but finally fled for their lives in a motorboat. The tower was automated shortly afterward, in the early 1960s.

DRUM POINT

Drum Point was first lighted on August 20, 1883. Located on the north side of the mouth of the Patuxent River, it was a hexagonal frame building on seven wrought-iron, ten-inch screw piles, similar to the lights at Hooper Strait and Janes Island. It was originally intended to be part of a set of range lights for the Patuxent River. In 1883, the Lighthouse Board noted in its annual report that "Congress provided, by act of August 7, 1882, for the establishment of two range-lights at the mouth of the Patuxent River....The smallness of the appropriation, as well as the absence of necessity for a range here, caused the board to erect a screw-pile lighthouse at Drum Point, which answers the present requirements for commerce. A second light, to complete the range, can be placed, if needed, on Sullivan Island, after an appropriation is made...." The second light in the range was never built. Drum Point originally showed a fixed red light of the fourth order.

The lighthouse was decommissioned in 1962 and stood abandoned on the point for twelve years. After years of negotiating, the Calvert County Historical Society acquired the lighthouse in 1974 and had it moved to its present site in Solomons. It is now open to the public at the Calvert Marine Museum.

GREAT SHOALS

Great Shoals, first lighted on August 15, 1884, marked the narrow deep-water channel into Monie Bay and the Wicomico River, on Maryland's Eastern Shore. It was built to support the increasing oyster trade in the area and to help guide vessels heading upriver to Salisbury. The square wooden-frame building sat atop simple iron piles that were driven into the ground.

This light and five other beacons on the Potomac River were blacked out and their fog bells silenced in 1942 as a wartime measure. The lights were later put back into operation.

The wooden house was demolished in 1966 and replaced with an automated light on top of the original lighthouse foundation.

CRAIGHILL CHANNEL UPPER RANGE

Originally called the New Cut-Off Channel Range for the Craighill Channel, it marked a new deep-water channel dredged in the Chesapeake Bay from the Craighill Channel to the mouth of the Patapsco River. The lights were completed on January 15, 1886.

The channel is near the original channel marked by the North Point Range in 1824. In fact, the board noted, "It was first proposed to use. . .the rear tower of the old North Point range as the front beacon of the new range, but a careful examination showed it to be entirely unsuitable....Plans were therefore prepared for a new tower, octagonal in shape, and built of brick, to stand upon the old stone foundation or pier, which is entirely secure. The rear beacon consists of an inner wooden shaft, covered with corrugated iron and supported by an iron skeleton frame, forming a frustum of a square pyramid, resting on stone and brick foundation piers. The dwellings are built on a convenient cottage plan, like those constructed at Cape Henry light-station, Virginia. Both lights are white, and shown from locomotive headlights; the front light is 25 feet and the rear light 65 feet above the water level."

For two years the keeper of the front range light passed over an adjacent property to reach his lighthouse, but in 1888, the owner of the adjoining land refused to allow him access, and the gate was moved to a position near the water, opening on the right-of-way owned by the government.

The front light had been connected to the shore by a small wooden bridge, but "a severe storm on August 28, 1893, carried away the bridge, built of timber and stone, connecting the front beacon with the shore, and washed out the strip of land originally purchased for a means of (traveling) between the beacon and the keeper's dwelling on shore. Hence it was deemed best to fit the beacon for occupancy by the keeper rather than to undertake to rebuild the bridge and purchase a new right-of-way," the board wrote in its 1894 report.

It is hard to imagine anyone living in this tiny structure, which was only about ten or twelve feet wide in an octagonal shape, but evidently it was done without too much fuss, for the board never mentions the living arrangements again.

Both dwellings have long since been demolished, though both beacons are still in service, fully automated.

OLD PLANTATION FLATS

Old Plantation Flats was located on the Eastern Shore of Virginia, at Plantation Inlet, south of Cape Charles City near the mouth of the Bay. It was first lighted on September 5, 1886.

The structure was a square screw pile, on five piles, showing a fixed white light of the fourth order, with a red cut to cover Inner Middle Ground and Middle Ground Shoals.

In January 1893, moving ice overturned and broke the lens. The light was discontinued temporarily. A spare fifth-order lens was substituted in February, the soonest the tender could get to the station because of heavy ice floes in the Bay. No damage to the structure was done by the ice.

In 1897, to increase the power of the light, the fifth-order lens was replaced by the fourth-order lens apparatus brought from the old Hog Island Light. In the winter of 1917–18, moving ice again caused damage, breaking two of the screw piles. In 1921, a new foundation of reinforced concrete and riprap was constructed.

The lighthouse survived until January 1962, when it was replaced by an automated light on the original lighthouse foundation.

GREAT WICOMICO RIVER

1915

Great Wicomico River Light, marking the entrance to the river, was first lighted on November 10, 1889. The lighthouse was a white wooden building, hexagonal in plan, resting upon seven iron piles (screwed into the shoal). The light, mounted in the black lantern, showed a fixed white light of the fourth order, with two red sectors covering shoals in the vicinity. A fog bell was struck by machinery. The house was similar to that of the Holland Island Bar Light. The lighthouse was torn down in 1967, and an automated light now stands on the foundation.

HOLLAND ISLAND BAR

1928

Holland Island Bar marked the approach to Kedges Strait, a narrow channel between South Marsh Island and Smith Island in the mid-Chesapeake Bay region.

In 1888, an appropriation of $35,000 was made to locate a lighthouse on this long and dangerous shoal. "It will be an important guide for both sailing vessels and steamers for a long distance both north and south of Kedge's Straits. It will also serve as a guide for vessels seeking an anchorage in Holland's Straits, and when supplied with a red sector it will, with the Solomon's Lump light, indicate the channel through Kedge's Straits," the Lighthouse Board wrote.

The structure was completed on November 25, 1889. It was a hexagonal frame dwelling on a screw-pile foundation, with a fixed white light of the fourth order. A fog bell was struck by machinery at intervals of ten seconds. The house was similar to that of the Great Wicomico River Light.

Holland Island was a rather unlucky lighthouse. It was the scene of a mysterious death in 1931 and was accidently fired upon by navy bombers in 1957 during weapons testing while still manned by coastguardsmen.

It was finally demolished in 1960. An automated light sits atop the old lighthouse foundation, still marking the channel.

COBB POINT BAR

Originally spelled Cob Point Bar, this lighthouse marked the mouth of the Wicomico River on the Potomac River. (There are three Wicomico Rivers in the mid-Bay region, all marked by lighthouses: the other two are Great Shoals on the Eastern Shore and Great Wicomico River, located just south of the Potomac and emptying directly into the Chesapeake Bay.)

The light was completed on December 25, 1889. The structure was a square wooden dwelling standing on five iron screw piles, with a fixed white light of the fourth order. Its fog bell was sounded by machinery ever fifteen seconds. The house was similar to that of Tangier Sound Light.

A need for the lighthouse was first noted in the annual reports of the Lighthouse Board in 1885: "Three steamboat lines run regularly into the Wicomico from the Potomac River, doing a heavy carrying trade in oysters, tobacco, and other productions. As many as 350 vessels have anchored at one time inside the bar. This is also a good harbor for refuge in storms or from drifting ice. The mouth of the river is, however, so nearly closed by the bars projecting from opposite sides that a vessel endeavoring to avoid one is in danger of being stranded upon the other. Hence, sailing vessels rarely attempt to leave or enter at night. In 1883, the steamer *Sue* in going out, by a mistake of one minute in the time of running, ran upon the bar at Cob Point. The light at Blackistone's

Island is nearly five miles distant and affords no guide to this location." An appropriation of $15,000 was made.

Cobb Point Bar Light burned in late 1939 when the keeper dropped a lighted cigarette into a cord of wood. The light was replaced by a mechanical bell.

TANGIER SOUND

Tangier Sound Light, first called Tangier Island Shoal, at the entrance to Tangier Sound, Virginia, was lighted in 1890. In 1887, the Lighthouse Board had pointed to the need for a lighthouse: "This shoal extends from the southern end of Tangier Island across the entrance of the sound in such way that in the absence of a light, vessels can not at night enter or leave the sound in safety. There has of late been a great increase of the commerce of this section." The screw-pile lighthouse was built at a cost of $25,000.

The fourth-order fixed white light was contained in a lantern resting on a square-framed building. It had a red sector covering the shoals south and east of Tangier Island. A fog bell was struck by machinery. The house was similar to that of Cobb Point Bar.

In 1914, the assistant keeper, William Asbury Crockett, died while sailing back to the lighthouse. The house was demolished in 1961, and an automated light was erected on the old foundation.

NEWPORT NEWS MIDDLE GROUND

Newport News Middle Ground is a caisson lighthouse built in Hampton Roads, Virginia, and first lighted on April 15, 1891.

The Lighthouse Board had reported a need for the lighthouse in 1887: "Vessels leaving the docks at Newport News drawing 24 feet of water invariably pass to the southward of the Middle Ground, and because of the several changes of course, masters now hesitate to leave their berths for sea on very dark or foggy nights. To obviate the necessity for thus losing much valuable time, a light-house and fog-signal should be established on the Middle Ground, near Newport News....The lighthouse will have to stand in about 17 feet of water at low tide or about 21 feet at high tide. It will be exposed to shocks from fields of running ice, and being in comparatively deep water will also be exposed to the danger of being run into by both steam and sailing vessels." The board recommended "an iron caisson, 35 feet in diameter, concrete-filled, surmounted by an iron lighthouse," at a cost of $50,000. "In July, 1891, the wooden caisson with four sections of the dredging shaft and two courses of the foundation cylinder was towed to the site and sunk."

The light was a fixed white of the fourth order, varied by a white flash every twenty seconds. The fog bell was struck by machinery, a double blow every fifteen seconds.

The lighthouse is built of iron, with a foundation cylinder which is 25 feet in diameter and 56 feet in height, some 15 feet of which shows above water. The iron tower is 29 feet high and 21 feet in diameter at the base, with a projecting circular gallery covered by a roof. It was automated in October 1954 and is still in use today.

SHARKFIN SHOAL

Sharkfin Shoal, at the entrance to Fishing Bay and the Nanticoke River on the Eastern Shore of Maryland, was lighted on August 1, 1892. A house on screw piles replaced Clay Island Lighthouse, which stood on land to the north of the channel.

In 1887 the Lighthouse Board reported, "The site of Clay Island lighthouse is being rapidly washed away, to prevent which, expensive works of protection would be needed. The structure is old and in need of repairs almost to the extent of rebuilding." The screw pile, with a house similar to that of Greenbury Point Shoal, was constructed for $25,000.

In 1964 the old structure was torn down and an automated beacon was erected on the foundation.

MARYLAND POINT

Maryland Point, on the Potomac River, was completed and lighted on December 15, 1892. In 1887, the Lighthouse Board noted in the annual report, "The channel of the river is quite narrow here and there is but ten feet of water on the apex of the shoal at low stages. Light-draught vessels can easily pass over the shoal, but vessels drawing more than 10 feet are liable to take the ground. The danger to vessels of heavier

draught is so great and there are so many plying on the river, that a light is needed here for the completion of the system decided on as necessary fully a dozen years ago." An appropriation of $50,000 was made on August 30, 1890.

The lighthouse was a hexagonal, wooden dwelling resting on seven wrought-iron screw piles, 40 feet long, and varying in diameter from 7 inches at the top to 10 inches at the bottom, or screw, end. The piles penetrated 13 feet into the shoal and were provided with circular disks, 5 feet in diameter, which rested on the surface of the shoal and augmented the bearing capacity of the screws. The light was a flashing white of the fourth order. The fog bell was struck by machinery, a double blow at 15-second intervals.

Maryland Point was demolished in the early 1960s.

PAGES ROCK

Pages Rock, located five miles from Yorktown, Virginia, on the York River, was first lighted on September 30, 1893. The wooden-frame hexagonal structure was built on sleeve piles. Wooden piles, 27½ feet long, were driven into the bottom and iron sleeves were placed around them.

As early as 1883, the Lighthouse Board noted in its annual report: "It is believed that the large and rapidly increasing commerce of this river is entitled to that assistance and additional security." In 1885, the board added, "The combination of railroads centering at West Point, at the head of the river, comprises more than 1,000 miles of road, and lines of steamers run at frequent intervals to Baltimore and northern ports."

An appropriation of $25,000 was made on March 3, 1891. The result of borings at the site showed "the foundation was not sufficiently firm to uphold a lighthouse on screw-piles. It therefore became necessary to adopt a structure depending for support upon wooden piles, which could be driven to a hard bearing at a point deeper than the screw-piles could be made to penetrate economically." The lighthouse was automated in 1951 and dismantled in 1967.

CEDAR POINT

Cedar Point Light marked the southern side of the mouth of the Patuxent River. Located on land, it was first lighted on October 31, 1896.

In 1888, the board pointed to the need for the lighthouse: "The harbor at the mouth of Patuxent River is the best on the western side of Chesapeake Bay. Vessels about to enter this harbor from the south pass close to Cedar Point, where the water is deep near the shore. In thick weather sounding is no safeguard, as the change from deep to shoal water is abrupt. The establishment of a light and fog-signal on Cedar Point would also be of much value to the general navigation of the bay, as most vessels pass near this point." The board requested $25,000.

The lens was of the fourth order, flashing red every five seconds. The lighthouse was a cottage-style dwelling, built of brick and wood. From one corner of the house rose a square tower, supporting a lantern. The dwelling was three stories high, including the basement, and the tower and lantern rose 50 feet above the ground. The focal plane of the light was 45 feet above mean high water. The fog bell and apparatus were placed in the upper room of a wooden structure, 35 feet high and 12 feet by 16 feet in plan, the first story of which contained a summer kitchen and the second floor, two storerooms. There was also a brick oil house, a frame boathouse, and a small outhouse.

The point eventually eroded, helped on by local dredging of sand from the area, and the lighthouse was left on an island by the 1920s, when it was abandoned. The cupola was moved ashore, and by 1996 part of the side of the brick house had collapsed. The U.S. Navy, which owns the property, is considering tearing it down to prevent injury to boaters.

HOOPER ISLAND

Hooper Island was first lighted on June 1, 1902, marking the east side of the Chesapeake Bay between Tar Bay and Hooper Strait. On July 1, 1898, Congress authorized $60,000 to build a caisson light and fog signal here.

In 1900, the contractor awarded the bid to erect the lighthouse failed to begin work on the project, and it was readvertised and given to the lowest bidder.

The light housed a lens of the fourth order, flashing white every fifteen seconds. The new stucture consists of a circular foundation pier, 33 feet in diameter, supporting a circular dwelling, a veranda, a watchroom, a circular cylinder, parapet, and a circular lantern. The iron dwelling is four stories high and in the form of a frustum of a cone, 18 feet in diameter at the base and 17 feet at the top.

The lighthouse was automated in the early 1960s and is still in use today.

POINT NO POINT

Point No Point Light, a caisson built on the west side of the Bay between the Potomac and Patuxent Rivers, served the simple task of filling a dark stretch of horizon when it was lighted on April 24, 1905.

In 1891, the Lighthouse Board noted, "There is a stretch of about 30 miles between the Cove Point and Smith Point lights which should be better lighted. For a part of the distance navigators are without a guide, where a deviation from their sailing course might carry vessels of heavy draught onto dangerous shoals. There are many of this class of vessel trading to Baltimore, and their number is increasing." Some $35,000 was appropriated for the lighthouse.

Work started on the wooden caisson August 11, 1902, but the contractor experienced many problems. The working pier was wrecked twice, and the caisson drifted away once.

The new light, completed on April 24, 1905, was of the fourth order, lighting the entire horizon and flashing white and red, alternately, at intervals of twenty seconds. A fog bell was struck a double blow by machinery every fifteen seconds. Point No Point was automated in April 1962.

BALTIMORE LIGHT

Baltimore Light, which marks the southern entrance to the Craighill Channel leading to the mouth of the Patapsco River, was the biggest caisson in the world when built and the most difficult lighthouse on the Chesapeake to construct. It was completed in 1908, thirteen years after the work first was started.

The lighthouse was proposed in 1890, and $60,000 was requested for its construction. In 1895, borings indicated that soft mud extended fifty-five feet below the surface of the shoal, and an additional $60,000 was requested for the project.

The caisson was towed to the site on September 19, 1904, but the project was abandoned by the contractors after the giant caisson turned over in a storm. The job was eventually completed by the insurance company.

Baltimore Light was automated in the 1960s and became the first atomic-powered lighthouse in 1964, when it was equipped with an isotopic power generator. The atomic generator was removed after two years and conventional power was restored.

RAGGED POINT

Ragged Point on the Potomac River was the last lighthouse built in a new location in the Chesapeake Bay; it was lighted on March 15, 1910. (The third Thimble Shoal was the last lighthouse *constructed* on the Chesapeake Bay, in 1914, after the second lighthouse at that site was rammed by a schooner and burned in 1909.)

In 1896, the Lighthouse Board stated in its annual report that a shoal off the west bank of the river at a short turning point needed to be marked by a light and bell.

The light was of the fourth order, flashing white every ten seconds and illuminating the entire horizon. A bell struck a double blow every ten seconds by machinery. The structure was a two-story wooden house, surrounded by a gallery and resting on a substructure of seven wrought-iron piles. The total cost of construction was $34,223.97.

Ragged Point was strafed by naval planes in the early 1960s during weapons testing (while still occupied by coastguardsmen) and was demolished shortly afterward.

CHESAPEAKE LIGHT STATION

Chesapeake Light Station began operation in September 1965, replacing *Chesapeake*, a lightship which had marked the entrance to the Bay for thirty-two years. Located fourteen and a half miles east of Cape Henry in the ocean, this station is a modern "platform," resembling an oil derrick and costing $1.7 million. Designed to last seventy-five years, it had a six-man crew—four on duty at all times—for a period of fifteen years before it was automated in October 1980.

Lightships

Lightships were originally called light-boats or light-vessels. Initially, a boat such as a schooner was used and a lantern was hoisted up the mast. Over time, a specialized vessel with high sides was developed to ride out bad weather. The early lightships were poor sailors, however, and often had to be towed to and from their posts.

In the list that follows, lightships are referred to by their location. Sometimes ships were given a name or number by the Lighthouse Board. In later years, however, the name of the shoal or site was usually painted in bold bright letters accross the sides of the lightship. When the vessel changed location, it received the name of the new site where it was stationed.

VIRGINIA

Craney Island, located at the entrance to the Elizabeth River in Hampton Roads, Virginia, 1820. This seventy-ton lightship was stationed briefly at Willoughbys Spit, but the location was too exposed and the ship was soon moved to Craney Island where it became the first permanent lightship in the country. Replaced by a lighthouse in 1859.

Willoughbys Spit, off Hampton Roads, Virginia, 1821. Replaced by Thimble Shoal Lighthouse in 1872.

Wolf Trap Shoals, near Gwynns Island, Virginia, 1821. Destroyed by rebels in 1861. Replaced by a lighthouse.

Upper Cedar Point, located on the Potomac River, below the Narrows and about forty-four miles below Mt. Vernon. Replaced by a lighthouse in 1867.

Lower Cedar Point, located in the Potomac River between Lower Cedar Point and Yates' Point, above Kettle Bottom, 1821. Destroyed by rebels in 1861. Replaced by a lighthouse.

Smith Point, 1831. The vessel was boarded, stripped, and removed by rebels, but Union soldiers later replaced it. On January 19, 1867, ice carried the ship away and it drifted for two days. It was put back on station, but lighthouse construction was already under way by 1867.

Windmill Point, 1834. The vessel was removed by rebels in 1861. A new vessel was stationed in 1868–69 before the lighthouse was completed in 1869.

Bowlers Rock, located in the Rappahannock River, 1835. Destroyed by rebels in 1861, and replaced by a lighthouse.

York Spit, 1855. Destroyed by rebels in April 1861. A lightship was reestablished in 1867 and stationed until the lighthouse was completed in 1870.

Cape Charles, located in the ocean beyond the Cape Charles Lighthouse, 1888. The ship was equipped with a steam-powered fog signal. On October 11, 1896, during a severe gale, Lightship No. 49 parted its moorings and drifted sixteen miles southeast of Cape Henry Light before the USS *Columbia* was able to get a line on it and tow it to Hampton Roads. The lightship survived the hurricane of August 1899, but in a severe gale on October 31, 1899, it strained so hard that the starboard chain stopper broke and carried away all the castings and connections. It was repaired and placed back on station.

Bush Bluff, located at the entrance to Norfolk on the Elizabeth River, 1888. The composite schooner *Drift*, of about eighty-seven tons gross burden, was borrowed from the Coast and Geodetic Survey to mark this station. "An appropriation of $20,000 was made in March, 1885, to place a lighthouse on Bush's Bluff, but it being found that the light would be of no use on the Bluff itself, Congress acted on August 4, 1886, to let the board place the house," the Lighthouse Board noted in 1887. "It was then found, by careful sounding, that the mud at the only place where the light would be of any use was 82 feet deep, and that it would cost $125,000 to construct a lighthouse on a foundation which would withstand the ice at that point. The board, therefore, suggests that the practicability of moving by dredging the mud shoal known as Bush's Bluff Shoal, or a part of it, be fully considered before entering upon the construction of a lighthouse at so great an expense." In 1888, the board recommended a lightship instead: "There being no present prospect that the dredging recommended will be undertaken, the board recommends the establishment of a lightship at this point, with steam fog-signal in duplicate, at $60,000. This shoal is a great inconvenience, as well as danger to the commerce entering and leaving Norfolk and Newport News. Much time and pains are expended in keeping clear of the shoal, and in spite of this, many vessels are caught upon it. A large steamer, the *D. H. Miller*, from Boston, grounded there lately and did not get off until the third day after, and then only with the help of three tugs and a large steamer. Several vessels belonging to the navy have run ashore on this shoal. Steamers of the Old Dominion Line have been ashore there some eight or ten times in the last five or six years, and the board is informed that schooners loaded with coal and drawing 18 feet of water frequently stick on this point. Several foreign vessels have grounded."

Tail of the Horse Shoe, located near the mouth of the Chesapeake between the two capes, 1900. Lightship No. 46 was received from the Fourth District in 1901 and soon thereafter overhauled. The zinc sheathing was removed, and the worm-eaten planks, parts of the keel, and the wood around the hawser pipe were cut out and replaced, a new sternpost was put in, and all sea connections were thoroughly repaired before it was placed on station.

Chesapeake, stationed off the mouth of the Chesapeake Bay, 1933. This lightship weathered three hurricanes— in 1933, 1936, and 1962—parting its moorings each time. It was replaced in 1965 by the Chesapeake Light Station, a seventy-five-foot platform lighthouse resembling an oil derrick. The platform was built five miles south of the location of the lightship. *Chesapeake* is currently a floating museum at the Inner Harbor in Baltimore.

MARYLAND
Hooper Strait, 1827. The ship was removed when the lighthouse was finished in 1967.

Janes Island, off the tail of Janes Bar at the entrance to the Little Annemessex River. Destroyed by rebels in 1861.

Choptank River, Benoni's Point, 1870. This lightship served for only one year while a lighthouse was being constructed.

Tenders

Violet - A wooden side-wheel steamer, built in 1861, about 231 tons gross burden. In 1890, it made 320 visits to lights, replaced and painted 560 buoys, built 24 beacons, and delivered 171 tons of coal, 100 cords of wood, keepers' rations, and other supplies. It steamed about 12,640 miles and consumed 593 tons of coal. In 1901, it was employed in supplying and inspecting lighthouses and working buoys.

Holly - An iron side-wheel steamer, built in 1881, rebuilt and sheathed with wood in 1898, about 367 tons gross burden. In 1890, it steamed about 14,000 miles, consuming 825 tons of coal. It made 342 visits to lighthouses and replaced and painted 421 buoys. It delivered 172 tons of coal, 107 cords of wood, keepers' rations, and miscellaneous supplies. In 1901, it was employed in supply, inspection, and attending of buoys and was in excellent condition. *Holly* steamed 10,374 miles and consumed about 794 tons of bituminous coal. It visited 264 lighthouses and vessels, delivered 152 tons of coal and 88 cords of wood, and inspected 131 light stations.

Jessamine - An iron side-wheel steamer, built in 1881, about 257 tons gross burden. In 1890, it was employed in the construction of lighthouses and repairs to stations. In May 1890, it was docked and its hull coated with American germicide paint to test its value as an anti-fouling composition. *Jessamine* steamed 5,495 miles and consumed 520 tons of coal. In 1901, it was used to inspect 39 light stations and two depots. It did borings, installed fog signals, and made repairs.

Nettle - A steam-launch, it assisted in construction of the lighthouses, both at the depot and at the sites, and in repairs. *Nettle* was transferred to the Third District on July 22, 1890.

Thistle - A wooden screw-steam tender, described as a steam tug, built in 1890 and purchased in May of that year; about 32 tons gross burden. It had been "apparent for some time that a vessel was needed with power sufficient to tow scows loaded with construction and repair materials, and with a lighter draught than the *Jessamine*, that would pass more readily through the inland route to the sounds of North Carolina [which was also part of the Fifth District, along with the Chesapeake Bay]. She is an efficient substitute for the *Jessamine* when the tender is not available for inspections and urgent repairs or construction," the Lighthouse Board reported. In 1901, *Thistle* was used in towing the working plant, materials, and repair party for work at various lighthouses.

Maple - A steel twin-screw steamer built in 1892, about 392 tons gross burden. It was employed in supplying and inspecting lighthouses and light vessels and in working on buoys. During an average year, it steamed 12,929 miles and consumed 1,312 tons of bituminous coal.

All photographs in the appendix are Coast Guard photos, courtesy of the National Archives, with the exception of the following: photographs of Blakistone Island, Sandy Point, Hawkins Point (Brewerton Range), Windmill Point, Choptank Light, Love Point, Craighill Channel Range Front Light, Solomons Lump, and Hooper Island are courtesy of the Chesapeake Bay Maritime Museum; the photograph of Chesapeake Light Station is by the author.

Concord Point Lighthouse.

The second Cape Henry Lighthouse was built in 1881 and automated in 1984.

Sources

One of the most important sources of information for this book was the *Report of the Lighthouse Board*, which was issued annually between 1853 and 1910, when the job of overseeing lighthouses in the United States was taken over by the U.S. Lighthouse Service. This agency issued a yearly *Report of the Commissioner of Lighthouses*, which was not nearly as detailed but, nevertheless, helpful. The U.S. Coast Guard took control of the lighthouses in 1939 and its records were used as references in this book as well.

Many documents housed at the National Archives were used as source material, including logbooks kept by lighthouse keepers and original letters written to the Lighthouse Board. Unfortunately, some letters were lost during a fire in 1921, making it difficult to verify what really happened in certain cases. When the original letters were not available, the index to letters, also maintained by the National Archives, was helpful in providing details of what the letters contained.

I wish to give special thanks to the following organizations, individuals, museums, and libraries for allowing me access to lighthouses and historical files and for assisting me in finding the material: Chief Warren Officer Dave Merrill, Group Hampton Roads, U.S. Coast Guard; Chief Warren Officer Mark Cowen, Group Baltimore, U.S. Coast Guard; the Rukert Terminals Corporation; Aberdeen Proving Ground, U.S. Army; John Romer, Patuxent Naval Air Station; the Living Classrooms Foundation; Pete Lesher, curator, Chesapeake Bay Maritime Museum; Mariners' Museum; Talbot County Free Library; the Special Collections and Archives Division of the Nimitz Library, U.S. Naval Academy; Mathews County, Virginia, Library; Maryland State Archives; the Maryland Court of Special Appeals, which maintains a complete copy of *Baltimore Sun* articles on microfilm for public access; Robert Hurry and Paul Berry, Calvert Marine Museum; the Kirn Memorial Library in Norfolk, Virginia; and the Enoch Pratt Memorial Library in Baltimore. Many of the newspaper and magazine articles listed below, as well as copies of the Lighthouse Board's annual reports, were found at these museums and libraries.

INTERVIEWS

- Celia Atwood, White Stone, Virginia
- Melba Barteau, Boerne, Texas, granddaughter of lighthouse keeper
- Olga Crouch, Turkey Point, Maryland, daughter of lighthouse keeper
- Alma Gatton, Scotland, Maryland, wife of Point Lookout Lighthouse keeper
- Bernadette Gesser, Baltimore, Maryland, relative of Thomas J. Steinhise, keeper
- Don Hammett, Point Lookout State Park ranger
- Frances Harstick, Cambridge, Maryland, visitor to lighthouse
- Mike Humphries, director of St. Clement's–Potomac River Museum
- Jane Jackstite, Havre de Grace, Maryland, Friends of the Concord Point Lighthouse
- Karl Eugene Kohler, Vienna, Virginia
- Alan Manuel, St. Marys County, former resident of Point Lookout Lighthouse
- Thelma Marshall, relative of Thomas J. Steinhise, keeper
- Lilian Milstead, relative of Thomas J. Steinhise, keeper
- Violet Taylor, relative of Thomas J. Steinhise, keeper
- Spencer Tracy, Salisbury, Maryland, grandson of Ulman Owens, keeper
- Harry Yeatman, St. Marys County, Maryland, son of Point Lookout Lighthouse keeper

DOCUMENTS

U.S. Department of Justice, Bureau of Investigation, report on Ulman Owens—Death on Government Reservation, March 24, 1931. Courtesy Spencer Tracy.

Calvert County, Maryland, Family Records, 1670–1929, compiled by Mildred Bowen O'Brien, Calvert Marine Museum Library.

United States vs. Schooner Malcom Baxter, Jr., *and the Tug* John Twohy, Jr., in the District Court of the United States for the Eastern District of Virginia.

U.S. Department of the Interior National Park Service, document written on Pooles Island Lighthouse for National Register of Historic Places.

Interview with Loretta Y. Goldsborough, December 29, 1979, conducted by Dave Bohaska and Clara Dixon for the Calvert Marine Museum in Solomons, Maryland.

Notes from the guest book of Drum Point Lighthouse, furnished by the Calvert Marine Museum Library.

BOOKS AND PAMPHLETS

deGast, Robert. *The Lighthouses of the Chesapeake.* Baltimore, Md.: The Johns Hopkins University Press, 1973.

"A History of Drum Point Lighthouse," Calvert Marine Museum Special Publication No. 1, June 1978.

"A Portrait of Deltaville," compiled by Zeta Epsilon Chapter, Beta Sigma Phi Sorority, Deltaville, Virginia, printed by The William Byrd Press, Richmond, Virginia, 1976.

Noble, Dennis. "The Coast Guard in the Southeast," Coast Guard Bicentennial Series, U.S. Coast Guard Public Affairs Staff.

"Lighthouses: Then and Now," Coast Guard publication, 1988–89.

NEWSPAPER AND MAGAZINE ARTICLES

"From Annapolis: An Expedition Sent to Retake the Smith Point Light-Ship," *Baltimore Sun,* May 18, 1861.

"The Light Ship Recovered," *Baltimore Sun,* May 20, 1861.

"The End of the Ice Blockade: Light-House Disaster," *Baltimore Sun,* January 15, 1877.

"Letter from Annapolis, *Baltimore Sun,* January 16, 1877.

"Thomas's Point Lighthouse in Trouble," *Baltimore Sun,* January 20, 1877.

"The Chesapeake Lighthouses," *Baltimore Sun,* January 22, 1877.

"Local Matters: Marine Diasters and Lighthouse Affairs," *Baltimore Sun,* January 26, 1877.

"Chesapeake Bay Light-Houses," *Baltimore Sun,* February 17, 1877.

"Cold Weather," *Easton Star,* January 4, 1881.

"The Ice Blockade," *Easton Star,* January 4, 1881.

"Light-House Matters," *Baltimore Sun,* January 22, 1881.

"Drift Ice in Chesapeake Bay," *Baltimore Sun,* January 22, 1881.

"The Choptank River Lighthouse," *Baltimore Sun,* January 28, 1881.

"Choptank River and Lighthouse," *Baltimore Sun,* January 29, 1881.

"Local Matters, Cold Weather and Ice," *Baltimore Sun,* February 4, 1881.

"Another Abandonment of Choptank Lighthouse," *Baltimore Sun,* Feburary 8, 1881.

"Ice Damages in the Chesapeake," *Baltimore Sun,* February 2, 1881.

"Local Record," *Easton Star,* February 15, 1881.

"Sharp's Island and Choptank Lighthouses," *Easton Star,* February 22, 1881.

"At Crisfield: A Party Will Undertake to Walk on the Ice to Tangier Island," *Baltimore Sun,* January 17, 1893.

"Extreme Cold in Caroline," *Baltimore Sun,* January 18, 1893.

"Fears for a Light-House Keeper," *Baltimore Sun,* January 20, 1893.

"Cruising through Ice: The Harbor, Patapsco River and Chesapeake Bay," *Baltimore Sun,* January 20, 1893.

"Eastern Shore of Virginia, Arctic Appearance of the Bay—Getting Oysters under Difficulties," *Baltimore Sun,* January 20, 1893.

"At Crisfield," *Baltimore Sun,* January 20, 1893.

"Across the Bay on the Ice," *Baltimore Sun,* January 20, 1893.

"Icebergs Near Cape Charles," *Baltimore Sun,* January 31, 1893.

"A Number of Spar Buoys Placed. The Wolf Trap Light-House Discovered Adrift," *Baltimore Sun,* February 1, 1893.

"News of the Port. Damage to Light-Houses by the Ice," *Baltimore Sun,* February 4, 1893.

"Light House Inspection," *Baltimore Sun,* February, 1893.

"Great Caisson for Lighthouse," *Baltimore American,* June 28, 1904.

"Two Rescued from Flaming Lighthouse," *Portsmouth Star,* December 27, 1909.

"High Winds Prevailing," *Portsmouth Star,* December 27, 1909.

"Christmas Storm Worst in Years," *Portsmouth Star,* December 27, 1909.

"News of the Shipping: Thimble Shoal Light Station Will be Total Wreck," *Baltimore Sun*, December 28, 1909.

"How Thimble Light Was Destroyed," *Baltimore Sun*, December 30, 1909.

"Assistant Keeper of Tangier Light Accidentally Killed," *Crisfield Times*, February 21, 1914.

"Narrow Escape in Storm," *Crisfield Times*, March 7, 1914.

"Crisfield Hit by Storm," *Crisfield Times*, March 7, 1914.

"Keeper Found Dead," *Baltimore Sun*, March 16, 1931.

"U.S. Probing Death of Light Keeper," *Baltimore Sun*, March 17, 1931.

"May Extend Probe at Holland Bar," *Baltimore Sun*, March 18, 1931.

"Light Keeper's Family Challenges Verdict," *Baltimore Sun*, March 18, 1931.

"Body of Light Keeper Exhumed," *Baltimore Sun*, March 20, 1931.

"Body of Lighthouse Keeper Exhumed as Authorities Investigate Strange Circumstances Connected with Death," *Crisfield Times*, March 21, 1931.

"More Agents Sent to Probe Owens' Death," *Baltimore Sun*, March 22, 1931.

"Fresh Clue Found in Keeper's Death," *Baltimore Sun*, March 24, 1931.

"Foul Play Theory in Death of Lighthouse Keeper Said to be Abandoned, New Evidence Found," *Baltimore Sun*, March 29, 1931.

"Murder Theory Doubted in Light Keeper's Death," *Baltimore Sun*, March 31, 1931.

"Death Probe Fails..." *Crisfield Times*, April 4, 1931.

"Report Death Due to Heart Trouble," *Crisfield Times*, April 18, 1931.

"U.S. Agencies Unite in New Death Probe," *Baltimore Sun*, May 18, 1931.

"Bond of 3 in Rum Case is Doubled," *Baltimore Evening Sun*, May 25, 1931.

"Wave Sinks Tug in Bay, 14 Rescued; Engineer of Vessel Is Drowned," *The Baltimore News*, August 21, 1933.

"7 Drown in Gale; Tug Sunk in Bay: Engineer Dies as Tug Sinks in Chesapeake," *Baltimore Evening Sun*, August 21, 1933.

"Storm Gaining; 8 Lives Lost in Coast Wrecks," *Baltimore Sun*, August 22, 1933.

"Evening Sun Spots: In Dark Times, He Keeps a Bright Spot for Mariners on the Bay," *Baltimore Evening Sun*, September 5, 1933.

"Heroic Rescue by the Keeper of Sevenfoot Knoll Light," 1936 newspaper clipping, courtesy Living Classrooms Foundation.

Dulaney, Carroll, *Baltimore News-Post*, February 28, 1936.

"To Visit Her Seven-Foot Knoll Lighthouse Birthplace Today," *Baltimore Sun*, May 14, 1939.

"Tells of 6-Hour Ordeal on Boat Disabled on Bay," *Baltimore Sun*, August, 1939.

"Cobb Island Lighthouse Soon Will Be Replaced," *Baltimore Sun*, January 3, 1940.

"Lighthouse at Back River, Historic County Landmark, Becomes Prey of Elements," *Newport News Daily Press*, August 11, 1940.

"Lighthouse," *Baltimore Evening Sun*, January 15, 1942.

"Modern Conveniences Boom to Only Woman Lighthouse Keeper," *U.S. Coast Guard Magazine*, circa 1944.

Taylor, Craig E., "Lighthouse Keeping," *Baltimore Sunday Sun*, October 13, 1946.

"Lighthouse Is Automatic," *Baltimore Sun*, May 7, 1948.

Moberly, Elizabeth H., "On The Beam in The Bay," *Baltimore Sunday Sun*, October 31, 1948.

Middleton, Arthur Pierce, "The Struggle for the Cape Henry Lighthouse, 1721–1791," reprinted from *The American Neptune*, vol. VIII, no. 1, 1948.

Blackford, Frank, "Old Cape Henry Lighthouse to Hold Fast," *Norfolk Virginian-Pilot*, July 2, 1950.

Hayne, Miriam, "Lighthouse Keeping, Like Light Housekeeping, Has Changed with the Times," *Richmond Times-Dispatch*, July 20, 1952.

Brown, Alexander C., "Aids to Mariner Make 'World's Greatest Harbor' Great–II," *Newport News Daily Press*, April 19, 1953.

Reppert, Ralph, "Vanishing America: The Keeper of The Light," *Baltimore Sun Magazine*, July 12, 1953.

"The Confederate Raid on the Blackistone Island Lighthouse," *Chronicles of St. Mary's*, vol. 1, no. 5, October 1953.

Sullivan, Frank, "Rumored Razing of Lighthouse at Cape Henry Denied by Association of State Antiquities," *Norfolk Virginian-Pilot*, June 23, 1954.

Wilkins, Guy, "New Wink at Middle Ground to Beguile Sailors in Autumn," *Norfolk Virginian-Pilot*, July 22, 1954.

"APVA To Begin Restoration of Old Cape Henry Lighthouse," *Norfolk Virginian-Pilot*, June 23, 1955.

Herman, Benjamin, "John O'Neill, Hero of Havre de Grace," *Baltimore Sun*, October 30, 1955.

Ritter, Larry Jerome, "Wolf's Trap Lighthouse Takes Name from a Wreck There 264 Years Ago," *Norfolk Virginian-Pilot and The Portsmouth Star*, December 4, 1955.

"Abandoned Lighthouse Gives Way to Flossy," *Newport News Times-Herald*, September 28, 1956.

"Rockets Hit Lighthouse," *Baltimore Sun*, February 20, 1957.

"The Week in Brief," *Baltimore Sunday Sun*, February 24, 1957.

Burgess, Robert H., "I Remember...The 'Tail of the Horseshoe,' " *Baltimore Sun*, November 17, 1957.

"Lighthouse at Cape Henry Repaired at $14,000 Cost," *Norfolk Virginian-Pilot*, February 18, 1958.

Gunther, Catherine O'Neill, "I Remember...Life at the Old Havre de Grace Lighthouse," *Baltimore Sun Magazine*, May 17, 1959.

Fenton, Frank J., "Schooner Crashes into Lighthouse," *Newport News Times-Herald*, November 16, 1959.

Marble, Robert L., "Lighthouse at Mouth of York Will Be Automatic Operation," *Newport News Daily Press*, February 21, 1960.

Williams, Jack, "Old Point Light Delights Visitors—Has Wonderful History," *Newport News Daily Press*, September 11, 1960.

"Old Plantation Light Automated," *Newport News Times-Herald*, January 13, 1962.

Evans, Philip E., "One of Maryland's Last Manned Lighthouses," *Baltimore Sun Magazine*, March 18, 1962.

"Lighthouse Nuclear Unit Due Tests," *Baltimore Sun*, January 16, 1963.

"Sandy Point Light to Go Automatic," *Newport News Times-Herald*, May 11, 1963.

Gaul, Christopher, article about Concord Light (no title), *Baltimore Evening Sun*, July 17, 1963.

Burgess, Robert H., "The Chesapeake's Vanishing Lighthouses," *Baltimore Sun Magazine*, October 20, 1963.

"Nuclear Reactor to Run Baltimore Light," *Baltimore Sun*, May 20, 1964.

"Baltimore Light First Atomic-Powered," *Baltimore Sun*, June, 1964.

"Most Lighthouses Fully Automatic," *The New York Times*, June 24, 1964.

Smith, Mary Wade, "Wolf Trap Light Has Stood through the Years as Mariners' Guide in Chesapeake," *Gloucester-Mathews News Gazette-Journal*, August 6, 1964.

"2 Old Lighthouses to Bow to Progress," *Richmond Times-Dispatch*, December 16, 1964.

Booth, Ed, "Maritime History Is Continued," *Richmond Times-Dispatch*, September 12, 1965.

Burgess, Robert H., "Bay Lightship Out—Tower In!" *Newport News Daily Press*, September 12, 1965.

"Mrs. Fannie Salter, 83, Lighthouse Keeper, Dies," *Norfolk Virginian-Pilot*, March 13, 1966.

Swaine, Mary, "Lighthouse Moved to Talbot," *Star Democrat*, November 16, 1966.

"75-Year-Old York Lighthouse Will Be Replaced By Steel Tower," *Newport News Daily Press*, December 4, 1966.

Carman, Lewis R., "I Remember: The Life of a Chesapeake Light-Keeper," *Baltimore Sun*, April 2, 1967.

Taylor, Zack, "Dismantled Screwpile Lights—Will They Beam or Burn?" *National Fisherman*, June 1967.

Burgess, Robert H., "The Passing of the Lighthouse Era," *Maryland Magazine*, Winter 1968, vol. 1, no. 2.

Wolf, Robert H., "The Guiding Light!" *Newport News Daily Press, New Dominion Magazine*, June 23, 1970.

"Bay Sentinels Are Automated," *Newport News Times-Herald*, November 11, 1971.

Holechek, John, "Old Lighthouses Fade Away," *Baltimore Sunday Sun*, November 4, 1973.

"Historic Lighthouse Approved for Sale," *Baltimore Sunday Sun*, October 6, 1974.

Frye, John, "Last Two Screwpile Lights May Survive a While Longer," *National Fisherman*, March 19, 1975.

"Lighthouse Moved to Solomons," *Prince Frederick Recorder*, March 27, 1975.

Foss, William O., "One Gets Used to Cape Henry Sand," *National Fisherman*, January 1978.

Wilson, Randy, "Vandals Hit Lighthouse," *Evening Capitol*, July 18, 1979.

Krzywicki, Fran, "Lights Out: Bay Beacons Falling Victim to Vandals," *Washington Post*, August 6, 1979.

"A Night at the Point," *Chronicles of St. Mary's*, April 1980.

"Automation Shines on Chesapeake Light," *Soundings*, May 1980.

Ewalt, Anna Weems, "Grandparents Living in a Lighthouse," *Baltimore Sun Magazine*, 1979.

Collins, Denis, "Lights Out For Guards," *Washington Post*, October 15, 1980.

"Ups and Downs, All Around," *Washington Post*, August 19, 1983.

Frankoski, Joseph, "The Old Point Comfort Light," *Chesapeake Bay Magazine*, April 1985.

Sword, Gerald J., "Point Lookout Lighthouse," *Chronicles of St. Mary's*, vol. 33, no. 5, May 1985.

"Lighthouse to Rise Again," *Washington Post*, July 6, 1985.

"Replica Recaptures Lighthouse's Glory Days," *Port of Baltimore*, December 1985.

"Lazaretto Lighthouse Replica Rising in Canton," *Baltimore Sun* (undated, circa 1985).

Waller, Jean, "Baltimore Wants Tourist Light," *Soundings*, February 1986.

Shisler, Michael, "Bay Spotlight: The Last Hurrah for Cove Point Light," *Chesapeake Bay Magazine*, April 1986.

Sands, John O., "Beacons of the Bay," *The Mariners' Museum Journal*, Summer 1986.

Homfeld, Max. F. (MD), "Clockwork Fog Signals," National Association of Watch and Clock Collectors, Inc., *Bulletin*, October 1986.

Noble, Dennis L., and Ralph E. Eshelman, "A Lighthouse for Drum Point," *The Keeper's Log*, Summer 1987.

Bergin, Layne, "Screwpile Lighthouse: From Britain to the Bay," *The Keeper's Log*, Summer 1987.

"Fannie May Salter Known as 'Md.'s Lady of the Lamp,'" *The Mariner*, August 21, 1987.

Cronin, William B., "Watts Island," *Chesapeake Bay Magazine*, July 1988.

"Lighthouse Renovated," *The Keeper's Log*, Fall 1988.

"Seven Foot Knoll Lighthouse to be Moved," *The Keeper's Log*, Fall 1988.

Goyette, Barbara, "Lighthouse Lift," *Chesapeake Bay Magazine*, January 1989.

McAllen, Bill, "The Last of the Bay's Working Cast-Iron Lighthouses is Saved," *Maryland Magazine*, Spring 1989.

Duncan, Scott, "Lighthouses of the Chesapeake," *Baltimore Sun*, August 5, 1989.

Norris, Joseph, "Lighthouses: Guardians of the Rivers," *St. Mary's Countian*, December 20, 1989.

Wheeler, Wayne, "The History of the Administration of the USLH Service," *The Keeper's Log*, Winter 1989 and Spring 1990.

Ballon, Marc, "Lighthouse Renewal Reunites Family," *The Maryland Gazette*, April 21, 1990.

Broadway, Bill, "Voices from the Past: The Keepers' Stories," *Washington Home*, August 16, 1990.

Thomas, Jennifer, "Point No Point's Lonely Outpost Now Houses Automated Light," *The Enterprise*, September 21, 1990.

Thomas, Jennifer, "13 Lamps Cast Light 11 Miles at Point Lookout," *The Enterprise*, September 26, 1990.

"Wreck of Lighthouse All That Remains of Cedar Point's Past," *The Enterprise*, July 30, 1993.

Clarke, Wendy Mitman, "Jones Point Lighthouse to Shine Again," *Soundings*, July 1993.

Bates, Steve, "Jones Point Light Flashes Back On," *Washington Post*, October 30, 1993.

Dodds, Richard J., "Drum Point Lighthouse—Its Origins Revisited," *Bugeye Times*, Winter 1993–94.

"Bright Lights, Big Lenses," *Nautical Collector*, July 1994.

DeFord, Susan, "Now History Beckons from the Beacon at Piney Point," *Washington Post*, November 10, 1994.

Hanks, Douglas III, "Coast Guard Eyes Lighthouse for Demolition," *Star Democrat*, 1996.

CLIPPINGS FROM THE FILES OF THE CALVERT MARINE MUSEUM

"The Last of the Lady Lighthouse Keepers," 1966.

Grant, Joseph R., "History of the Turkey Point Lighthouse."

"Drum Pt. Lighthouse Reminiscences."

"Commissioners Deed Drum Point Lighthouse to Historical Society," November 1974.

Bilek, Babette, "The Ghosts of Pt. Lookout Light."

"Navy Acquires Former Cedar Point Lighthouse Site."

CLIPPINGS FROM THE FILES OF THE CHESAPEAKE BAY MARITIME MUSEUM

Henderson, Randi, "O'Neill's Heroism Wins Lighthouse."

Burgess, Robert H., "I Remember...The Lazaretto Point Lighthouse," *Baltimore Sun*.

"So Long, Thomas Point Light."

CLIPPINGS FROM THE FILES OF THE MATHEWS COUNTY, VIRGINIA, LIBRARY

Diggs, Martin, "New Point Lighthouse," Summer 1969.

"New Point Light Built before 1810; Famous Landmark," *History and Progress*, Mathews County, Virginia.

Young, Edwin P., "At New Point Light Fifty Years Ago," 1978.

South, Jeff, "Residents of Mathews Restore Their 176-year-old Lighthouse," *Ledger-Star*.

Sandy Point Lighthouse, located just one-half mile off the shore of Sandy Point State Park, has become a favorite part of the landscape for boaters, sunbathers, and visitors to the park.

Numbers in bold designate photographs.

A

Aberdeen Proving Ground, **132**, 133
Absecon Lighthouse, N.J., 48, 51
acetylene-gas beacons, 106, 109
Addie M. Lawrence, 85
Alexandria, Va., **42**
Annapolis, 130
Annapolis, Md., 26, 32, 41, 60, 139, 148
Annapolis Harbor, 41, 139
Apache, 123
Applegarth, C. H., 61
Argand, Jean Robert, 10
Argand wick lamp, 10
Arundel Corporation, 45, 123, 151
Association for the Preservation of Virginia Antiquities, 138
Atlantic City, N.J., 51
Atlantic City Naval Air Station, 131
Atomic Energy Commission, 137
Atwood, Celia, 135, 136
Atwood, Dr. Wallace, 135, 136
August Storm of 1933, 41, **44**, 119-23, 144, 154, 155

B

B. Mohawk, 85
Bache, Lt. George M., 13
Back Creek, **134**
Back River, 13
Back River Lighthouse, 14, 15, 27, 42, 43, 109, 163
Baker, Captain, 32
Baltimore, 6, 11, 12, 18, 20, 27, 32, 37, 67, 73-80, 86, 91, 106, 117, 120, **121**, **122**, 123, 127-29, 135, 136, 138, 147, 151, 155, 156
Baltimore Harbor, 31, 69, 74, 79, 119
Baltimore, 53

Baltimore American, 69, 73, 79, 80, 86
Baltimore and Philadelphia Steamboat Company, 129
Baltimore Lighthouse, 71, 73, 75, 79, 80, *94*, 137, 149, **149**, 178, 179
Barney, Capt. Willis B., 11, 12
Barteau, Melba Crouch, 130. *See also* Frances Melba Crouch
Bayside Wharf, 41
bell machinery, 99-103
Bells Rock Lighthouse, 86, 109, 174
Berg, Erik, 143
Berg, Laura, 143
Bethlehem Steel, **80**
Betterton Beach, 129
Billys Island, 32
Bishops Head, 59
Blackbeard, 4
Blades, Joseph, 120, 123
Blakistone Island, 44
Blakistone Island Lighthouse, 12, 23, 26-28, 109, 165
blockade, 24
Bloodsworth, Garland, 113, 114, 117
Bloody Point Lighthouse, 60, 71, 74, **87**, 89, 90, 137, **148**, **156**, 174
Bloody Point Range Lights, 47, 48
Bodkin Island, 11
Bodkin Island Lighthouse, 11, 15, 18, 39, 74, 161
Boenning, Carl J., 135, 138
Bolling, Capt. James T., 29, 34, 65
Bolling, Eva, 34
Bolling, Knolie, 31, 34
Boston, Mass., 83
Boston Harbor Outer Light, 101
Borroughs, Elsey, 7
Bowlers Rock, 26
Bowlers Rock Lighthouse, 170
Bowlers Rock Lightship, 179
Breton Bay, 4, 23
Brewerton Channel, 79
Brewerton Channel Range Lights, 76, 78, 109, 170
Brumfield, Georgiana Crouch, 127

Bull's Bay, S.C., 24
Bureau of Lighthouses. *See* U.S. Bureau of Lighthouses
Burginal, Eugene, 33
Bush Bluff Lightship, 55, 91, 180
Bush River, 133
Butler, keeper, 35

C

caisson, 35, 38, 56, 69-73, 79, 80, 149
definition of, 37
first, 37
California Rock, 96
Callahan, C. J., 117
Calvert Cliffs, 12
Calvert County, 41, 67, 156
Calvert County Commissioners, 151
Calvert County Historical Society, **134**, 152
Calvert Marine Museum, 67, **67**, 91, 100, **102**, 141, 148, 152, 156, 157
Cambridge, Md., 32, 53
Cape Canaveral, Fla., 47
Cape Charles, 26, 39, 59, **62**, 83, 90
Cape Charles City, 109, 111, 137
Cape Charles Lighthouse, 12, 26, 39, 41, 45, 50, 125, 138, 162
Cape Charles Lightship, 179
Cape Henry, 3-7, 83, 86, 97
Cape Henry Lighthouse, **2**, **4-6**, 4-7, 11, 25, 27, 45, 102, 108, 128, 138, 139, 159, 160
Cape Romain, S.C., 24
lighthouse, 48
Carman, Lewis R., 83, 87, 89-91
catoptric system, 10
Cecil County Clerk of the Court, 130
Cedar Point, 66
Cedar Point Lighthouse, 45, **46**, 66, 90, 91, 156, **157**, 177, 178
Friends of, 156
Chappell, Thomas C., 78
Charles H. Warner, 91

Charleston, S.C., 23, 24, 50

Charleston Lighthouse, 51

Cherrystone Inlet Lighthouse, 26, 59, 109, 168

Chesapeake and Delaware Canal, 100, 126, **126**, 130

Chesapeake Bay, 5, 6, 13, 15, 17, 25, 27, 28, 47, 48, 50, 53, 76, 83, 102, 106, 109, 114

Chesapeake Bay Maritime Museum, **18**, **32**, **139**, **150**, 151-52, **152**

Chesapeake Light Station, 179

Chesapeake Lightship, 25, 180

Chester River, 37

Choptank River, 53, 109

Choptank River Lighthouse, 57, 105, 109, 171

Choptank River Lightship, 180

Chronicles of St. Marys, 143

Civil Service Commission, 127

Civil War, 23-29, 74, 77, 101, 102, 131, 142, 143, 145

Claxton, Alexander, 9, 13, 17

Clay Island Lighthouse, 44, 164

Coast Guard. *See* U.S. Coast Guard

Cobb Point Bar Lighthouse, 63, 109, 176

Cockburn, Adm. George, 9, 10

Cole, Captain, 59

Collins, Captain, 59

colza oil, 6

Concord Point, 10, 45

Concord Point Lighthouse, 9, 10, 12, **12**, **16**, 45, 109, **110**, 148, 154, 161, 162

Friends of, 155

Confederate, **22**, 25-27, 143

Congress, 15, 17, 41, 63, 74, 79, 80, 152

Congressional Medal, 123

Conowingo Dam, 45

Conway, Capt. Alexander S., 31, 33, 34

Cooks Point, 92

Coolidge, President Calvin, 128

Cooper, John, 96

Cooper, Lewis, 96

Coppuck, Evans and, 11

Cornwall, John S., 31, 33, 34

Coulbourne, Dr. George C., 117

Coulbourne, Dr. W. H., 116, 117

Cove Point Lighthouse, 12, **14**, **19**, 41, 45, **49**, 50, 63, **101**, 139, 156, 162, 163

Craighill Channel, 76, 79

Craighill Channel Range Lights, 35, **72**, 77, 172, 173

front light, 37, 38, **81**, 149

back light, **82**

Craighill Channel Upper Range Lights, **76**, 77, **77**, **80**, 175

Craney Island, 13

Craney Island Lighthouse, **25**, 27, 109, 169

Craney Island Light-Boat, 17, 179

Crisfield, 34, 53, 91, 93, 95, 109, 114, 116, 117

Crisfield Times, 111

Crockett, Capt. William Asbury, 93, 95

Crouch, Frances Melba, 100. *See also* Melba Barteau

Crouch, James, 100, 128, 129

Crouch, John, 127

Crouch, Olga, 89, 100, 125, 127-130, **129**

Crouch, Rebecca Sherwood, 127

Crystal Beach, 130

Culkold Point, 76

Curtis Bay, 147

D

Daines, John, 4

Daisy Archer, 53

Daisy, Dr. W. O., 95

Daley, John J., 119

Dames Quarter, Md., 117

Dafuskie Island, S.C., 47, 48

Daugherty, Sheriff Luther, 114

Davis, Ann, 142

Davis Creek, 54

Davis, W. H., Jr., 91

Davis Palmer, 83

Deal Island, 59, 93

Deep Water Shoal Lighthouse, 20, 21, 27, 137, 167

Delaware, 28

Delmarva, 26

Democrat, Cambridge, 33

Department of Commerce, 103, 106

Diggs, Rev. Wilbur, 89

Donohoo, John, **8**, 11, 12, **14**, 23, 44, 74, **124**, **132**, 133, **145**, 153, 155

Dorchester County, 31, 32, 34, 111, 151

Dorsey, Mary, 67

Dorsey, Maude, 67

Dorsey, William, 67

Doyle, Arnold W., 131

Drum Point, 45, 65, 66, 67

Drum Point Lighthouse, **31**, 45, 50, 63-67, **64**, **66**, **67**, 91, 99, 100, **115**, 119, **134**, 148, 151-53, 174

Dunmore, Governor Lord, 5

Dutch Gap Canal Lights, 173

E

earthquake, 47-51

Eastern Bay, 31

Eastern Shore, 112

Eastern Shore of Maryland, 12, 31, 33, 34, 59, 76, 92, 129

Eastern Shore of Virginia, 26

Eastville, Va., 59

Edward L. Martin, 41

Edwards, Pamela, 27, 142

electricity, 107, 108

experiments with, 106

Elizabeth River, 13, 26, 55

Elk River, 126, 130

Ellis, J. M., 91

Eminizer, A. J., 123

Empire Construction Company, 155

Encyclopaedia Britannica, 128

erosion, 6, 7, 39-46

Europe, 10

Evans and Coppuck, 11

Evans, J. D., 55

Ewalt, Anna Weems, 63, 65-67, **66**, 153

Ewalt, G. Walther, 152

Express, 143

F

Farrell, David L., 131

Federal Bureau of Investigation, 116, 117

fish oil, 6

Fishing Battery Island, 43

Fishing Battery Island Lighthouse, 12, **40**, 43, 44, **108-9**, 166

Fishing Bay, 44

Fifth District, 17, 19, 105, 107

Flaherty & Lande, 70, 71, 73, 79

Flaherty, William H., 70

Fog Point Lighthouse, 12, 15, 162

fog signals, types of, 101-3

Fort Carroll Lighthouse, **26**, **28**, 166

Fort George, 4
Fort McHenry, 74
Fort McHenry channel, 79
Fort McHenry Range Lights, 79, 80
Fort Monroe, 4, **22**, **24**, 26, 27
Fort Story, 45
Fort Washington Bell Tower, 148, 153, **154-55**, 168
Fowey, HMS, 5
Frances, 59
Frances Scott Key Bridge, 155
Fresnel, Augustin Jean, 10
Fresnel lens, 10-12, **16**, 17, 20, 24, 48, 63, 106, 126, 135, 148, 154
fuel, 6
Fulcher, Thomas L., 85

G
Garner, H. J., 114
Gatton, Alma, 101, 142-45
Gatton, George, 138, 142
Galesville, 89
Gaston, **55**
Gedneys, Channel, N.J., 106
George, Mrs. Luther, 53, 54
Georgetown, S.C., 24
Georgia, 47
ghosts, 141-45
Gibson Island, 11, 29, 73, 137, 149
Gloucester County, Va., 154
Godfrey, Arthur, 91
Goeshy, Beatrice, 99
Goeshy, William, 99
Goldsborough, Loretta Y., 89, 91
Goldsmith, Capt. John M., 27
Great Annemessex River, 55
Great Britain, 9
Great Charleston Earthquake, 47-51
Great Shoals Lighthouse, 174
Great Wicomico River, 26, 69
Great Wicomico River Lighthouse, 175
Greenbury Point Lighthouse, 12, 20, 41, 165
Gunter, William, 54, 57
Gwynns Island, 25
H
Hallets Point, N.Y., 106
Hammersla, Carl J., 89

Hampton Roads, 4, 7, 9, 13, 19, **24**, **25-27**, 47, 54, 55, 83, **84**, 86, 137, **158**
Hannibal, 131
Hanson, John, 153
Harford County, Maryland, 9
Harrison, Percy, 120
Hartge, Deputy Commander E. A., 53
Hartwig, Milton, 147, 149
Hart-Miller Island, 76
Harwood, Colonel, 32, 33
Havre de Grace, 9-12, 45, 109, **110**, 148, 154
Hawkins, Eva Bolling, 34
Hawkins Point, 78
    lighthouse, 76, 78, 109
Hawkins Point Farm, 78
Heliotrope, 32
Higginson, F. J., 35
Hilton Head Range Light, S.C., 51
Hog Island, Va., 26
Hog Island Lighthouse, 125
Holland Island, 105
Holland Island Bar Lighthouse, 61, 83, 87, 90, 91, 105, 111-14, **115**, 131, 137, 175, 176
Holly, 65, 180
Holzer, Dr. Hans, 142
Hooper Island Lighthouse, 61, 74, **88**, 97, 137, 178
Hooper islands, **88**
Hooper Strait Lighthouse, 31-34, **32**, 50, 111, **139**, **150**, 151, 152, **152**, 155, 169
Hooper Strait Lightship, 180
House of Burgesses, 4
Hudgins, Capt. Arthur, 89
Hudgins, Capt. Filmore, 89
Hudgins, Miles, 93
Humphries, Mike, 142
Hunley, G. C., 92
Hunter, Comdr. T. T., 23, 24
Hunting Island, S.C., 24
Hurricane Barbara, 138
Hurricane Connie, 145
Hurricane Diane, 145
Hurricane Flossy, 42
Hurricane Hazel, 154
hydrogen sulfide gas, 70
I
icebreakers, 130

Inner Harbor, Baltimore, **25**, **118**, **122-23**, 155

J
James River, 20, 21, 27, 32, 44, 45, 48, 137
Jane, 90
Janes Island Lighthouse, 34, 53, 55, 91, 109, 169, 170
Janes Island Lightship, 180
Jarvis, John T., 87
Jessamine, **65**, 180
Jesuit priests, 4
John Twohy Jr., 83, 85
Johnson, G. G., 90
Jones Point Lighthouse, **42**, 45, 133, 153, 167
Jordan Point Lighthouse, 44, 45, 109, 167
Juniper, 92

K
Kedges Strait, 55
Kellen, Gordon, 55
Kenmore, 85
Kent Island, 31, 37, 71, **87**, 89
kerosene, 6
Kirschner, Capt. Ralph, 120
    Ralph, Jr., 121
Kirwin, assistant keeper, 56
Koch, Rebecca Sedwick, 67
Kraske, Henry P., 123

L
lard oil, 6
Latrobe, 130
Latrobe, B. H., 6
Lady Baltimore, 92
Lamberts Point Lighthouse, 19, 20, 171, 172
lamp, Aladdin mantle, 126
Lancaster Grays, 26
Lazaretto Point Depot, 20, 77, 155, 156
Lazaretto Point Lighthouse, 12, 20, 74, 77, **78**, 79, 81, 91, 106, 109, 163, 164
Leading Point, 76
Lee, Thomas, 5
lens
    nonrevolving, 112
    revolving, **19**
Lewis, Winslow, 9, 10, 12, 17, 42, 43
Lexington Park, 156
light, incandescent oil vapor, 113

lighting apparatus (or lighting
system), 9-12, 17
Lighthouse Board. *See* U.S.
Lighthouse Board
lighthouse depot, 20, 77
lighthouses
atomic-powered, 137
automation of, 108, 109
condition of, 15, 17
construction of, 6-7, 11, 12, 14,
17-20
construction problems of, 12, 13
cost of, 17
first, 3, 6
manned, number of, 139
number of, 6, 7, 10, 11, 14, 18, 28
pile, 38
number of, 7, 54
rebuilding of, 39
reproduction of, 155, 156
vandalism of, 148
lightship (or light-vessel), 13, 14,
25, 25-28, 43, 55, 106, 107,
179, 180
Little Watts Island, 44, 96
Living Classrooms Foundation,
155
Long Shoal Lighthouse, N.C., 92
Love Point Lighthouse, 37, 172
Lower Cedar Point, 26, 169, 179
Lusby, Elizabeth, 127
Lusby, Robert, 127
Lynnhaven, 4

M
Maidstone, 10
Malcolm Baxter Jr., 83, 85
Malinowski, Theodore, 123
Manohanock, 117
Manuel, Alan, 141, 142
Manuel, Sue Winter, 141, 142
Maple, 87, 91, 181
Marchant, Larry, 55, 59, 60
Marlborough, 9
Mariners' Museum, 155
Marion, Md., 117
Marshall, Archie C., 120, 123
Martin Company, 137
Mary E. Fouble, 91
Mary L. Colburn, 86
Marydel, 113
Maryland, 5, 11
first lighthouse in, 11, 74
first screw-pile lighthouse in, 18
Maryland Commission for
Psychic Research, 142

Maryland Point Lighthouse, 137,
177
Mathias Point Lighthouse, 137,
173
Mathews County, Va., 41, 45, 54,
89, 125, 127
Mathews County Historical
Society, 154
McDorican, W. F., 105
McWilliams, Jerome, 23, 27-28
Merrimac, CSS, 26, 29
Miller, Captain, 29
Miles River, 151
Mitchell, Alexander, 18
Mobjack Bay, 7, 14, 25, 41, 109,
125
Monitor, USS, 26, 29
Moore, H. S., 91
Morgan, John E., 91
Morrill, 54
Morris Island, S.C., 51
Morris, Judge, 78
Mount Vernon Chapter of the
Daughters of the
American Revolution, 133
Mulberry Tree Papers, 65
Murphy, Captain, 32

N
Nansemond River Lighthouse,
109, 174
Nanticoke River, 44
National Geographic, 128
National Park Service, 133
National Register of Historic
Places, 139, 152
Naval Academy, U.S., 41
Naval Air Test and Evaluation
Museum, 156
Naval Hospital Beacon, 25, 27, 60,
166
Navy Commissioners, Honorable
Board of, 9, 13
Navy Department, 103, 106
Navy Point, **32**, 151
Nelms, William, 7
Nettle, 181
Nettie Champion, 83
New Cut-Off Channel Range
Lights, 76, 77, 175. *See also*
Craighill Channel Upper
Range
New England, 5, 83
New Point, 41, 42
New Point Comfort, 7, 119

New Point Comfort Lighthouse,
14, 25, 41, 42, **44**, 45, **104**,
109, 138, 154, 161
Newport News Middle Ground,
137, **158**, 176, 177
New York Eighth Artillery, 26
New York Bay, 50
New York City, 83
New York Harbor, 47, 48, 108
New York Thirteenth Regiment,
26
Newtown Manor House, 4
Norfolk, Va., 25, 27, 32, 34, 83
North Carolina, 17
North Point, 76, 77
North Point Range Lights, 11, 15,
74, 77, 161
Northeast, Md., **124**, 128
Lions Club of, 156
Northumberland County, Va., 55
Norvell, Maggie, 128

O
Ocean City, Md., 119
Old Plantation Flats Lighthouse,
54, 56, 57, 90, 111, 137, 175
Old Point Comfort, 4, 7, 9, 26
Old Point Comfort Lighthouse, 7,
15, **22**, **24**, 45, 47, **50**, 160
Old Road Bay, 77
O'Neill, John, 9, 10
O'Neill, Matilda, 10
optical system, 9-13
Orchid, 86
Owens, Ella, 112, 117
Owens, Myrtie, 112
Owens, Ulman, 111-14, 116, 117
Oxford, Md., 57, 105, 109
oyster dredging, 93
oyster navy, 53

P
Pages Rock Lighthouse, 20, 56,
91, 137, 177
parabolic reflectors, 10, 11, 17
paranormal, 142, 143
Parkburst, Guy, 117
Patapsco River, 11, 15, 18, **26**, 31,
35, 37, 72, 74, 76, 77-79, 91,
109, 119, **121**, 149, 155
Patuxent River Naval Air Station,
131, 156

Patuxent River, 45, **46**, 63, 66, 92, 99, 152, 156, **157**
Paw Paw Cove, 35
Pearce, Capt. W. Irving, 83
Perryville, Md., 100
Pertner, Charles H., 91
pile lighthouses 20, 38. *See also* screw pile, sleeve pile
Piney Point Lighthouse, 12, 45, 99, 144, **146**, 153, **153**, 164
pirates, 4, 5
Pleasonton, Stephen, 10, 12-14, 17
Pocomoke Sound, 93
Poe, Edgar Allan, 74
Point Breeze, 120, 122, 123
Point Comfort, 5. *See also* Old Point Comfort
Point Lookout, 28, 45
Point Lookout Lighthouse, 12, 27, 101, 138, **140**, **143**, **145**, 140-45, 153, 163
    prisoner-of-war camp at, 27, 143
Point Lookout State Park, **140**, 142
Point No Point Lighthouse, **60**, 71, 74, 91, **97**, **113**, 137, 139, 144, 147, 178
Point of Shoals Lighthouse, 20, 27, 48, 109, 137, 167
Pooles Island, 12, 133
Pooles Island Lighthouse, 11, 12, **132**, 133, 161
Porter, Captain W. H., 55
Potato Battery, 9
Potomac River, 4, 6, 7, 11-13, 23, 25-27, **42**, 43, 45, 55, 56, 63, **68**, 69, 91, 101, 109, 131, 137, **140**, 142, 144, 148, 153, **154-55**
Port Deposit granite, 11
Portsmouth, Va., 54, 155
Pratt, Stephen M., 135, 151
Price, keeper, 57
Princess Anne Militia, 25
Prohibition, 114
Prudence, 85
Pungoteague Creek Lighthouse, 20, 21, 167
Purcell, Gilbert, 135

R
R. T. Runkett, 86
Racoon Key, S.C., 48

radio fog signals, 106, 107, 108
    compass stations, 107
    direction finders, 108
    waves, 103
Ragged Point Lighthouse, 56, 80, 131, 137, 179
range lights, 11, 15, 35, **72**, 74
    definition of, 28
rapeseed, 6
Rappahannock River, 3, 5, 26, **55**, 71, 135
reflector system. *See* parabolic reflectors
Report of the Officers Constituting the Light-House Board, 17
Revolutionary War, 5, 6
Reynolds, John, 59
Rhoda M. Parker, 93
Rhode River, 139
Riley, Eugene S., 91
Rogers, Rear Admiral Ins., USN, 35
Roosevelt, President Franklin D., 90, 91
Roosevelt, James, 90
Rukert, Norman ("Cap"), Sr., 156
Rukert, Norman G., 155, 156
Rukert Terminals Corporation, **78**, 155, 156
rumrunners, 114, 116, 117

S
St. Clements Bay, 4, 23
St. Clements Island, 23, 44
St. Clement's Island–Potomac River Museum, 142, 156
St. Jerome Creek, 71, 97
St. Marys County, 23, 142, 153, 156
St. Marys County Department of Parks and Recreation, Museum, 153, **153**
St. Marys County Historical Society, 143
St. Michaels, **18**, **32**, **150**, 151,**152**
St. Patricks Creek, 27
Salter, Bradley, 125, 127, 129, 130
Salter, Clarence W., 89, 125-27, **129**
Salter, Fannie May, 100, 101, 125-30, **129**
Salter, Mabel, 125, 128
Salter, Olga. *See* Olga Crouch
Sandy Point, 76, 148

Sandy Point Lighthouse, 38, **52**, **56**, **58**, 59, **90**, 137, 148, 168, 169
Sarah, 123
Scotland, Md., 135, 151
Scott, William T., 131
screw pile, **18**, 31
    cost of, 21
    description of, 18, 19
    destruction of, 21
    number of, 21, 28, 38
    uses of disks with, 20
secession, 23
Sevenfoot Knoll Lighthouse, 18, 29, 74, **118**, **121-23**, 119-23, 148, 155, 167, 168
Severn, 91
Severn River, 53, 139
Sharkfin Shoal Lighthouse, 44, 59, 177
Sharps Island, 7, 43
Sharps Island Lighthouse, 15, 35, **36**, 38, **38**, 39, 43, 71, 165
shipwreck, 143
Shockley, Jesse M. W., 92
Shores, Minnie, 112, 117
Silver Lifesaving Award, 123
siren, steam-powered, 102
sleeve pile, definition of, 20, 31
Smith Island, Md., 12, 15, 55, 131, 136
Smith Island, Va., 26, 39, 41, 51, 138
Smith, John, 135
Smith Point, 7, 43, 114
Smith Point Lighthouse, 7, 11, 13, 15, 17, 39, 43, 55-57, 59, **68**, 69-71, 80, **92**, 93, 113, 139, 160
Smith Point Lightship, 26, 27, 179
Snug Harbor, 89
Solomons, 65, 99, 134, 141
Solomons Lump Lighthouse, 50, 55, 56, 70, 71, 113, 114, **115**, **136**, 173
Somers Cove Lighthouse, 109, 170
Somerset County, 112, 117
South Carolina, 23, 47, 48, 50, 51
South River, 32, 139
sperm oil, 6
Spanish-American War, 106
Sparrows Point, 77
Sponselles, Margaret Carey, 99, 100
Spotwood, Gov. Alexander, 3, 4
steamboat, 17, 28

Patuxent River, 45, **46**, 63, 66, 92, 99, 152, 156, **157**
Paw Paw Cove, 35
Pearce, Capt. W. Irving, 83
Perryville, Md., 100
Pertner, Charles H., 91
pile lighthouses 20, 38. *See also* screw pile, sleeve pile
Piney Point Lighthouse, 12, 45, 99, 144, **146**, 153, **153**, 164
pirates, 4, 5
Pleasonton, Stephen, 10, 12-14, 17
Pocomoke Sound, 93
Poe, Edgar Allan, 74
Point Breeze, 120, 122, 123
Point Comfort, 5. *See also* Old Point Comfort
Point Lookout, 28, 45
Point Lookout Lighthouse, 12, 27, 101, 138, **140**, **143**, **145**, 140-45, 153, 163
    prisoner-of-war camp at, 27, 143
Point Lookout State Park, **140**, 142
Point No Point Lighthouse, **60**, 71, 74, 91, **97**, **113**, 137, 139, 144, 147, 178
Point of Shoals Lighthouse, 20, 27, 48, 109, 137, 167
Pooles Island, 12, 133
Pooles Island Lighthouse, 11, 12, **132**, 133, 161
Porter, Captain W. H., 55
Potato Battery, 9
Potomac River, 4, 6, 7, 11-13, 23, 25-27, **42**, 43, 45, 55, 56, 63, **68**, 69, 91, 101, 109, 131, 137, **140**, 142, 144, 148, 153, **154-55**
Port Deposit granite, 11
Portsmouth, Va., 54, 155
Pratt, Stephen M., 135, 151
Price, keeper, 57
Princess Anne Militia, 25
Prohibition, 114
Prudence, 85
Pungoteague Creek Lighthouse, 20, 21, 167
Purcell, Gilbert, 135

R
R. T. Runkett, 86
Racoon Key, S.C., 48

radio fog signals, 106, 107, 108
    compass stations, 107
    direction finders, 108
    waves, 103
Ragged Point Lighthouse, 56, 80, 131, 137, 179
range lights, 11, 15, 35, **72**, 74
    definition of, 28
rapeseed, 6
Rappahannock River, 3, 5, 26, **55**, 71, 135
reflector system. *See* parabolic reflectors
Report of the Officers Constituting the Light-House Board, 17
Revolutionary War, 5, 6
Reynolds, John, 59
Rhoda M. Parker, 93
Rhode River, 139
Riley, Eugene S., 91
Rogers, Rear Admiral Ins., USN, 35
Roosevelt, President Franklin D., 90, 91
Roosevelt, James, 90
Rukert, Norman ("Cap"), Sr., 156
Rukert, Norman G., 155, 156
Rukert Terminals Corporation, **78**, 155, 156
rumrunners, 114, 116, 117

S
St. Clements Bay, 4, 23
St. Clements Island, 23, 44
St. Clement's Island–Potomac River Museum, 142, 156
St. Jerome Creek, 71, 97
St. Marys County, 23, 142, 153, 156
St. Marys County Department of Parks and Recreation, Museum, 153, **153**
St. Marys County Historical Society, 143
St. Michaels, **18**, **32**, **150**, 151, **152**
St. Patricks Creek, 27
Salter, Bradley, 125, 127, 129, 130
Salter, Clarence W., 89, 125-27, **129**
Salter, Fannie May, 100, 101, 125-30, **129**
Salter, Mabel, 125, 128
Salter, Olga. *See* Olga Crouch
Sandy Point, 76, 148

Sandy Point Lighthouse, 38, **52**, **56**, **58**, 59, **90**, 137, 148, 168, 169
Sarah, 123
Scotland, Md., 135, 151
Scott, William T., 131
screw pile, **18**, 31
    cost of, 21
    description of, 18, 19
    destruction of, 21
    number of, 21, 28, 38
    uses of disks with, 20
secession, 23
Sevenfoot Knoll Lighthouse, 18, 29, 74, **118**, **121-23**, 119-23, 148, 155, 167, 168
Severn, 91
Severn River, 53, 139
Sharkfin Shoal Lighthouse, 44, 59, 177
Sharps Island, 7, 43
Sharps Island Lighthouse, 15, 35, **36**, 38, **38**, 39, 43, 71, 165
shipwreck, 143
Shockley, Jesse M. W., 92
Shores, Minnie, 112, 117
Silver Lifesaving Award, 123
siren, steam-powered, 102
sleeve pile, definition of, 20, 31
Smith Island, Md., 12, 15, 55, 131, 136
Smith Island, Va., 26, 39, 41, 51, 138
Smith, John, 135
Smith Point, 7, 43, 114
Smith Point Lighthouse, 7, 11, 13, 15, 17, 39, 43, 55-57, 59, **68**, 69-71, 80, **92**, 93, 113, 139, 160
Smith Point Lightship, 26, 27, 179
Snug Harbor, 89
Solomons, 65, 99, 134, 141
Solomons Lump Lighthouse, 50, 55, 56, 70, 71, 113, 114, **115**, **136**, 173
Somers Cove Lighthouse, 109, 170
Somerset County, 112, 117
South Carolina, 23, 47, 48, 50, 51
South River, 32, 139
sperm oil, 6
Spanish-American War, 106
Sparrows Point, 77
Sponselles, Margaret Carey, 99, 100
Spotwood, Gov. Alexander, 3, 4
steamboat, 17, 28

Steinhise, Earl, 119-21, 123
Steinhise, Thomas J., 119-23, 155
Sterling, Henry, 113, 114
Sterling, Royce, 113
Stevens, Frank, 123
Stevens, George M., and
    Company, 101
Stingray Point Lighthouse, 55, 59,
    135, 137, 168
Stirling, Yates, 57, 59
Stowe, Cale B., 99, 100
Stowe, Myrtle, 99, 100
Sun, Baltimore, 29, 33, 34, 53, 59,
    60, 83, 87, 131, 135, 138
Susquehanna River, 9, 11, **40**, 43,
    45
Swan, 27
Sword, Gerald, 142, 143

T
Tail of the Horse Shoe, 27, 83, 180
Tangier Island, 93, 95-97, 137
Tangier Sound, 31, 53, 55, 93, 96,
    109
Tangier Sound Lighthouse, 61, 86,
    92, 93, 95-97, 120, 137, 176
Tarr, Charles L., 35
Thimble Shoal Lighthouse, 19,
    50, 54, 71, 80, 83-86, *84*, **86**,
    172
Thistle, 181
Thomas, Barney, 95-97
Thomas, Capt. Edward L., 93, 95
Thomas, John William, 54
Thomas, Joseph B., 85
Thomas Point Lighthouse, 11-13,
    39, 161
Thomas Point Shoal Lighthouse,
    7, **21**, 29, **30**, 32-34, **34**, 38,
    96, **98**, 139, 161
Tidewater Construction
    Corporation, 155
Tilghman Island, 35
Tolson, John T., 91
Todd, Capt. William C., 111
Todd, Ulysses, 112, 114, 116
Tred Avon River, 109
Tryal, 3
Tue Marshes Lighthouse, 18, 137,
    173
Tulip, 32
Turkey Point Lighthouse, **8**, 12,
    45, 100, 101, **124**, **126-27**,
    129, 125-30, 148, 156, 164
Tyler, C. C., 105
Tyler, John Tawes, 114

U
Union, 25-27
    hospital, 143
U.S. Army, **132**, 133
U.S. Bureau of Lighthouses, 45,
    80, 90, 105
U.S. circuit court, 78
U.S. Coast Guard, 45, 56, 109,
    114, 117, 123, 130, 131,
    135-39, 147-49, 154, 156,
    156, 157
U.S. Coast Guard Depot, 135, 138
U.S. Coast Guard Magazine, 100
U.S. Fish Commission, 43
U.S. Geological Survey, 48
U.S. Lighthouse Board, 12, 14, 15,
    16, 23, 29, 32, 34, 35, 38, 39,
    41, 43, 45, 48, 56, 57, 59, 63,
    64, 71, 74, 77-80, 85, 102,
    103, 105, 106, 125
    establishment of, 17
    annual reports of, 13, 20, 24-28,
    39, 48
U.S. Naval District, Fifth, 11
U.S. Navy, 13, **145**, 156
U.S. Public Health Service
    Hospital, 127, 129
U.S. Treasury Department, 10
Upper Cedar Point, 13
Upper Cedar Point Lighthouse,
    137, 169
Upper Cedar Point Lightship, 179
Upper Craighill Channel Range.
    See Craighill Channel Upper
    Range

V
Valliant, W. E., Fertilizer
    Company, 113
Violet, 180
Virginia, 3, 5, 11
Virginia, warship, 26
Virginia, tugboat, 85
Virginia Council, 5
Virginia Legislature, 5
*Virginia Pilot and the
    Portsmouth Star,* 53

W
Waackaack Station, N.J., 50
War of 1812, 9, 10, *22*
Warner, Donald M., 131
Washington, D.C., 23
Washington, President George, 6,
    128
Watts Island, 96

Watts Island Lighthouse, 12, 44,
    96, 109, 164
Webster's Store, 99
Weems, Alice, 63, 65-67
Weems, Anne, 65
Weems, James Loch, 63, **64**, 65-67
Weems, Mary, 63, 65
Weller, U.S. Senator O. E., 128
Wells, Isaac D., Jr., 85
Wescott, William R., 59
West River, 53, 139
Whippoorwill, 114, 117
White, Hiram, 89, 90
White Shoals Lighthouse, 20, 27,
    137, 167
White, Tom, 60
Wible, George M., 91
William Woodward, 26
Williams, Ferdinand, 55, 57
Williams, James Bennett, 55, 57
Williams, Nathaniel F., 6
Williams, Capt. W. S., 85
Willis, G. M., Sr., 91
Willoughbys Spit, 13, 179
Wilson, J., 109
Windmill Point, 25, 135
Windmill Point Lighthouse, 135,
    137, 170
Windmill Point Lightship, 179
Wingate, G. B., 61
Winnie and Estelle, 114
Wolf Trap Lighthouse, 53, 54, **54**,
    56, 91, 139, 171
Wolf Trap Lightship, 179
Wolf Trap Shoals, 13, 25
Woodbury, Honorable Levi, 13
World War I, 91, 105-7, 133
World War II, 87, 100, 130, 133

Y
Yeatman, Harry, 144, 145
Yeatman, Herbert, 142
Yeatman, Percy, 142
Yeatman, William M., 91, 143
Yeatman, William, Jr., 142
Yeatman, William III (Bill), 142
Young, Edwin P., 41
York River, 5, 13, 18, 20, 25, 56,
    86, 91, 125, 137
York Spit, 9, 13
York Spit Lighthouse, 89, 92, 125,
    137, 171
York Spit Lightship, 25, 179
Yorktown, 86